Praise for *How to be a Craftivist*

'Craft is often thought of as domestic, belonging to a private world. Corbett brings it into the public sphere and shows us its transformational potential. Craftivism isn't a gimmick. From politicians to CEOs, Corbett's campaigns have changed the hardest of hearts and minds. This book doesn't tell you what to care about, it shows you a different way to care. Here is an irresistible invitation to a kinder, more beautiful world, where the gentle are heroes and thoughtful creativity reigns.'

Lily Caprani, Deputy Executive Director, Unicef UK

'Sarah's approach to craftivism makes us more imaginative, rebuilds our attention spans, enables conversation, recovers dexterity, connects us to our ancestors, makes us smile, enables us to feel change is possible. We owe Sarah Corbett a deep debt of gratitude for showing us how it's done. A vital piece of the world-changer's jigsaw.'

Rob Hopkins, Founder of the Transition movement

'This book is an antidote to the dire state the world is in, teaching us how to create a more beautiful, gentle, loving world with activism that matches.'

Charlie Craggs, Founder of Nails Transphobia

'Who wants to be a whining, complaining "activist"? This book offers a better way, with creativity and a sense of collaboration to some of the most pressing issues humanity faces. Give it a read.'

Jolyon Rubinstein, actor, writer, producer and director,
including 'The Revolution Will Be Televised'

'At a time when activism is no longer seen as a fringe activity, and more and more people are seeking ways to speak out, Sarah Corbett's methods of Craftivism are especially relevant. Sarah proves that the effectiveness of a message doesn't have to rely solely on loud volume and displays of power. Craftivism's strength comes through unwavering kindness and gentleness when spoken in the unexpected, but familiar, language of craft.'

Jenny Hart, Founder of Sublime Stitching

'Sarah's creative and original activism has been a huge inspiration. Totally in line both with Fashion Revolution's ethos and my personal passions, it has been a pleasure to walk alongside her on this journey. This book is essential reading for all those who want to join the collective walk towards a more intelligent fashion consumption, which will lead to a better, safer, cleaner and more transparent fashion industry.'

Orsola de Castro, Founder and Creative Director of Fashion Revolution

'This book is for every quiet soul who wants to bring positive change into the world but doesn't feel well-suited to traditional forms of activism. Corbett shows us what is possible through the art of gentle protest, and how messages for change can be communicated through beautiful, lovingly-made craft objects. Smart, compassionate and engaging, Corbett's book is filled with practical advice and inspirational ideas – the perfect introduction for all budding craftivists.'

Sarah Campbell, Head of Learning Programmes, Victoria and Albert Museum

'Sarah's gentle and powerful approach to activism is relevant more than ever in the world we are living in: why not follow Sarah's lead with this book and help to change the world too.'

Harriet Vine, Co-founder of Tatty Devine

'We know craft can fuel almost magical results – whether as a restorative hobby, a fulfilling career or as the innovative spark to industry or technological break-through. Now, Sarah Corbett's wonderful book shows us how craft and making can be the perfect tool for those who want to make a difference to our world in a gentle way. She combines tools with encouragement that will inspire even the most circumspect of us to find our voice and be part of creating a better world.'

Nicky Dewar, Head of Learning and Talent Development, Crafts Council

'Move over William Morris – here comes Sarah Corbett with an inspiring twenty-first century manifesto for transforming craft into a tool for social change. *How to be a Craftivist* manages that rare feat of stitching together the personal and the political in a way that is both convincing and empowering.'

Roman Krznaric, author of *Carpe Diem Regained* and *Empathy*

'A compelling and intimate portrait that expands our understanding of activism at a time when new forms of protest are more needed than ever.'

Micah White, Co-founder of Occupy Wall Street and author of *The End of Protest: A New Playbook for Revolution*

'This is a wonderful book which will cheer your spirits and lift your soul at a time of austerity and global anxiety over peace and social injustice. It is strategic and significant in terms of its international reach and its intelligent summaries of how slow and mindful craftivism can be open-hearted, modest, peaceful, good-natured and loving.'

Janis Jefferies, Professor of Visual Arts, Goldsmiths University

'I defy you not to be both charmed and inspired by one of the most creative "how to" guides you're likely to come across, jam-packed as it is with practical advice, telling insights, and informed in every line by compassion and a refreshingly different transformational energy.'

Jonathon Porritt CBE, Founder Director, Forum for the Future

'An empowering book, Sarah Corbett brilliantly elucidates ways of making a difference in our world today through the strategic use of craft, making and design as embodied and mindful approaches to activism and long-term transformation.'
Jane Pirone, Dean, School of Design Strategies, Parsons School of Design

'Sarah Corbett shows us the extraordinary relationship between doing and being.'
Milton Glaser, celebrated graphic designer and creator of the I ♥ NY logo

'I loved this book. First, it made me sit up and wonder why I wasn't doing more. Then it showed me that protest can be clever, artful, gentle, AND persuasive. Now I'm telling everyone I know about the art of gentle protest and making it part of my positive psychology curriculum to help transform the world we live in. Sarah Corbett has shown us how to use our talents and strengths in a new way to make a difference.'
Professor Stephen Joseph, editor of *Positive Psychology in Practice: Promoting Human Flourishing in Work, Health, Education and Everyday Life*

'Equal parts inspiration and provocation, this book is for anyone struggling with fury and frustration at the state of the world. The brilliant Sarah Corbett shows how to make a creative, articulate stand in support of all we hold dear.'
Margaret Heffernan, CEO and author of *Willful Blindness* and *A Bigger Prize*

'Sarah Corbett shows how the craft and gentleness of making can be united with world-changing political action. She demonstrates that small, thoughtful shifts in how we do things in our lives can lead to vital transformations. She has powerful ideas about grace, kindness and giving gifts. This is an inspiring and brilliant book.'
David Gauntlett, Professor of Creativity and Design and author of *Making is Connecting*

'In a troubling and troubled world, Sarah Corbett makes the case for a gentle and humane form of activism with force and feeling.'
Douglas Alexander, former UK Member of Parliament & Secretary of State for International Development 2007–10

'Sarah makes social protest appealing and accessible to quiet crafters, helping us to speak out about issues by using creativity and kindness.'
Tilly Walnes, Director, Tilly and the Buttons

'Sarah Corbett's Craftivism is inspiring proof that small quiet actions can foster the transformational change we have all been hoping for.'
John Thackara, Senior Fellow at the Royal College of Art and author of *How to Thrive in the Next Economy: Designing Tomorrow's World Today*

'*How to be a Craftivist* demonstrates that with beautifully crafted design and carefully crafted activation strategies, smart ideas win over dumb ideas and justice wins over injustice. In these times of information overload, competing with beauty is not a luxury – it is a necessity if you want to engage hearts and minds and inspire action.'
Bruce Mau, award-winning designer and author

Sarah P. Corbett is an award-winning activist, author and Ashoka Fellow. She grew up in an activist family and has worked as a professional campaigner for over a decade. Corbett set up the global Craftivist Collective in 2009 providing craftivism (craft + activism) products and services for individuals, groups and organisations around the world using her unique 'Gentle Protest' methodology. She received an Honorary Fellowship from Goldsmiths, University of London in 2022 for her contribution to design activism and public engagement. Corbett's TEDxTalk 'Activism Needs Introverts' was chosen as a TED Talk of the Day on TED.com. In 2024, Unbound published her most recent book, *The Craftivist Collective Handbook*, which features twenty Gentle Protest projects that can help people make a positive difference.

@Craftivists

BY THE SAME AUTHOR

A Little Book of Craftivism
Canary Craftivists Manual
The Craftivist Collective Handbook

How to be a

CRAFTIVIST

The art of
gentle protest

Sarah P. Corbett

unbound

First published in 2017
This paperback edition published in 2024

Unbound
c/o TC Group, 6th Floor King's House, 9-10 Haymarket, London, SW1Y 4BP
www.unbound.com

© Sarah P. Corbett, 2017
Illustrations © Jill Tytherleigh

With special thanks to Trust Greenbelt who have kindly sponsored the illustrations in this book.

While every effort has been made to trace the owners of copyright material reproduced herein, the publisher would like to apologise for any omissions and will be pleased to incorporate missing acknowledgments in any further editions.

Text design by Ellipsis

A CIP record for this book is available from the British Library

ISBN 978-1-78965-183-6 (paperback)
ISBN 978-1-78352-407-5 (hardback)
ISBN 978-1-78352-408-2 (ebook)

Printed and bound in Great Britain by Clays Ltd, Elcograf S.p.A.

1 3 5 7 9 8 6 4 2

MIX
Paper | Supporting
responsible forestry
FSC
www.fsc.org FSC® C018072

For everyone who wants to help improve our wonderful world
in a beautiful, gentle and loving way.

Contents

Part IV: Power in the Public Sphere

Introduction

*If we want our world to be a more beautiful, kind and fair place,
then shouldn't our activism be more beautiful, kind and fair?*

The world is amazing. There is so much loveliness in nature, in people, in
craft, in creativity. But I know that we can make it even more beautiful,
and more kind and more fair. I have been an activist since I was three,
but a few years ago I burnt out and felt that I didn't fit in. I was going
to give up. Then I discovered I could use craft in my activism. I became
a craftivist.

This book is here to help you become not just a craftivist, but the most
effective craftivist possible. To become someone who channels their anger
at injustice and their passion for a better world into creative objects and
activities. And those crafted objects can then help play a part in tackling the
root causes of injustice and help create long-lasting positive change. Yes, it's
a big claim but after nine years of delivering workshops and events offline to
over 15,000 people worldwide, as well as working with organisations ranging
from charities to art institutions to universities and creative companies, I can
say with my hand on my heart that craftivism can be truly transformational,
both personally and politically.

In this book, you will learn how to use the process of making to
engage deeply and critically with the issues you care about on your own or
in a group. I will show you how every detail of your creation is important

from the colour you use, the fonts, the size, messaging and presentation. You will see how craftivism street art and public activities can not only intrigue passers-by but can engage even more people, reaching different audiences online around the world, creating thoughts, conversations and action in places social justice isn't often discussed. Throughout the book I will share with you what I've learnt from my own experience, from the feedback of others, the successes, challenges and hazards to be aware of. There will be case studies to learn from and skills you can transfer into other parts of your life.

Unlike some forms of activism and craftivism, my approach is not aggressive, loud or transactional, but focuses on a gentle art of protesting, threading humility through all that we create and do. Gentleness is not a weak form of protesting, it's not mild or non-assertive. It requires self-control when what we feel is anger or sadness when we see injustice. It requires thoughtfulness to understand the context of the situation and empathy to help understand people's views and actions. We need tact to know what's the best way to tackle the problem and we need concern for all involved.

If you want to do it well, craftivism isn't fast and easy. I often refer to our work as 'slow and mindful activism'. Injustices tend to be complex tapestries with no quick fix or one individual to blame. They can involve many problems woven together that we need to address in different ways and craftivism can be one of the tools to go alongside other forms of activism in the activism toolbox. A tool for slow, kind and intriguing activism. It's a craft that needs honing like any other skill. I want to help you fulfil your potential as a craftivist as you help tackle injustice and seek to create a better world.

My story

I'd always been an activist. I grew up in a low-income area of Liverpool in the 1980s in an activist family. I was taken to protests from the age of three and was present with local residents trying to save good local housing from demolition. I will never forget a family trip to South Africa in 1991. I was eight and Nelson Mandela had been released from prison the previous year. For three weeks we were visiting churches and communities who had worked to end apartheid.

At secondary school to my surprise I was voted head girl and successfully campaigned for lockers for the students (annoyingly we lost our campaign to eradicate 'gym knickers' from the sports kit!). At university I campaigned on global issues and spent the first seven years of my adult career working for large charities as a professional activist and movement-builder. I've grown up watching and learning how campaigns can be won or lost, what the tipping points can be, and how to address the root causes of poverty and injustice, not just the symptoms.

But by 2008 I felt like a burnt-out activist. I'm an introvert; so going to marches and meetings drained me. I didn't like shouting, demonising people or telling people what to do, and I didn't feel as though I fitted into some groups. And so much of my work as a professional campaigner and as an activist in my own time was online and not very creative. I really missed using my hands to create and make things.

In the summer of 2008 I picked up a cross-stitch craft kit from a local shop to stitch on a train journey when I felt too travel-sick to work. I immediately experienced how stitching could help address some of my difficulties with traditional forms of activism. Stitching calmed me down, helped me think through issues more clearly and I was able to be creative with my hands. It felt empowering. I discovered that the act of stitching in public led to people asking me questions about the injustice issue I was stitching about. My local politician had been ignoring my petitions and requests to take particular actions against injustice, so I hand-embroidered a message on to a handkerchief, asking her not to blow her chance of making a positive difference in her powerful position. I gave it to her as a gift to show that I wanted to encourage, support and help her tackle injustices as a critical friend not fight her as an aggressive enemy.

It worked (see Chapter 8). My actions of making small, provocative but not preachy cross-stitched mini banners to hang up in public places to engage passers-by were not only being seen, enjoyed and discussed but to my surprise people were sharing images of them online, creating even more conversation.

I found the word 'craftivism' by googling 'craft and activism' and I wanted to see if there were any people combining the two. Betsy Greer coined the term 'craftivism' in 2003 and defines it as 'a way of looking at life where voicing opinions through creativity makes your voice stronger, your compassion deeper'.[1]

At the time I couldn't find any craftivism projects to do or groups I could join and so I contacted Betsy to ask if there were any guidelines to follow. She said that there were not and gave me her blessing to create my own craftivism projects. I founded the Craftivist Collective in 2009 after people wanted to join in with my projects. It started off as a local group in London and is now a growing worldwide network of craftivists. Over the years I've been constantly learning, in this ever-changing world, where and how craft can be a powerful tool for positive change, as well as where and how people can use it in their own situation.

This book is not focusing on which issues to care about the most. It's about how to be a craftivist. I am aware that some people may use it on campaigns that I may not agree with. But my goal is to inspire and empower you to take a stand against injustice and increase your skills needed to engage in craftivism effectively.

I hope you will read this book with an open heart and open mind. I hope it inspires and empowers you to have a go in making our world an even more beautiful, kind and fair place for everyone. Being a craftivist can sound like a novel gimmick but it can also be world-changing, one stitch at a time...

Part I

Definitions

1
Craftivism

There comes a point where we need to stop just pulling people out of the river. We need to go upstream and find out why they're falling in.

— Desmond Tutu

When I tell people I'm a craftivist, I tend to get confused looks, or people assume that it's simply just a mash-up of 'craft' and 'activist'. Which it is, sort of. It can also be much more than that. I want to use this chapter to set out exactly what I mean by 'craftivist' and 'craftivism' and how I see it as an effective and inclusive tool for changing systemic injustice. So before we think about threading our needles and tackling that craftivism project, let's take a look at the different forms of activism, what my approach to craftivism is and how we can use it to try and change our world for the better.

I see the word 'craftivism' like the word 'punk'. The bands The Clash, Sex Pistols, Ramones, Blondie and so many others have their own unique sound yet they are all seen as part of the punk music scene. And just like punk music, there are many different forms that craftivism takes.

Craftivism as a word and a concept may have only been around since 2003 when Betsy Greer came up with it, but craft has been used as a form of activism for many years. Arpilleras (small hand-stitched pieces) were made by groups of women known as 'arpilleristas' in Chile during the military dictatorship (1973–90) not only as a source of income but also to express their grief and anger, to immortalise their deceased, exiled or disappeared loved ones. Many of these arpilleras were smuggled out of Chile and used by Amnesty International to help build public and political pressure to bring down Pinochet for his atrocities. Back at the turn of the twentieth century, many suffragettes created outfits and fashion accessories in their brand colours of purple, white and green to show they were part of a movement demanding votes for women. And to go back even further, throughout the nineteenth and twentieth centuries, trade unions and the Labour movement started commissioning large embroidered banners to display at political marches worldwide. Rozsika Parker in her seminal book *The Subversive Stitch*, first published in 1984, wrote about needlework creating space for freedom for women as well as being a performance that restricted women in social conversation. The quilting bee, for example, often served as a subversive space for promoting women's suffrage, financial independence, to carry political messages or to raise money for their cause while appearing to be a group of women just chatting while they made objects for their home. These are just some of the examples often described as craftivism.

Some people believe that the act of crafting itself is political because it is going against the grain of mass production while others believe the act must be attached explicitly to a political message to be called craftivism. It is often difficult and confusing to find a clear definition of craftivism. Greer wrote on her website craftivism.com:

But then I remembered that there is no rule book for craftivism (outside of the fact it should fall inside of those tenets and be handmade and make the world better) and that's why I created it to be the amorphous blob that it is. So it can evolve and change so it can involve all interested parties.[1]

It's great to give people freedom but when it comes to tackling complicated social injustices people are at the centre of our work; so we have to be careful not to victimise or demonise people or oversimplify issues. And to do this I believe that we do need direction. It can feel overwhelming if there are so many different examples of craftivism with no one saying what the guidelines are to work within. It can be daunting, or worse, disempowering for some people, like having a blank canvas and not knowing where to start. I want this book to empower you in your craftivism and help you to be a craftivist. Therefore let's start this journey by going back to the words 'craft' and 'activism' and their meanings, and for me to be clear on what I believe effective craftivism is. I know, you're probably itching to get on with the fun part – the crafting – but we want to do more than just make pretty things, if we want our pretty things to actually tackle injustice and help create long-lasting positive change, if – in other words – we want to make craftivist objects rather than simply craft, then we need to discuss what craft is, what activism is, and how they come together to make not just craftivism but effective craftivism.*

Craft definition

The word 'craft' can be used in so many different ways. There is high craft, low craft, reproductive craft and conceptual craft. It can

---

* If you don't agree with my definition, please don't stop reading this book. I'm giving my opinion and perspective so that it offers you something to respond to and reflect on.

be used for unique handmade objects as well as to describe mass-produced industrial products. It is a noun, a verb and a metaphor. I agree with woodworker Peter Korn when he calls the word craft a 'moving target'[2] in his book *Why We Make Things and Why It Matters: The Education of a Craftsman*. He also says that 'Craft is a cultural construct that evolves in response to changing mindsets and conditions of society.'

Our modern understanding of craft as a form of production or a type of object originated with the Arts and Crafts Movement in Britain 130 years ago. John Ruskin, William Morris and the Arts and Craft Movement informed what we understand to be 'craft': beautiful and useful objects that merge practical skills with political utopianism, often idealised as a model of honest, high-quality and fulfilling work, in contrast to mechanised production and industrial capitalism.

On the other hand, craft is often used in a dismissive way to describe women crafting clothes for family and other items in private, an activity that does not receive the same respect as male-dominated activities in public. Worse still, for some of us the word still has ties to keeping women in subservient roles in society throughout history.

In this book, I focus on how to use craft as a tool and method to bring about or work towards positive social change now and in the future. Because today's craft is not just about fulfilling a function and it's often cheaper to buy mass-produced goods, many craft objects focus more on aesthetics as much as – or even more than – the function. This contemporary context of how we understand the word 'craft' will shape our craftivism so that our work can be as effective as possible and help us communicate effective craftivism to others. Also be aware that this book focuses on examples and case studies mostly created and delivered in a Western context where residents can mostly speak freely, where people are not struggling in a war-torn country and democracy is, for the most part, in operation.

We've looked at the word 'craft' in general, now let's look at it in detail.

Craft as a verb: 'to exercise skill in making (an object), typically by hand'*

For the purposes of this book, I'm going to say that to craft something involves skill in making things mostly by hand not machine. Take a handmade chair for example. The more knowledgeable and skilled the chair-maker, the more durable, high quality and comfortable it will be, and therefore the more effective it is at being a chair. The chair-maker might make many chairs that look very different aesthetically but the function of the chair is always executed to the best of their ability. We should see craftivism in the same way: craftivism is designed to fit a purpose and this purpose is activism to make our world a more just place for all. Craft for craftivism prioritises problem-solving injustice issues over play, but that doesn't stop your craftivism from being fun and fulfilling too!

Craft as a noun: 'an activity involving skill in making things by hand'

The makers of most non-art, non-manufactured objects are called craftspeople. This title can extend beyond people making things with their hands. For example, a craftsperson can also be a lawyer crafting a contract, a mathematician creating a new equation or an actor performing on stage. These craftspeople work hard to hone their craft to be as effective as possible in achieving their goal. Good intentions aren't enough: craftspeople need knowledge, skill and experience to be great at their craft. Craftivists do too.

---

* All definitions in this chapter are courtesy of *The Concise Oxford Dictionary*, 2006.

Craft as a metaphor

Before the Arts and Crafts Movement, 'craft' was used mostly to describe shrewdness and manipulation, as in 'witchcraft'. Craft can be defined as 'skill used in deceiving others'. For example you can be 'crafty'. Our craftivism shouldn't be about manipulation but we should look to see how to use craft in activism in the most impactful way, using creative thinking, shrewdness and emotional intelligence. Craft and words relating to craft objects and activities can serve as metaphors to help us with our craftivism work. It can be useful for us as a skill in developing what the pragmatist and philosopher Richard Rorty describes as 'a hopeful, melioristic, experimental frame of mind'.[3]

Activism isn't always easy, there aren't many quick-to-win campaigns and often you can't clearly see the change you are making (see Chapter 18). We can use craft-related language to help motivate ourselves and others using tangible images for often fuzzy activism achievements. For example, we can make, thread and weave our values through all that we do. Stitch by stitch we can make a difference. Sometimes we need to unravel an unjust system before we can sew it back together and sometimes we simply need to make do and mend a situation rather than create a revolution. Injustices can be seen as messy and tangled up threads; we need to see how they are connected before we can pull them apart and see where we can untangle them. Veteran activist Aidan Ricketts uses a craft metaphor in his *Activists' Handbook* that can be a helpful message for us:

> Strategy is a key consideration in all campaign work; it is the golden thread that can stitch together the elements of a public interest issue into an effective and successful campaign.[4]

Now that we've seen how craft can be used as a noun, verb and metaphor, let's look at activism, see how it is defined and how we can translate that into our gentle protest approach to effective craftivism.

Activism: 'The policy or action of using vigorous campaigning to bring about political or social change'

Activism is taking action to change something from A to B. To create long-lasting social change we need knowledge of A and B, a thoughtful strategy to get from A to B, and the curiosity to ask why injustices are happening. Activists need to be curious; questioning where the power lies and then using the power we have to change the status quo, structures and cultures that are causing the injustice. There are lots of different tactics in activism but at its core we are focusing on the causes of injustice and how to stop them from the root up, or from as close to the root as possible.

In the charity sector we refer to three areas for tackling social injustice: emergency relief, advocacy and development. Emergency relief is providing urgent necessities to help people stay alive and stay safe such as medical supplies, food and shelter. Advocacy is about gaining public support for, or the recommendation of, a particular cause or policy to tackle injustice. That could be campaigning for a change in law globally, nationally or locally in governments or business, shifting cultures as well as changing individuals' behaviours or habits. Development focuses on working with – not for – communities to develop resources and identify actions people can take to fulfil their potential, which could be developing a healthcare structure in rural Ghana to tackle high maternal mortality, building a well in a community so people don't have to travel miles for clean water, or creating pamphlets and lesson plans in the UK for school teachers to use to tackle bullying.

Often people confuse these areas and see donation as activism. Let's use Desmond Tutu's quote at the head of this chapter as a useful tool to explain what activism is: emergency relief would be helping to pull people out of the river; activism would be going upstream to find out why they are falling in *and* coming up with a plan to change the system at play so that people don't fall in anymore. We should never stop trying to pull people out of the river but if we don't act to change the system then there will always be people who need to be pulled out. We need advocacy development and relief, but we also need to see that they are at different places in the stream.

Awareness-raising is often discussed as part of an activism narrative. Shining a spotlight on injustice can be a very useful part of an activism campaign. Raising awareness of an issue can encourage people to join a movement for change, to use their power to demand change from power-holders, and to shift the culture that causes people to fall in the river. However, we need to see it as one element of activism, one channel of activism, not activism as a whole. There are some beautiful examples of street art and handmade performance props, such as puppets or costumes, being used to raise awareness of an injustice or oppression or poverty. However, we need to be careful that our awareness-raising also encourages people into effective action to solve the injustices – or at least encourages them to question *why* these injustices are happening, rather than simply seeing that they *are* happening – and, furthermore, to disrupt the status quo. We can raise awareness of climate change but without strategies to change the situation, we might actually disempower people because we are not offering ways they can help our world go from global warming to global cooling.

And consider the suffrage movement of the early part of the twentieth century. Votes for women did not come about by awareness-raising or donations alone. Donations often helped fund and sustain many campaign actions and meetings, awareness helped keep the issue in the public sphere, but the suffragettes also had to be explicit in their protest message against women not being able to vote and have a clear ask in their campaign: a change in the law to solve the injustice.

My worry is that if we call actions of fundraising, donation or awareness-raising 'activism' then we are diluting the potential of the word activism and confusing people about what activism is and can be.

14

Worse, we are stopping people from having the courage to stand up, protest against injustice and demand change by offering them more comfortable actions to take instead. Activism can be difficult to plan, create and continue to do. It can be uncomfortable to stand above the parapet at times. It's not often glamorous. But it is vital. Malala Yousafzai isn't campaigning to ease the pain of girls around the world who have no access to education and to ask people to make toys for them. She is asking us to stand alongside her and girls across the world to campaign for change in existing structures and mindsets so that all girls will receive an education and an opportunity to fulfil their potential. What a powerful and positive movement to be part of!

Activism is practised in a variety of ways: writing letters or writing in to the comments section of a newspaper; signing petitions; shareholder activism; boycotting; holding local meetings; bringing a case to court; attending a protest march to meet with political or business leaders to bring about change; or even challenging your friend who makes racist comments to question themselves and encouraging them to stop. We don't just need to think about what activism is but what type of activism we should focus on for each campaign we take part in so that we can use our time, skills and knowledge in the most efficient way.

Effective activism

Effectiveness is doing the most good with whatever resources you have. Let's all try to make the most difference we can. Determining whether something is effective means recognising that some ways of doing good are better than others. There are so many problems in the world it's difficult to know which ones to focus on. You'll have to make some hard decisions on where to focus your time and energy and accept that you can't do it all. Associate Professor of Philosophy at Lincoln College, Oxford, William MacAskill is the founder and president of 80,000 Hours and author of *Doing Good Better: Effective Altruism and a Radical New*

Way to Make a Difference. He recommends five key questions that can help us with our activism. I find them really useful:

1. How many people benefit, and by how much?
2. Is this the most effective thing you can do?
3. Is this area neglected?
4. What would have happened otherwise?
5. What are the chances of success and how good would success be?

We also need to make sure we are doing our activism ethically. Injustices affect some people directly in harmful ways and so we have to be very sensitive and emotionally intelligent when tackling the issues so that we are not adding to their pain or shame. We should make sure we are in solidarity with those affected by injustice so that people don't feel judged or pitied but supported. Lilla Watson, activist, academic and artist, says that the following quote is a collective belief born from the activist groups she was a part of: 'If you have come here to help me, you are wasting your time. But if you have come because your liberation is bound up with mine, then let us work together.'

Growing up in Everton I saw people coming in with big hearts who wanted to help tackle the problems in our area; from poverty, bad health and bad housing to the increasing gang culture and drugs problems. They offered clothing, bedding and other relief but sadly would not often make time to find out *why* our community struggled with these issues and how to work *with* us to fix the system upstream so more people did not fall into poverty or other problems. It's easy to support a cause when there's nothing on the line, but what if you actually had to sacrifice something in order to support the cause? That is what support means: to bear the weight of something.

For us in Everton we didn't want pity or to be patronised. We wanted people to join us in campaigning effectively to the local council and government for a health centre, better housing, less discrimination and education to help us get ourselves out of poverty so that we didn't need hand-outs. We saved and improved local housing with the help of lawyers, politicians, journalists, religious leaders, local people typing up minutes of meetings, people taking shifts squatting to save good local houses from demolition,* and people who made great cups of tea. For a community in rural Kenya, support might be in the shape of UK citizens campaigning to their prime minister and other citizens campaigning to their world leader to cancel the international debt that is crippling countries in the developing world so that the Kenyan government can then use that money to pay for free education for all and free maternal healthcare. For children working in sweatshops in Bangladesh, support might mean UK citizens pressuring the clothing companies they work for to clean up their production processes. You will see throughout this book how to use craft in your activism in effective ways.

My approach to craftivism

When we see injustice it's often difficult to look away towards the more wonderful world we want to live in. We see atrocities and our whole being wants to fix it and feels bad for looking away. But the world is how it is because people envisioned it.

Visualisation is a powerful tool, and craftivism should start with envisioning the sort of world we want to live in. Doing this first will help alert you to the opportunities that exist to achieve it. With a goal in focus, subconsciously your brain sets off a 'search pattern' in your mind that will look for opportunities to bring your vision to reality. Being angry at injustice is a good thing. It can spur us into action but chronic

---

* If you're interested, the proposal to demolish the buildings was in order to create a larger park that no one wanted, would have made the area more unsafe and would have separated families from each other. We won and the houses still exist.

anger can lead to burn-out or inaction because your brain focuses on the injustices rather than striving for the possible solutions. Focus on the world you want to help craft, not the one you want to eliminate. This not only will inspire and empower you but envisioning a better world inspires and empowers others to join in and commit to our campaigns. It's more attractive and powerful for you and others to share dreams not complaints and it's more sustainable and joyful. Martin Luther King did not say, 'I have a complaint'. He said, 'I have a dream', and went on to share with us the details of that dream so we could all visualise and strive for it.

Craft is our tool for activism not our taskmaster. We focus on long-term transformation not quick short-term transactions of relief. Our approach to craftivism focuses on handicrafts that use slow, repetitive hand actions so that we can also use the act of crafting to meditate and think critically about the social injustice we are tackling and the strategy we need to overcome it. Using craft materials that are small, delicate and soft creates a comforting space, which helps us to ask ourselves and others uncomfortable questions about how to tackle injustice issues. There may be elements of the methodology shared in this book that can be transferred to other craft activities and objects but in my experience hand-embroidery and paper crafts are the most effective ways to enable all or most of the strengths of craftivism to appear.

Strategic thinking needs to saturate every aspect of our craftivism practice. It is all very well having a good cause, good information and good intentions, but to be effective craftivists we need to coordinate all of this into an effective strategy. To conceive and effectively implement a deliberate strategy requires considerable forethought and planning and necessitates a real understanding of what strategy entails. There are, unfortunately, not normally two simple sides to a campaign. It's often a complex web of people and needs different supporters or activities at different times to influence different elements of the change we are striving for. Sometimes we need to focus on mobilising and influencing public opinion, sometimes we need to focus on publicly challenging societal attitudes or behaviours, sometimes we need to engage quietly with power-holders one-to-one or in small groups, and we always need to anticipate and possibly counter opposing reactions.

We need to see our craftivism tools, craftivism methods and project objects as part of the activism toolkit, not to replace other forms but to be used where they can be most effective and needed. We need to be led more by our passion for positive change in the world than our love of craft, and we need to work critically to be as effective as possible in our craftivism so as not to create harm.

Like any activism, our approach to craftivism does not guarantee success; some elements will impact some people more than others and vice versa. Your hard work may not win over everyone but knowing that each project has been planned, strategised, critiqued, honed, seen as a piece of the jigsaw complementing other actions rather than trying to solve the problem alone, means it is more likely that you will be effective. Where we live shapes our work, so be aware of this when reading and transferring the skills learnt into your own environment.

Good intentions are only the start

There are times when craftivism will not be the right approach for your campaign, or not the right approach at a particular time. Strategic consideration is needed for when to use craftivism and when not to. Our craftivism work should always be rooted in principles of love, respect, solidarity, collaboration and forgiveness, not for combat, shaming or selfishness. Our craftivism should always stand up against injustice but also work with stakeholders to find and promote solutions as well. And we should never lose our vision for a world that can sustain itself, where everyone can fulfil their potential and live in harmony. Our approach to craftivism should be built on foundations of gentle protest.

DEFINITIONS

Now you're done with the tough bit! I hope you're ready to get started and see how you, your craft materials and your crafty thoughts can help to change the world for the better.

2
Gentle Protest

Our greatest strength lies in the gentleness and tenderness of
our heart.

— Rumi

There are brilliant things about our world and there are also things we
should protest against. But it's often not easy. I was in South Africa in
1991 for a few weeks with my family and I attended a local school for
a day as part of the trip. Mandela had been freed from prison the year
before and apartheid had officially ended. It was a time of transition
for everyone. I was eight years old. In the afternoon the teacher asked a
question. I put my hand up. A fellow classmate had her hand up before
me – quite a few seconds before me. The teacher ignored her and asked
me for my answer. I looked at my classmate then my teacher, and said,
confused, 'Her hand was up first, Miss.' The teacher replied aggressively,

'What is your answer?' I gave my answer and the lesson carried on. I vividly remember feeling a strong sense of injustice. For the rest of the day (and even now) I felt embarrassed that I didn't do anything to protest. I didn't know what to do. I couldn't shout at the teacher; I couldn't tell her off. I was eight! I knew it was wrong that the teacher was discriminating against some of my peers in the classroom because of the colour of their skin. We fuel inequality when we don't protest against situations like this one. My protest wouldn't have fixed the systemic issue but injustice shouldn't continue because we don't know how to protest effectively. I wish I had known a gentle way to protest against the teacher's action.

Many people are turned off by political protests. Tactics of aggression, confrontation, shaming, bullying, demonising and violence (threats, physical and emotional violence) can be used in protests to intimidate, terrorise and undermine people.

Sadly, violent protests are often what people see in the media, even when the majority of protests are mostly peaceful. No wonder I hear from craftivists and others around the world who feel they can't protest because they don't want to be abusive, they don't want to upset people or be judgemental. Quiet, shy or introverted craftivists tell me that protesting is a big and uncomfortable leap for them because they don't feel confident about speaking in public. I tell them that you don't need public speaking to protest. You don't need to be loud. We need to stop seeing protest as only being about shouting in a crowd and start having the kind of smaller conversations that actually connect to fellow human beings, and help to influence them gently.

'Gentle protest' sounds like an oxymoron. Gentleness brings to mind something soft and mild. 'Gentle protest' sounds attractive but also hopelessly naive and idealistic. But in fact, protesting gently can be hugely effective. Nelson Mandela went to jail believing in violence as a successful agent for change. Twenty-seven years later, he and others had slowly and carefully honed their skills in non-violence to turn one of the most vicious and prejudiced governments in the world into a democracy working *with* those who had oppressed them.

Throughout history, gentleness has threaded through many effective campaigns for social change and I believe that to be effective social changemakers, we craftivists should focus on honing our craft of craftivism specifically in the art of gentle protest.

Protest

The negative connotation of the word 'protest' is sadly inevitable. Even when protests present their argument in a positive form, e.g. environmentalists seeking to preserve forests, they are often portrayed by the media and others as 'anti-logging' rather than 'pro-forest'. It can be frustrating that doing good is framed as anti-bad. It just doesn't sound as attractive, does it? However, to reach our goal of a better world, we need to protest against the systems causing the injustice, not just focus on the vision of the world we want. We have to show our disapproval of and objection to the actions, power systems or mindsets that allow injustice to continue. Acknowledging why injustice is happening helps us learn what to do in response and shines a spotlight on the problems so that everyone knows what to avoid and we don't slip back into the injustice.

I don't enjoy protesting. Most people don't. It's scary speaking out against someone or something. When the injustice is part of the status quo, it's easier to remain silent when the majority of people are also silent.

It can also be dangerous to protest at times. It can feel harder to protest against friends or groups we admire than someone we dislike. My default thought is to hope someone else nearby is willing to stand up and speak out against harm happening so I don't have to. However, when we see or hear something that fuels injustice we have a responsibility to challenge it and keep challenging it until it's clear that the actions are wrong and shouldn't happen, whether that's sexism, racism or tax avoidance. I hope one day that we don't have to protest. But until that day comes, we should not shy away from protesting against harmful actions. We need to stop the tides of injustice continuing.

Protests are an important part of the activism toolkit. They can be delivered in many different ways and on different scales: public meetings, rallies, marches, occupations, and blockades, as well as private meetings, spontaneous conversations and many more ways in which you can share your protest. The unifying factor is that they are protesting against something. Protests, unlike rallies, don't always have to be supported by large numbers of people. There are numerous examples of effective one-person protests – Rosa Parks sitting down on the bus in the American Civil Rights campaign – or small group protests – two people protesting against being sued by McDonald's for libel for distributing fact sheets that made several allegations against the company. Protests can happen on private or on public property such as corporate offices, shareholder meetings, parks, as well as online. A protest can be a group of people speaking out against an entire government or a business on the high street. Or protest can be at a dinner party when the person next to you says a harmful comment and you quietly challenge their words and talk through the need for a change on the issue. Protest is a vital part of improving our world. However, it's worth pointing out two types of activism that can be detrimental in achieving the results you want.

Angry activism

Before I figured out how to protest gently and effectively, I would get so angry and then become emotionally exhausted. Seeing injustice happen, locally or globally, should make us feel angry and want to stand up against it. Anger is one of the strongest emotions we have and it can give us courage to take action. But reacting in anger isn't always effective if we don't take the time to channel that anger into a wiser strategy. Despite our good intentions, unless we invest time in research, our angry activism can lead to trouble. Quick outbursts can create confrontation and conflict.

I can understand how people's anger can turn violent. We can feed off other protesters' emotions and energy and then release it through shouting disrespectful messages or acting violently against a person or property. Aggression triggers the fight-or-flight response in both parties – not a safe space for communication and collaboration. But if we are asking people to treat others and our planet with respect, then isn't it contradictory to do it in an aggressive way?

Angry actions can put people off from joining your cause because, often without realising, you are intimidating them. People may see a tired, unhappy, unloving and busy activist who they don't want to become or to engage with. My anger at injustice was eating away at me and no one wants to join a campaign where those involved look exhausted and depressed. We know from an early age that if we want long-term support we need to encourage people to work with us, not bully them into submission. No one likes being told what to do. So why, when it comes to activism, do we often try to impose our will upon others, order them around, or even bully them?

Robotic activism

My response to seeing injustice wasn't to use physical violence, it was to sign lots of petitions, host lots of stalls, go on lots of marches – a scattered approach to activism, rather than a focused one. Without realising, I turned myself into an activist robot. Of course we should sometimes act fast against injustice. If a government is trying to slip in a law without the public knowing then we quickly need to shine a spotlight on it so that people are aware and can challenge it. The quickest way to do this is by signing a petition or grabbing media attention through a stunt. However, there were so many injustices in the world I cared deeply about, it was hard to choose which to ignore and which to prioritise. I wanted to help and so I would go to lots of meetings, chair some of them, write up the minutes for others, plan events and stunts, write and send press releases. I struggled to keep on top of the many email petitions from different organisations titled 'Urgent: we need your support' or 'Stop this law being passed NOW', but I also struggled to ignore them. They were so demanding and it was overwhelming.

To cope, I often became numb to the issues so that I could get as much done as possible without feeling emotionally drained or starting to think too much. It was easier to do lots of quick transactions rather than think through what were the root causes of this injustice and what would be the best use of my time. I felt that I was showing my solidarity with those affected, and I didn't have to slow down and think about whether what I was doing was strategic: that required asking myself potentially uncomfortable questions. Maybe I was wearing my busyness as a badge of honour, or using it as if to say, 'Look I'm so busy saving the world, I don't have time to think!'

Not only had I turned into an activist robot, I became worried that I was treating other people as robots too. For example, I would focus on getting as many signatures on a petition as possible. If people asked me for more information, I didn't see that as a great opportunity to discuss the issue with them and help them engage more deeply with the campaign, I saw it as a waste of time that I could be using to get more signatures. I wasn't encouraging people to think through the reasons why these injustices were happening, and how we could try to be part of the solution to the problem in different ways. In my heart, it didn't sit right that the action I was asking people to do – sign a petition – was so easy because I knew that the easier something is, the less likely we are to reflect on it, take ownership of it, or even remember it! I began doubting my effectiveness as an activist. I was wondering whether people truly cared about the petition they had signed, and the small level of commitment involved made me question whether customers or constituents would see the issue as something that would affect their consumer or voting choices.

Uncomfortable with angry activism, and having become burnt-out by robotic activism, I began to see that the most effective way to protest is gently. Let me explain what I mean by gentleness before I explain what I mean by the art of gentle protest.

Gentleness

Gentleness can describe the character of an individual or group. Positive descriptions for a gentle temperament include being kind, open-hearted, modest, calm, peaceful, good-natured and loving. Gentle traits aren't necessarily to do with being shy, quiet or unconfident: extroverts and people who often act loudly can share these aspects too. Extroverts get their energy from being around other people, while introverts get their energy from being by themselves. Gentle can mean demure and graceful but it can also be used to describe someone as passive or submissive, someone who doesn't engage with their own opinion, thought or action. In this book we are focusing on three specific positive characteristics of gentleness, not the negative interpretations.

A gentle approach to life is an active one – it's not about being passive and letting the world go by. To engage with people gently is to be thoughtful about your actions, consider carefully the most effective approach to each situation and keep an eye on the details so nothing is neglected or rushed. Practising self-control is important in gentle activism. For example, it might be that you've noticed you need to control outbursts in a particular situation and discipline yourself to be quieter, to show respect for others. When you see an atrocity happen, you might need to move from shock and confusion to using empathy to understand the situation and work out how to respond to it in the best, most effective way. In the case of craftivists, approaching injustice with aggressive anger is unhelpful for our protest. A more effective way to protest is through compassion and empathy for all involved: the victim, perpetrators and everyone in the process, recognising that human beings are fragile and should be handled with care.

A second gentle approach to protest uses emotional intelligence to engage with others effectively. In his book *Emotional Intelligence: Why It Can Matter More Than IQ*, psychologist Dr Daniel Goleman wrote:

> Those who are at the mercy of impulse – who lack self-control – suffer a moral deficiency: the ability to control impulse is the base of will and character. By the same token, the root of altruism lies in empathy, the ability to read emotions in others; lacking a sense of another's need or despair, there is no caring. And if there are any two moral stances that our times call for, they are precisely these, self-restraint and compassion.[1]

To be emotionally intelligent in our actions is a skill that requires willpower, discipline and commitment. It's not enough to learn emotional intelligence, we have to practise it, and take responsibility for our approach.

One unusual but useful way of describing gentleness comes from the philosopher Aristotle. In *The Nicomachean Ethics*, Aristotle's philosophical enquiry into virtue, character and the good life, he challenges us to manage our emotional life with intelligence. With this in mind he explains gentleness as a compromise between excessive anger and excessive indifference. A gentle approach doesn't reject anger but asks us to use it appropriately. We shouldn't be angry when it's inappropriate and unhelpful, but it would be wrong not to be angry (in the right, controlled way) if that is the most helpful and appropriate approach for the situation:

> Anybody can be angry – that is easy, but to be angry with the right person and to the right degree and at the right time and for the right purpose, and in the right way – that is not within everybody's power and is not easy.

I agree with Aristotle that an appropriate anger is difficult and doesn't always come naturally, but most of us can do it if we see gentleness as a skill to practise, a craft to hone.

A third way I want to use the word 'gentle' is to describe how we use the power we have. Protests are usually against the abuse of, or unequal distribution of, power. Where we have opportunity, ability or capacity to do something, our power is in the way we choose to act. Sometimes we have lots of power, sometimes we have only a small amount, but we always have some. How we use our power positively to influence people or events is what we are addressing here.

The nature of power can be defined as a person's (or organisation's) ability to get the job done. But in our culture it's often bound up with notions of force and aggression that sometimes spill over into abuse. As activists, we can try to force, manipulate, abuse or use intimidation tactics to make something happen or we can move towards a more gentle and effective approach to power: to support, nurture and encourage change through others, through collaboration and cooperation, education, discussion or persuasion. Being gentle in the way we use power can lift people up to take the action that is needed. Sometimes it's more effective to find a gentle way to help other people deliver the change we need in the world to fix the causes of injustice than trying to do it all ourselves.

Empowering other people requires humility. It upends and overturns all the power plays that have hurt us and others and that fuel cynicism. Being humble in heart stops you from fighting for power with an 'opponent'. Humility helps you resist trying to win arguments. Humility helps you listen to people you disagree with and see where they are coming from without having to agree or disagree with them. Humility helps you let your opponent take action without acknowledging your influence and without taking ownership of their decision, which in the long run can be more effective. Humility helps you see what's best for the situation, not what's best for yourself.

Using power gently moves you from the habit of thinking you need to be a leader to becoming a facilitator and friend, working with people to get things done together carefully, respectfully and lovingly, where possible. Sometimes, of course, the person or people won't budge and it is not possible to work with them. Then other strategies are needed.

The art of gentle protest

I believe that the most effective way to be a craftivist is through the art of gentle protest. It's a way that we can – alone or in a group – effectively protest against harmful structures, attract people to protest, and reflect on the way we want our world to be, challenging injustice and harm through values of love, kindness and humility. A gentle protest approach is in line with our goal of doing activism in a beautiful, kind and fair way that models the world we want to live in.

There is a place for disagreement and it's often unavoidable, even using our 'gentle protest' approach. Sometimes there's a deliberate need to generate some disagreement to bring some issues to the public. Some of the great religious and political figures of history have been protesters and human progress owes much to their effort, and the effort of the many we do not know of. We need to be careful to be a gentle protester not a rebel. 'The rebel' tends to be unreceptive, rigid and unwilling to listen. The art of gentle protest requires you don't maintain conflict but you focus on a path towards resolution. The value of conflict is the opportunity it creates for debate, discussion and exploring new approaches; it is rarely constructive on its own. Scilla Elworthy, three-time Nobel Peace Prize nominee and a recipient of the Niwano Peace Prize, said:

At the beginning, I was so outraged at the dangers they were exposing us to that I just wanted to argue and blame them and make them wrong. Totally ineffective. In order to develop a dialogue for change, we have to deal with our anger. It's OK to be angry with things (such as the nuclear weapons) but it is hopeless to be angry with people. They are human beings too just like the rest of us and they are doing what they think is right. And that's the basis we have to talk with them.[2]

Violence is not only inhumane; it also can be ineffective. It is always worth remembering to treat people how you would like to be treated – with dignity and respect – whether they are the oppressor or oppressed. It's easy to take the moral high ground if we're not the ones making the decision. Our craftivism can help us protest gently and effectively against actions, not people; policies not personalities. It can create opportunities to open our own hearts and see where we fit into the injustice and whether we need to confront our own presumptions or practices as well as protest against other people's actions and the parts they play in systems of injustice. If we protest gently, we can help create community rather than conflict. Through craftivism, we can overcome barriers and borders and create honest connection where there was isolation.

Sometimes our protests using craftivism are direct, sometimes they are more subtle, but they should always be created to engage all involved with kindness, decency and thoughtfulness. For example, when we do something that is harmful or thoughtless, and someone close to us says, 'I'm not angry, I'm just disappointed,' their words are powerful. It sinks into our heart and mind much more than when someone shouts at us – because what they are saying is that they love us, believe that we can do better, and that we know better than to repeat our mistakes. That's the gentle approach I'm talking about, one where we show love and we value someone, and believe that everyone can make the world a better place. We want to support people to be their best selves, helping not harming others. This requires us to be hopeful and open-minded. We shouldn't assume that a businessperson will 'only be interested in the money'. We should probe to uncover a broader range of values in a person. Gentle protest is not about condemning the things people have done in the past but opening up conversation to see how we can all work towards creating a better future. This is what the anti-apartheid movement achieved: oppressed people forgave and worked with their oppressors for peace and reconciliation. Both sides knew it was the only way for long-lasting change. The process was not about making sure people knew they were wrong but about people knowing they were valued and cared about; not about proving who was right or pointing out people's faults, but seeing how they could be helped to acknowledge and fix the injustice; not putting forward a robust argument but building a relationship so that everyone could change the situation together.

A gentle protest approach to craftivism will work differently for different people in different situations. Sometimes what's best for one person is not best for another. Sometimes it might be best to use your craftivism to offer a solution, other times it's better to encourage and help people find solutions themselves. For one person a quiet chat might be most appropriate, whereas a bold but gentle confrontation might work best for someone else. The impact can be different for everyone.

With a gentle approach to protest threaded through all of our craftivism work we will focus on what is causing injustice and how we can help to fix it to stop more people and our planet being harmed. In our planning and in our crafting we can use our craftivism as a tool calmly and carefully to reflect on and understand the injustice issue more, empathise with all those involved, and work out how to engage with those with the power to change it in an emotionally intelligent way. These questions are not always welcome but our intriguing, fragile and attractive craftivism objects can help our protest become a gentle and effective one.

Be gentle until the end. When people are being unkind to you, stay gentle with them. When you are being provoked to react, don't react. When you are asked something by someone with the intention to trap or trip you up, be wise and maybe stay silent.

You have power – learn how to use it

If I could go back in time to the classroom in South Africa, I would go up to the teacher after class calmly and ask respectfully but in a confused tone why I was asked to answer the question and the other student was not (maybe she asked me because I was a guest, but the tone and body language didn't suggest that). I hope I would have been able to show my protest against racism but also understand that a mixed school was a new situation for her and her students. I hope I would be able to protest in a gentle, loving way to challenge my teacher without her feeling I was competing for power or judging her. I wish I had known there was a gentler way to protest against racism in that classroom.

When learning of the different gentle ways we can protest against injustice using craftivism, we can see ourselves like a beautiful horse in its prime. We are not wild dogs led by our emotions, barking in anger and showing sharp teeth to anyone who looks. A well-trained, elegant horse knows how to use their power. Sometimes they carry people towards justice on their back, sometimes they lead the way, and sometimes they are led by others. Sometimes they work the land unglamorously, pulling the heavy plough, sometimes they courageously take a leap over a barrier to reach their goal. Whatever they do, they do it with elegance and controlled strength.

PART II

Power in the Process

3
Slow Activism

Slow but steady wins the race.

— Aesop

'Don't forget to be the tortoise. Breathe. Slow down.'

That's what I often say at workshops I deliver. From New York to Norway, slowing down seems to be the first challenge for people at my workshops. People start things in the wrong order because they skip the instructions. They're surprised when embroidery thread breaks after being separated too forcefully. You can feel the frustration in the room when it takes makers more than three times to thread their needle successfully. But my approach to craftivism needs time and a steady hand to tackle injustice with care, thoughtfulness and sensitivity. You can't rush these things. You've got to slow down.

It's not surprising people struggle. I struggle. Perhaps you do too, at times. We live in such a fast-paced world, trying to keep up with our emails, the news, trends, our social-media streams, our friends, wherever they may be. It's exhausting just thinking about it. But channelling your inner tortoise is a vital part of how to be an effective craftivist. Strategic planning, creative thinking and building relationships all take time and, if rushed, are impossible to fulfil. Craftivism (and activism) needs all these things: slowness is vital. A slow pace should be threaded through all of your craftivism work so that it is produced with care, courage and consideration.

Fast-paced world

It's harder than it sounds. We live in a world where the average attention span of an adult has gone from twelve seconds in the year 2000 to eight seconds in 2015. We have less concentration than a goldfish! Mobile phones have transformed the way many of us live. The average person spends more time each day looking at their devices than sleeping. Our culture seems to admire people more who are, or just look, busy.

For many, work absorbs most of our waking hours, with life fitted in around our schedules. Modern technology was supposed to mean we could work less but...oops, we are working more. How do we find time to rest, see family and friends, exercise, eat well, have a hobby, never mind find time to squeeze in campaigning to improve our world? It can feel impossible. In our culture time is often seen as money and deadlines rule our lives. I'm not saying that deadlines aren't good – they can focus our minds and give us drive to perform great things. But we can only do this short-term: many of us feel stuck in a bottomless pit of permanent deadlines and it's rewiring how we live. We treat time like another commodity and sometimes even feel we need to justify how we are spending our free time.

The free time we do find is often interrupted by FOMO (fear of missing out) so we fill it with socialising, weekend trips, courses, cultural events, or bingeing on box sets. Some even Instagram a picture of themselves chilling out and reading a book instead of just reading it – I've been guilty of that!

Always being connected and busy can lead to depression and chronic fatigue. Slow activities like walking, meditation, yoga, gardening and handicrafts are increasingly prescribed by psychologists, therapists and even business consultants to promote health and well-being.

If you never stop doing, you will never recharge your batteries. A fast-paced life stops us functioning to the best of our abilities: concentration starts to wander, information struggles to sink in and, ironically, things then take longer than they should. You lose your temper more easily. The joy dissolves and everything feels like a chore. This fast-paced living is taking its toll on our health, community and society.

Carl Honoré, one of the world's most respected advocates of the Slow Movement, wrote in his book *In Praise of Slow*:

> The recession is a jolting reminder that the way we have been living is unsustainable. The pursuit of fast growth, fast profit and fast consumption has brought the world to its knees. It has made us unhappy and unhealthy. [...] More and more of us are coming around to the idea that we need to reinvent the way we run our economies and societies from the ground up. Slowing down will be a big part of that change.[1]

The Slow Movement

The Slow Movement started as a protest. In 1986, Carlo Petrini began protesting against the opening of the fast-food chain McDonald's near the Spanish Steps in Rome, sparking the creation of the Slow Food Movement, opposed to the fast-food culture, and encouraging the use of regional, organic produce and preserving traditional foods.

At the core of the Slow Movement is the philosophy of wanting to do well and to do good. Quality is the priority, not quantity; sustainability, not speed; ethically produced, not cheaply made. It is a celebration of the time, energy and care that has gone into each product or action. There are slow movements in fashion, childcare, gardening, even photography and science. Surely we should apply this approach to more aspects of our life?

Research shows that overwork is the enemy of efficiency, productivity and creativity; the Slow Movement not only helps individuals live a healthier and more enjoyable life, but also helps communities create effective, ethical and attractive models of living. It's not about doing everything at a snail's pace; instead, it's about making time to reflect and to think critically about the pace we need to go at to do everything as well as possible, rather than as fast as possible. From travelling to cooking, the movement gently protests against a culture of speed, size and surplus. The Slow Movement challenges the notion that if we want to hang on to our jobs, stay relevant, and be valued, then we need to speed up. Each slow action gently asks us to stop multitasking, slow down, do less, buy less, drive less, unplug more, walk more, sleep more. Meditate, pray or do yoga. The movement is gently and quietly encouraging people to take a look, have a think, and to join in when they are ready on their own terms. I wanted slow activism to do the same.

So why, when it comes to campaigning for a healthier, happier and fairer world for all, is much of our activism planning and response rushed when injustices are often complicated and tangled up in many areas of life? Surely in times of urgency we need to slow down so that we can come up with the most robust plan for our protest?

As previously mentioned, I was a burnt-out activist a few years ago. There are lots of reasons why many traditional forms of activism drained me but one big reason was that I was doing too much too fast. I just didn't stop or slow down. I craved a form of 'slow activism'. I was searching for slow activists or slow-activism techniques to learn from, but I couldn't find any.

Crafting slowly

One day in the spring of 2008, I took a long train journey. I was working on a project funded by the UK Department for International Development enabling 5,000 eighteen- to twenty-four-year-olds to go overseas for ten weeks to a Lower Income Country in the global south to help alleviate poverty. It was an amazing job. I loved working with organisations to recruit young people who would benefit from the project. I enjoyed preparing them for their trips, and teaching them about how development programmes can help people get themselves out of poverty. I loved supporting these volunteers after their trip to express their experience in their own creative ways once they were back in their own communities and were trying to engage more people in social justice. What I didn't love were the long hours and travel needed to do my job. I would try to work on the train but would feel travel-sick reading, writing or typing.

I was looking around a shop one weekend when I spotted a small square cross-stitch kit. I missed painting and using my hands to make things. The kit was small, affordable, and fitted in my pocket. I decided to take it on my next train journey.

I had never done cross-stitch before. Immediately, I needed to slow down because I had to read the instructions so that I didn't mess up. It required my hands and head to work together in a way I hadn't asked them to for a long time. I had to cut the thread to a particular length (the length from my index finger to my shoulder) so that it wasn't too long and wouldn't get tangled up. But I also had to cut it so that it wasn't too short or I would be giving myself extra work rethreading the needle. I learnt that embroidery thread is different to thread for a sewing machine. You get six strands of thread in each embroidery floss, and you choose, or are told by the instructions in the kit, to use the optimum amount of strands that complement your design and size. I had to separate my thread into two groups of three strands. The first time I separated the thread it felt like it took hours because I was so used to doing everything at speed. I needed to give it my full attention and watch the thread separate, and I had to make sure it wasn't attached to anything that might cause a knot. I had to let the thread unravel at its own pace. I naturally slowed down to count the number of crosses to stitch and to count the grid pattern on the fabric to see where to start the stitches. I had to make sure that I didn't pull the thread so tight that the stitches bunched up and warped the design. I am faster now, but hand embroidery cannot be too rushed or even the most experienced and skilled person will make mistakes.

The craft kit was accessible for beginners like me but it wasn't so easy to do that I couldn't be proud of my efforts; with every stitch created, realisation dawned. I had been looking to incorporate what I had learnt about the Slow Movement into my activism. I wanted to join this growing movement and teach others how it could inform and enhance activism. I realised that stitching could be the tool I was looking for to help me develop the form of slow activism that I was craving.

Keep your head

I don't think craftivism as a form of 'slow activism' should replace 'fast' activism. We will always need rapid responses and we should take part in them. However, many social injustices that are deeply ingrained in our culture demand a more complex, long-term and multi-faceted solution. The entrenched causes of systematic or cultural harms need to be identified, and take time, thought and a clever strategy before they are changed. When our work is about improving the world for everyone and protecting it from harm, then it's important we get the campaigning right. We also need to slow down so that we can keep our heads when many around us may be losing theirs. No one gets it completely right. As craftivists we should be kind to ourselves, and do one thing at a time. We should embed slow moments and rituals into our schedule, and prioritise face-to-face time with people so that we connect more meaningfully. Slowing down helps us feel energised and more ready to demand a better world for all.

Remember who won the race between the tortoise and the hare...

The tortoise, unlike the hare, won by moving forward one step at a time, never giving up and never being distracted from his goal. You can't do mindfulness quickly. So hold that image of the tortoise as we go into the next chapter where I explain the importance of being a mindful craftivist.

4
Mindful Activism

An unexamined life is not worth living.

– Socrates

Jess was a craftivist. I had met her in her home town of Stockholm at an event where I was interviewed by Swedish journalist Frida Engström. Jess sat on the front row with a large piece of fabric she was working on. After the event, I asked Jess what she had been stitching. She showed me her banner. It said in Swedish 'The Swedish Democrats is a racist party'. She was going to put it in the centre of a square near her home where a racist group regularly met. And then Jess told me, in no uncertain terms:

> I don't agree with your craftivism. We need to be angry. We need to fight against hateful people. We need to shout loudly that

injustice is happening. We need to grab people's attention: so our craftivism banners should be big and angry.

I admitted that I do often question my methods when there is so much harm happening in the world and I asked her what she hoped the banner would achieve. She said she wasn't sure but someone needed to stand up against racism. Had she put herself in her target audience's shoes to imagine the response it would create? I asked. She went quiet, then said:

I'm angry and tired...I can't work because of health problems and craft is one of the few things I can do; so I want to use my craft for good. But I'm worried that I'm not being a good role model for my child because she just sees my anger and hate and exhaustion at fighting the world's problems...I have to find another way to be a craftivist.

She told me that she had already booked in to one of my evening workshops the following week and then asked if she could also book in a one-to-one Wellmaking Clinic session (see p. 285) to talk through her craftivism plans and how she could improve on them. Jess remained sceptical of the effectiveness of some of my gentle methods but we both agreed that we would see if the workshop and session might be of some help to her and her work, as well as to my own.

After the sessions Jess emailed me to say:

During your craftivism workshop I noticed the unhealthy amount of anger I was bringing to my craftivism work. I thought about how standing on the barricades shouting at injustices not only made me angry and tired, but also that hate only brings more hate. Since our last meeting I've felt a bit afraid that my concerns about doing things in the best way possible may stop me from doing them at all. I guess I just want to feel that I'm actually making some sort of change in the world, not just making pretty things and spreading them around for fame and glory. It comes down to the patience again, I guess. Be the tortoise! I am very grateful for your help in becoming more self-aware so I don't burn out and so I can challenge myself to be a better craftivist. This gentle approach to craftivism has made me a peaceful and happy activist and a better role model for my child, teaching her a good way to change the world.

Mindful of our baggage

We all bring personal baggage to situations. Mindfulness helps us to pay attention to the baggage and assumptions we have. We can use the repetitive and meditative nature of craft to notice what feelings and thoughts we are threading through the craftivism project we are making.

Ellen J. Langer, Harvard Professor of Psychology and author of the book *Mindfulness*, writes: 'When you're mindless the past is over-determining the present. You're trapped in a rigid perspective, oblivious to alternative perspectives.'[1]

In the sense in which I am using the word, mindfulness is a form of discovery and insight about ourselves, without judgement. My favourite explanation of mindfulness is to imagine our brains are like snow globes. When we are on autopilot, anxious or stressed, our brains end up like a shaken snow globe with snowflakes everywhere. You can't see where you are, or where you are headed. Mindfulness is being aware of what is happening around you, the blizzard of snow, not trying to think your way out of it but giving time and space for clarity and calm to descend so the snow can settle and you can then see what is important and what may be clouding your judgement.

Mindful of our motivations

What is the main motivation for our craftivism? Love of craft or a passion for justice? Is our goal to be celebrated for saving people from their struggles or is our motivation to be in solidarity with those directly affected by injustice? As craftivists we need to be mindful of how we are framing our own craftivism projects to ourselves, or offering the craftivism project to others. Are you asking people to get involved by encouraging them to be kind and stand up for equality for all, or are you saying that they can join a cool group to save the world? These small differences in language can have a big effect. You might end up with more people wanting to get involved if you push the personal rewards they will receive but in the long term that can be unhelpful in our goal of a more kind and fairer world for all.

When we are campaigning on behalf of people directly affected by poverty or human rights injustices, we have to be mindful of the impact we can have, for good or ill. We need to set aside our own baggage when dealing with people and social injustices: pitying people is patronising, stigmatising injustices is judgemental, and neither are useful when trying to help. Instead, we should work with others in support and mutual respect. 'We' are not saving 'them' – we all are seeking liberation together.

Mindful of our emotional tendencies

In so many ways we have achieved so much as a human race. But when it comes to emotional development, our primitive selves are often still in charge. Do you know what emotional tendencies you have? We all have them, they can change and it's not a weakness to acknowledge what they can be, it's a strength. Are you too embarrassed to try projects in case they turn out badly? Do you hate confrontation and so avoid challenging friends if they say or do something harmful to others? Are you crippled by doubt or cynicism when it comes to being the change you wish to see in the world? Our emotions can lead to self-fulfilling prophecies, so it's worth paying attention to them. It's helpful, before we start crafting, to be aware of the emotions that will effect our planning and the process of our craftivism.

Craft can be a soothing tool to help us connect with our emotions rather than distract ourselves from them. An American degree student discovered during one of our workshops that: 'Working slowly helped calm my anxious thoughts.'

But craft isn't always easy, and can be just as frustrating as it is calming at times. Its difficulties can tell us a lot about our emotional tendencies. If we stitch fast and rough then our fabric may become bunched up rather than flat – it may be that we need to learn patience. If we want to scream on our fifth attempt at threading our needle, we may need to work on our anger management. If we spend too much time looking at the work of other craftivists next to us in a room or online then we may need to acknowledge our competitive side. If our natural tendency is to give up after making a mistake, or if we are determined to 'beat' the project and finish it too quickly, that will show in our crafting. Use some of your making activity to notice the emotions you are putting into your craftivism work. As one craftivist noticed during one of my workshops: 'Concentration is a lot harder than it seems.'

Mindful of our presumptions

Expert opinion repeatedly states that household budgets are not comparable to government budget. Personal debt is different to state debt. From Nobel Prize-winner Paul Krugman to Cambridge University's world-renowned Dr Ha-Joon Chang, the vast majority of university-taught economists regularly remind the media that comparing household budgets to government budgets demonstrates a fundamental misunderstanding of the subject. But to me that just doesn't seem to make sense! Money is money. I have to remind myself regularly that my gut instinct here is wrong.

We might presume that in order to fix a particular injustice there is a clear answer or action to take, but we might be wrong. Are you correct in who you think is the main person causing the injustice, or could it be someone else? You might be convinced that you have no involvement in a particular injustice but you may find that your pension, for example, is funding the systemic problem. Should we fight fire with fire or is there a gentler way to solve the problem? Is bigger always best? Is loud always better than quiet? It's not always clear what the solutions are, and they are often different for different situations.

These questions and more need to be reflected on (see next chapter) and critiqued, but first of all we need to be mindful of our thinking, aware of whether we are genuinely questioning or if we are on autopilot. I sometimes darn a friend's jumper to help me think through my craftivism project planning; the repetitive hand actions help my thinking.

Mindful of our physical selves

Activism has a habit of burning people out. It can be hard physical work protesting, and it can be easy to let yourself become very emotionally caught up in the injustices. We need to keep protesting but not by being mindless robots. For three years before stitching I hadn't made time to listen to my body, I had just been ploughing on through life and work, focusing all of my attention on my brain. In some ways I thought it was narcissistic to give attention to my body when improving our world needed our brains to change laws, cultures and ways of thinking.

How we feel in our body can be a physical manifestation of our thoughts. How we relate to our thoughts can affect how we relate to other people. And how we relate to people can mirror how we react to the world. If our bodies are tight and rigid, our thoughts may be inflexible too. So it's helpful to be aware of our physical selves if we want to improve our world. I have a habit of being too much in my head, but unlike any other activity I had tried, the physical touch of craft got me out of my head and into the now. It helped me notice that, like so many other activists, I was in danger of burning out: my posture was awful and my body was tired and weak. I realised I needed to address this physical issue if I wanted to carry on campaigning and encouraging others to join in – no one wants to join a group where its members look drained or stressed! Another craftivist, mindful of how much they had enjoyed the workshop, wrote down their feedback: 'Inspired! My heart swells and my eyes open.'

Stitchable Changemakers project*

I created the 'Stitchable Changemakers' craftivism project to learn how others have improved our world and to think through how we can take forward that learning in our own lives. The five changemakers are great role models, teaching us how they have threaded their values through all that they do in their different situations. Changemakers aren't superheroes but sometimes we forget that. They are all very human people who made themselves extraordinary by using their passion, talents and opportunities to protest against injustice in a gentle and effective way.

The 'Stitchable Changemakers' kits are letterpress-printed thick cards with dot-to-dot portraits of five very different changemakers (three women and two men, just to challenge gender inequality in the world!). I encourage people to pick the changemaker that most resonates with them, (more information on each changemaker is printed on the back of the card), or to choose the quote that challenges them the most and that will encourage them to live well and care for others.

On a separate card there are clear instructions to slow down and pierce each hole before stitching: craftivists can get their anger out through this step. Then, whether people do it in a group or on their own, they use

* www.craftivist-collective.com/project-stitchable-changemakers

the repetitive action of backstitch to meditate on how the changemakers they chose made a difference, and then how the craftivist can thread their values through all that they think, say and do.

This activity is a useful craftivism project to do to remember that changing the world starts with seeing if we need to change ourselves and our actions. I encourage craftivists to display their finished portrait somewhere visible to remind them to be a changemaker. People often share their creation online to encourage others to be mindful activists.

The text on the back of each card connected to each changemaker says:

'We were scared, but our fear was not as strong as our courage'

Malala Yousafzai wrote what was originally an anonymous blog for the BBC about going to school as a girl in Mingora, Pakistan under the Taliban rule. The Taliban issued a death threat against her, resulting in a shot to the head from a gunman when she was travelling home from school. Malala used the media attention she received from this traumatic experience to mobilise people around the world to campaign for all girls to have access to education.

Have you directly been affected by an injustice that you could speak about and campaign for it not to happen to others?

'The best way to predict the future is to create it'

Abraham Lincoln is known for his human and humane personality and as an emancipator of people in slavery. He rose from humble beginnings to become a lawyer and then US president and never gave up on eradicating slavery. He was mostly self-educated, became a gifted storyteller and the poet and essayist Ralph Waldo Emerson described Abe as a man who did not 'offend by superiority'.

Where can you help break down systems of oppression of others using humility and patience?

'It takes a great deal of bravery to stand up to our enemies, but just as much to stand up to our friends'

J. K. Rowling, one of the most successful contemporary authors in the world, speaks out publicly against suffering, injustice and discrimination, often using 140 characters or less on Twitter to powerful effect. Her work has inspired other changemakers too, such as the Harry Potter Alliance, which fights bigotry, violence and the abuse of power and won the campaign it set up asking Warner Bros to make all Harry Potter chocolate Fair Trade.

Do you have an existing supporter-base or know someone who does and can you use it to provoke action against injustice?

'My humanity is bound up in yours, for we can only be human together'

Desmond Tutu, a South African Anglican bishop, was a leading social-rights activist and an opponent of apartheid. Tutu continues to travel to share his vision of a world where people are valued for who they are and not for external factors that are often used to marginalise people. He has built bridges between many people through his peace and reconciliation work around the world and is an incredible role model in the art of forgiveness. His optimism, laughter and dance moves are infectious: he's a great reminder to be a joyful activist.

Is there an injustice where you can help encourage the forgiveness that is needed before change can be created by all those involved?

'With the new day comes new strength and new thoughts'

Eleanor Roosevelt, the wife of President Franklin D. Roosevelt, was an introvert who became one of the most outspoken First Ladies in the White House. Harnessing her powerful position she became politically active by writing a newspaper column, giving press conferences, lectures, speaking out on women's rights, poverty, racism and drafting the UN Bill on Human Rights. She became a spokesperson in the UN, overcoming her shyness, and was known for her graciousness and sincerity of purpose.

Are you in a position that you can harness for positive change, such as improving the ethics of your workplace from within or using your relationships with potentially powerful people to help them use their influence for good?

The project encouraged and challenged me in many different ways. One example is that it caused me to slow down when engaging in activism. Now, before I fire off that email or angry post on Facebook, I take time to think, pray and consider how to engage in a strong yet respectful way.

– Craftivist Elizabeth

Be a mindful craftivist

The advantage of mindfulness is in the noticing. Being self-aware of your motives, the emotional baggage and presumptions you bring to your craftivism project, as well as using your craft activity to acknowledge your physical and emotional health, is a form of self-care. Mindfulness isn't about feeling good, it's more about being able to relate to emotions. Handicrafts can help you stay calm and comfort you if you are struggling to examine your own life. If you don't want to acknowledge what you may bring to your craftivism, I understand that. But it's worth knowing that the majority of what we express is non-verbal: we can't hide our emotions from other people even if we try. When craftivists are stressed or are struggling emotionally I sometimes encourage them to take time out and just stroke their thread or fabric for a bit: it can be soothing. It also offers a chance to have a chuckle at my suggestion and to do something that might seem silly, and helps to loosen people up before they carry on engaging deeply in the project.

I use some of my crafting time to exercise mindfulness and that has made it easier to practice mindfulness at other times of the day too: I try and live more responsibly, from wearing ethical clothes where possible and turning lights off when I don't need them, to moving my money to a bank that doesn't invest in the arms trade. I am careful not to deliver too many workshops with no breaks so I don't burn out and I'm content in knowing that I'm not the right person to deliver certain roles, such as front-line social work, but I'm better in other areas. I channel my inner Desmond Tutu when I'm struggling to listen to people I disagree with, and I remember Eleanor Roosevelt when I make a speech about something I care about but my throat is dry with nerves.

Let's be mindful craftivists so that we can do our craftivism work with focus, clarity and skill. Not only will the quality of our work increase but we will also be more connected to our work. We will be more careful in our creations and we will create them without burning out. We are more likely to take ownership of what we have made because of the investment of time and energy we have woven into it and therefore will want to use it with courage to protest against injustices that are difficult to stand up against and easier to shy away from.

5
Crafterthoughts

We must combine the toughness of the serpent with the softness
of the dove. A tough mind and tender heart.

– Martin Luther King

Many of us makers love becoming absorbed in what we are making. It's
a wonderful way to forget our worries and the troubles in the world; an
opportunity to do something with our hands while we watch television
or hang out with friends. It's fun. Other distractions fade into the
background and critical voices are hushed. It feels effortless, liberating,
even superhuman. Bliss. But is this mindset the right one when we are
trying to become mindful craftivists? Our craftivism should be thoughtful
not thoughtless. It should be about engagement not distraction,
thoughtful in the construction as well as to the beauty of the finished
object. We can use our craft as a tool to 'unself' – come out of yourself

– and facilitate some worthwhile thoughts on our chosen issue to better our world and support vulnerable people in a thoughtful way.

It's tempting to assume that we are naturally shrewdly objective in our thinking. But left to ourselves, much of our thinking can be biased, distorted, partial, overgeneralised, self-deceptive, susceptible to some common fallacies, rigid, uninformed or prejudiced.* On the other hand, critical thinking analyses, assesses and reconstructs a subject or problem. It can be difficult at first, because critical thinking is self-directed, self-disciplined, self-monitored thinking. We need to train ourselves in it and overcome our natural human impulse to think only of ourselves or our close friends and family. We need to make time to understand and empathise with those directly affected by the issue. Critical thinking would guard us against over-simplifying our project or lazily labelling those involved in the situation.

It won't be easy: heart and head work are hard work but the quality of our craftivism can depend very much on the quality of our 'crafterthoughts'.

Power in the planning: crafterthoughts before you start making

Good intentions are only the start. Just like a furniture maker, preparation is vital so that we don't end up with a craftivist's version of a wobbly chair. The quality achieved at each stage is dependent on the care with which the craftsperson has accomplished every previous step.

Read around the subject as much as you can (without using that as a procrastination tool!): the facts, the arguments on both sides, case studies and stories from those directly affected. Ask experts for their advice, research organisations to see how your work can support their current

---

* Yikes, that's depressing, isn't it? Bear with me and keep reading, please, there is a happy ending.

protest campaign, use this book's suggestions. The more conscientious we are the more constructive our craftivism project can be. Yes, there are always external factors that will affect the outcome of a project (and often you won't know the full effect of your piece of craftivism, see Chapter 18 for more on this) but that shouldn't stop us taking care with our planning.

We should look at the resources we are going to use and be careful not to be part of 'greenwashing', the practice of deceptively marketing a product as environmentally friendly with imagery and colour palette (lots of green!) even though there has been no attempt made at lowering the environmental impact of its production. A fashion brand might ask you to 'upcycle' their offcuts of fabric to use in your craftivism so that they can then promote it as part of their corporate responsibility agenda. But you might not be able to use their super-thick denim to create an effective craftivism project. Don't be misled by 'goodwashing' too, which helps skyrocket sales of products by creating emotive marketing content that moves us and makes us feel we are backing a trustworthy brand. For example, a global coffee chain might give you £500 to deliver a community event for them and they spend £5000 documenting and sharing it with the public to show they are supporting a community while at the same time they may be decreasing maternity leave for their workers.

There might be a project that encourages us to craft a teddy that will be sent to a community in some distant country to bring smiles to the children. But do the children really want your teddy? Could your action have connotations of colonialism? How is sending a teddy challenging structures of injustice? Have you thought about why these children are not smiling and if we can help campaign in solidarity with them to fix the problem at its roots? Have the community leaders been asked what they really want? It is respectful to ask, and will make the gift so much more helpful and effective if the teddies are useful tools for change. Let's be honest about what is craft and what is craftivism and communicate the difference clearly.

I have created kits* for people to construct that have a strategy already in place. The kits are, as much as possible, ethically made, use donated fabrics where possible and include tips on how to deliver the project on your own or in a group, with step-by-step instructions, 'crafterthought' questions to reflect on whilst you craft and suggestions for messages to use. You don't have to plan out your own project from scratch but can get straight into thinking through making. However, if you are coming up with your own craftivist project you will need to make time to prepare and critique your plan from its initial motivation to delivery.

Some questions to help create 'crafterthoughts':

1. What are the causes of the injustice you are seeking to address?
2. What are groups, organisations or people already doing to tackle the injustice and can you help strengthen their campaign rather than create something alone or competing with theirs?
3. What time, energy, skill can you realistically offer this project and issue?
4. Is craft the best tool for your protest in this situation?
5. What is the key message or action you want people to engage with and is it clear enough for them to understand?
6. Who should you target to tackle this issue? A politician, a businessperson, fashionistas, sports-lovers?
7. Are you treating the victims, perpetrators and everyone else in between with dignity?
8. How can you use resources that are ethical and environmentally friendly rather than cheap and harmful where possible?
9. What is the best thing to make to engage your audience?
10. If you have been given the opportunity to bring craftivism into an

* www.craftivist-collective.com/shop

event, what project can you do to provoke the most thought, and hopefully action, on a particular issue within the limited time?

Thinking with things: crafterthoughts during the process

I see my craftivism activity as being like a wooden spoon, stirring thoughts around my brain. Through using my hands, I can use the time needed to reflect critically on the research I have done, and work out how we should campaign against the issue and turn that information into a type of wisdom soup. If we don't have much knowledge about the issue and don't understand its context, then we won't be able to gain much wisdom because we won't have the necessary information to make decisions about our activism.

Clinicians and neuroscientists are increasingly showing that doing a physical activity (like craft) whilst thinking about difficult subjects can help us cope with the feelings of being overwhelmed, disempowered, angry or depressed when we see injustice in our world.

As craftivists, we can gain wisdom from engaging with global injustices and looking for answers to problems while we craft, engaging our hands, heart and head. I often keep a 'crafterthoughts' notebook next to me when crafting, so that if new questions, answers, connections or comments pop up in my brain I can write them down to reflect on later. I recommend your craftivism projects take at least thirty minutes so that you have time to reflect on the issue you are addressing during your making. Don't worry about finishing your project in one sitting; it can actually be more beneficial to do it in a few sittings so that your brain can have a rest, settle and come back to the issue with a new perspective. Sleep can really help your subconscious do some of the work of stirring your thoughts too and turning them into wise reflection. Don't be surprised if you wake up with little epiphanies, discoveries or answers to problems you were reflecting over while stitching the previous evening.

Thinking with things can help us take charge of our own mind and life. With such a comforting activity, we can grapple with uncomfortable and difficult questions and take ownership of what we are making. We needn't be passive or uncritical, we can use our time crafting to question our own craftivism pieces.

The first ten minutes I just felt frustrated at my terrible handiwork...I had to unpick my terrible stitching and start from scratch. But having to go back and start from scratch was the most important moment. It made me stop, and I mean really stop, and think about what I was doing. In other words, it allowed me to be a fuller me as it didn't stop my critical thinking to function. If anything, it makes my brain work better. It paces it, leaving space for even more connections.

– Craftivist Holly making the project 'A Heart For Your Sleeve'

Big numbers, such as the number of people in poverty, can be too large to fully grasp. We can become numb to them. Some of our making-time can be used to exercise empathy. Empathy needs sensitive questioning, what cultural thinker and author Roman Krznaric in his book *Empathy: Why It Matters, and How to Get It* calls 'outrospection'. Empathy is one of the fundamental ways we understand and relate to one another: the way your heart hurts when your friend goes through a break-up; the exhilaration when the underdog wins first place; the shame when the CEO of an oil company answers questions on a massive oil spill. Try to understand why the perpetrators are involved in atrocities, as well as empathising with the victims affected by the injustice you are engaging with.

**Here is my thought process for a craftivism project
I was asked to create for a workshop**

For the Victoria and Albert Museum (V&A) in London, UK I was asked to deliver a craftivism workshop for adults to drop in to any time between 11 a.m. and 4 p.m. on the Sunday of Refugee Week. I had to be realistic about how much we could achieve in the time, space and budget, with a maximum of ten craftivist volunteers, and with people coming in and out, which could be disruptive. I didn't want to create lots of physical waste that might be difficult to recycle or end up in a landfill by ordering in lots of cheap but toxic resources. I knew that it was not possible for the Craftivist Collective or the V&A to keep hold of or showcase the finished products people made and so that had to be factored in too.

I contacted Refugee Week staff to find out more about their current campaign and how we could complement and support it during this event. After research and reflection I decided that the best use of this opportunity was to create an activity to understand and empathise with refugees, their rights as refugees, how people become refugees, what they may have gone through to get to their destination, the struggles they face in new countries and a space to think through how we can campaign for better treatment of refugees in the UK, from our government, individuals and society. It's important as craftivists that we look for and listen to the views and experiences of those directly affected by the issue and so I asked Refugee Week for case studies with quotes in from refugees that I could use, as well as campaign resources for people to take away with them with more information on how they could protest against the sometimes inhumane treatment of refugees in the UK.

I cut cream-coloured stiff canvas into luggage-tag-shaped pieces. I machine sewed the edges of each tag with a zigzag stitch so they didn't fray and punched out a hole in each one to fit a metal eyelet in for ribbon to go through. That way participants could use or display their tag once they had finished with it. I asked people to write their signature large enough to cover the canvas using the pens provided. Our signature is often used to show our identity and existence, to access resources and places, to show a sign of commitment or action. It seemed a useful symbol to help people engage, connect and empathise with others on a difficult journey. Participants were then asked to stitch over their signature in a simple backstitch. I asked attendees to pick one of three different refugee stories to read and then to reflect on the story while stitching and to put themselves in the shoes of a refugee, imagining they were carrying a bag with their luggage tag on it. Some of these stories can be pretty harrowing so I tried to pick stories that worked for people of all ages, had hope, and showed dignity and strength in the person of refugee status and were possible to engage with for twenty minutes minimum if people couldn't stay longer than that. You could take your tag, needle and thread home with you alongside resources from Refugee Week in a little paper bag to finish off your work and to continue to reflect on the story and the issue.

Participants were also given 'crafterthought' questions to reflect on while stitching:

1. What does the word 'home' mean to you?
2. How do you feel about the case study you have just read?
3. Do you think refugees are given fair treatment in the UK?
4. Can you think of some of the labels used by the UK press to describe refugees?
5. Did you know that 'fish and chips' was introduced by mixing the traditions of Protestant refugees from France and Jewish refugees from Portugal?!

I asked Refugee Week staff to check my craftivism project plan before delivering it to see if they were happy with its content and delivery methods and if they thought their refugee-status friends would be happy with it. They know best when it comes to the issue at hand and how our work can support theirs. My goal for this project was to encourage empathy, which would help people to connect to refugees whether on the news or walking down our streets. I hoped it would lead to a better understanding of refugee rights, and give people the confidence to speak up when someone says a harmful comment stereotyping all refugees, as well as valuing the positive impact refugees have brought to the UK. I also asked them to think about what to do about companies that can be part of the problem, for example by stimulating global warming that can lead to water wars, civil unrest and ultimately many refugee crises.

The activity did not change the world and didn't claim to, but hopefully it offered some time and space at the gallery to help people learn and understand how they can support refugees during such a difficult time in their lives. We had over 150 people attend throughout the day. The vast majority stayed longer than twenty minutes, the average participation time was an hour and sometimes even three hours! People stitched alone with their thoughts as well as chatting to friends or strangers about the issue and case studies. Craftivists shared their #crafterthoughts and put images of their finished tags on social media to continue the conversation elsewhere. The vast majority of tags were taken away with pride and people still email or tell me in person that they have their luggage tag hung on their bags to provoke conversation and to be in solidarity with refugees. The tags remind the craftivists to protest against any mistreatment.

A tough mind and a tender heart

It's important as craftivists to have, in Martin Luther King's words, both 'a tough mind and a tender heart'. It can sometimes feel as if head and heart are competing with each other but it's so important to make sure that all our thoughts and actions are rooted in love for others. The more preparation and thought we put in, the better our craftivism will be. Our plan needs to be flexible, but we still need a plan. We shouldn't waste the opportunity of using the power of the craft process to learn, grow and engage.

Critical thinking is a discipline, and can sometimes be an

uncomfortable process. Happily, the handicrafts we use can create a comforting and safe space for contemplation and reflection. Craft can help us be critical of our own thinking and the issue we are addressing without inducing hopelessness or depression. Crafting can give us time to stop and think over an issue. It's a great framework to engage more deeply on the issue you are protesting against and to reflect on the issues to help you become a more powerful advocate for change.

Our 'crafterthoughts' should acknowledge the complexities of injustice, empathise with those involved, and think critically about where we can make the most difference using our talents, actions and opportunities. We are not going to change the world by thinking or empathy alone, but we can't effectively practise our gentle protests without them. We should make time to turn our knowledge into practical wisdom. We should question what we are doing to support vulnerable people, and question the information that is being presented to us: can it be trusted? How will we respond to it? The more we work on our critical thinking, the better our piece of craftivism will become.

Using your crafting time to connect to the issue more deeply and to decide how best to stand up against injustice and to promote change is surely far more fulfilling than crafting something without a thought in your head.

6
Communal Crafting

If you want to go quickly, go alone. If you want to go far, go together.

— African proverb

Today we can connect to millions of people, anywhere and at any time online. But this new feeling of connectivity will never quite replace the feeling of being physically present with others. I set up the Craftivist Collective in 2009 after strangers and friends asked if they could join in with my craftivism projects. Since then I've delivered craftivism workshops to over 10,000 people around the world. Although the attendees of these gatherings are often within very different situations, there are trends that come out of each communal craftivism session that can help us all become more skilled in the art of gentle protest.

As a traditional activist I used to go to lots of meetings where we would sit together and plan protest actions. Naturally, the louder, more confident people would speak up. Silence was far from encouraged. We didn't create space to deepen our engagement in the injustices we were protesting against, to learn more about the macro and micro levels of the injustice, reflect on the issues, discuss our views and understanding, or to discover the multiple ways we could tackle these issues personally and collectively. We were too busy preparing and delivering actions. Sitting around a table with the sole intention of discussing and planning can be intimidating for many of us. For introverts like me it is also tiring because of the constant interaction with others. I couldn't find somewhere that would offer a safe space for quiet, structured discussion, discovery and deep reflection. That was until I started doing craftivism communally.

There are a variety of ways to deliver communal crafting sessions: a public 'stitch-in', for example, is a great way to engage members of the public and media outlets in raising consciousness and in mobilising people (see more on this in Chapter 14). Offering a drop-in activity at an existing event can attract a new audience to your campaign and to craftivism. In this chapter I will focus on the power of doing craftivism with others, and how it can help us to engage more deeply, critically, and with growing confidence on our craftivism project. This type of focused craftivism gathering is usually done best in a small, intimate and structured workshop that lasts at least one hour and is led by a facilitator.

A place for change

Travelling to the venue often helps me to get in the right headspace for the session. Attending a gathering is an opportunity to reflect with other people about a cause. And being in a place with others can take you away from the distractions of everyday life and provide a disciplined structure to engage more fully in the issue discussed.

These benefits can come from joining any activism group but I felt there was something missing from the ones I had joined over the years.

Typically we met in back rooms of cafes, shops or any other room we could find for free. These rooms, not often used by others, could be cold in temperature and colour, and tended to be uninspiring and unloved: it felt sometimes as if we had been put there as a punishment for doing something bad when in fact we were volunteering our time to try and do something good!

Visualisation is a great tool for when we want to achieve something: imagining the end result helps our brains to figure out practical ways to reach our goals. As craftivists we want to help create a more beautiful, kind and fair world for all. If we only show ourselves what we are protesting against, our mind will focus on these problems and not on how to manifest a better world. Therefore, we should try and turn our gatherings into examples of how we want our world to be: a place of beauty, kindness and respect for others. It is not a luxury to make a space look and feel special for the group: it's a wise investment of time and thought and will enhance everyone's experience. People should feel positive and excited when they arrive at the space, feel cared for and valued so they want to stay there, get comfortable and engage deeply in often distressing social injustices through the act of craftivism, and finally leave inspired, empowered and confident to make the world a gorgeous place for everyone.

We should create a place that is safe, enabling, and exudes a supportive atmosphere, so empathy with those attending is fundamental when planning and preparing the space. Think about light: it should not be so dark that people struggle to see their craft. Windows and natural light can lift people's moods. The space shouldn't be so warm that people feel groggy or so cold that they feel uncomfortable: a bit of ventilation always helps to keep the space feeling fresh. The room should be somewhere without too many distractions or too much noise. The ideal size for a discussion group is twelve people or fewer so that people feel comfortable to speak up but do not create subgroups easily. The larger the group, the harder it is to manage, the less safe it feels, and there will be more distractions. One way of tackling big groups is by seating the group around a circular table (or square if that's not possible). This also flattens any sense of hierarchy. King Arthur had the right idea. That might be one table in a small room or lots of tables cabaret-style in a larger room for big groups, and I often bring fabric to cover the communal tables to brighten up a space. Colour affects mood, behaviour and stress levels. I tend to use a warm yellow since yellow helps create joy and orange is a colour of stimulation and enthusiasm. Soft furnishings like cushions for the chairs can add comfort. Homemade bunting or decorations can give the room a positive atmosphere, which will help to avoid any of the group's members feeling depressed or ineffective when discussing what they want to protest against. Flowers or plants not only help cleanse the room with oxygen, produce a lovely smell, and subliminally remind us to care for our planet, but visually their colours and symmetrical shapes can be calming: nature is a powerful tool to help create a safe space so that we can encourage ourselves to get the most out of a session. Be careful of too much stimulus, however, as it will distract people from the purpose of the gathering

Most of the resources can be displayed attractively on the tables to interest people when they arrive. Having limited resources can be beneficial: enough scissors for one between two means people have to share, connect, have an excuse to talk to each other, or at least smile when passing the scissors. Whenever you can, use resources that are either borrowed or ethically sourced. There are ways of getting what is needed without people feeling guilt-tripped into giving you free stuff. The kits or instructions can be held back until after you have explained the session outline: people rushing ahead is no help. A display area of craftivism projects and examples on a small side table for people to rummage through helps the person who arrives early and is nervous or shy about talking to people before the session starts: they can see what projects we

70

make and also pass the time while they wait for the beginning of the workshop. You're also offering an opportunity that can aid conversation with others who are rummaging.

Small details – like having clear arrows to the toilets, snacks and where to collect their craft resources if needed – show thoughtfulness about participants' needs. A sign outside saying to passers-by 'Shhh, craftivism workshop in process' for the attendees to see as they arrive can help put them in the correct mindset without having to be spoon-fed this information. It also helps passers-by to be mindful not to disrupt the session (as well as intrigue them, too).

Participants can feel valued and excited if they're asked to help set up: they might feel like they're helping to create the communal space by bringing resources such as wildflowers to put in jam jars with some water in for a table display. Your gathering is an opportunity to attract people who might be too frightened to go to an activism meeting. Offering volunteer roles can also help fearful people feel supported. It can help prevent people who are nervous, undecided, or coming alone from cancelling at the last minute. For example, I spoke to a very shy person who had attended one of my talks. She said: 'Without being a volunteer I honestly don't think I would have had the courage to go along alone. The workshop was great, I met lovely people, and felt useful and helpful.'

Background music can also enhance the calm feeling you are creating without it becoming overpowering. Dr Catherine Loveday, a neuropsychologist who focuses on music and memory at the University of Westminster says:

For craftivism gatherings I recommend repetitive music to get into a contemplative zone. Slow music is calming. Lyrics can be distracting for your work but songs with specific association can sometimes help. For example 'Chariots of Fire' for people of my generation is something that makes you feel like anything is possible. Film soundtracks can be really good because they are designed to create emotion without distracting too much.*

I delivered one workshop where they let me borrow their turntable: I brought a vinyl of the album *Chilly Gonzales – Solo Piano II*. It was great to see people come in, spot the vinyl playing, smile and quietly find a space to settle in. It really did seem to make the space that bit more special.

Having fruit and juice or water in the centre of each table for people to share is visually attractive and encourages a sense of communal sharing as well as engaging our sense of taste. When it comes to food and drink, vegan options keep the carbon footprint down and ethics up. Best are products sourced from ethical companies where people get a decent wage and pension and where the environment is not harmed. Care over resource sourcing is another way to show how we are a part of the change we wish to see in the world. I've been to events where we discuss human rights injustices but are offered highly unethical drinks and food where the companies are known to treat their employees badly and to pollute the environment: that can leave a bad taste in your mouth (!) and can discredit any work with the attendees.

The more thoughtfully prepared the environment is, the more chance the space will have of being a fruitful place for people to delve into the issues concerned and discover new ways of being an active citizen in the future. People will remember the session more, feel valued, and hopefully see that our world can be a good place if we put our minds to it. People at the end of the session may want to capture the space in a photograph as a memory of the gathering and to share with their friends on social media to show what they have been up to. This intrigues more people to

---

* You can use my playlist here: open.spotify.com/playlist/7guCQOffJkWp8rRdl9mNEF

look into what craftivism is, and can create more conversations afterwards outside of the workshop.*

> I was apprehensive but walking into the prepared space I immediately felt welcomed, comfortable and focused. It was a lovely night with lovely people, full of hope, passion for change, and practical actions we could take.

> – Craftivist Gavin

I advertise my workshops on social media, my newsletter and website but I also make sure that I target particular groups who live nearby or who I know are influential with the power-holders of the cause we are working on. Saying the event is open to anyone makes it feel less special or attractive. The events are open to everyone but I also recommend making time and effort contacting people with bespoke invites saying why you think they will benefit from your workshop and how you will benefit from their involvement can make people feel much more valued and excited to attend and help your workshop fulfil its potential to help create positive change.

Craft is your social lubricant

If you're thinking of holding a craftivism event, make sure to welcome participants as they arrive. There might also be volunteers on hand if it is a large group around a few small tables (remember twelve around each table maximum, if possible) who can help people with the technical steps of the activity as well as gently keep the conversations on the chosen topic. At the start of the session, when everyone is seated and ready, introduce yourself, the structure, and the goals of the session. I always

---

* See some of our workshops on YouTube Craftivist Collective for tips: www.youtube.com/user/craftivistcollective

enjoy reminding people that 'this is all about slow activism so if you finish it by the end of the session then you've done it wrong!' It helps break the ice, takes away any stress or competitiveness in the room and creates giggles.

If the gathering is twelve people or fewer, encourage people to introduce themselves and talk about their motivations for attending. This is a great way for people to connect with anyone who has similar motives, or skills and experiences that might help them with their craftivism and maybe even keep in touch to support each other in the future as craftivists. Then the host can hand out the craftivism kits or instructions to go with the resources on the table. The group can then open up their kits and I encourage them to read their instructions alone silently while the instrumental background music may be turned up a little. After five minutes, or when it looks like everyone has read the information, the music can be turned down and the group asked if the project makes sense in terms of purpose and process and whether anyone has any questions. Once everyone is happy the crafting can get started.

Making things together helps people open up to each other. They're not just learning how to become a craftivist, they're learning about the people they are with: who is frustrated, who is a calming influence, who is an experienced crafter or campaigner, and who has insight or different views about the issue being discussed. Making objects together is a natural subject for chat, freeing people from the necessity of talking about themselves. People often think out loud about the message or colour choice in their craftivism project, or their struggle with a particular step that others can help with. The question 'What are you making?' rather than 'What should we do?' turns a blunt question to a reflective one, learning from each other's thinking and creation.

In the group, objects in progress serve as sites around which talk about social injustice can be discussed without distraction (the kit's crafterthoughts can help too). Discussing the making of a craftivism project, sharing feedback and ideas can have an effect on what is produced, increasing the quality of the product more than if it were worked on alone. I know my work improves when I'm with other people for part of the making process.

You can't sustain eye contact with people when you are trying to craft something with your hands. You have to look down once in a while to see what you are doing and make sure you are not making a mistake. This might sound odd to mention but we need reduced eye contact to comfort us when we are sad, when we are accessing internal thoughts or emotions or when we feel shameful. Reflecting on the many facets of the injustice we are protesting against to see where we can help create lasting solutions is an emotional and intellectual process where reduced eye contact is needed at times to help us think for ourselves. Too much eye contact with people can feel hostile or intimidating, especially if you disagree with someone, and you might end up saying something you regret. Reducing eye contact is less confrontational, and it helps people who may be feeling sad or upset about the injustice their craft project is tackling to continue to interact and not close themselves off. Craftivists don't have to talk to take part in the session, and having something to do while listening or thinking can help to absorb the information. The role of crafted objects and making together create a condition for ease and un-pressured social interaction. Craftivist Wendy noted the benefits that craft brought when she went along to a meeting in Glasgow: 'I really liked that I could come and talk or not talk. I could make myself a bit separate and stay in my shell but still listen to other people's conversations without the pressure to join in. It helped me engage more deeply in the issue we were tackling through our craftivism project.'

Encouraging an environment where people feel safe, and are free to talk or not talk, often acts as a catalyst for people to be their true selves, opening up to their neighbours or a small group without having to look up. I'm surprised how much people open up to each other about their views, experiences, even flaws they have become aware of during the session and want to work on. The making process acts as a social lubricant to challenge the craftivists, and to encourage them to explore issues and thoughts they hadn't explored before – or at least not in depth. For example, in one craftivism session, while making mini banners during London Fashion Week, we talked about how sweatshops affected their workers, which led organically on to how the process affects our planet, how some of us had never thought about who made our clothes or the supply chain before; we discussed how stressed the designers must feel having to create twelve collections a year, rather than four because of the demand from profit-driven companies, how we often felt the stresses of having to look good and wear fashionable clothes, the status you're given because of what you buy and wear, and how we can protest against these harmful structures and cultures.

Facilitators need to keep people on topic. If handled well the session can create space for 'thawing out', helping people open up to new experiences and thoughts, challenge their views, and remove any walls to allow them to open up and be vulnerable with others.* Sometimes, if we are more than halfway through a session and people are starting to discuss other issues, I ask everyone to stop talking, tell them I am going to play one instrumental song ('Hunted By A Freak' by Mogwai) and that they have to try and answer some of the 'crafterthought' questions on their instruction sheet for the duration of the song. I ask them to pretend they have blinkers over their eyes so that they only focus on their own work and their crafterthought sheets in front of them. After the song has played I then congratulate them for their silence and ask if anyone wants to share what they were thinking about, why they are stitching a particular message, or if their

---

* Make sure people don't use the session inappropriately for a therapy session – do encourage them to seek help from professionals for this.

reasons for coming are being fulfilled and what they will do after this workshop. As well as offering new content for discussion, it also offers a little taster session to show people how they can use music to help them structure their time to finish off their craftivism alone somewhere after the session.

Fifteen minutes before the end of the session I encourage people to think through what resources they need to pack into their kit to take home to finish their project, such as extra coloured thread or embellishments like buttons, sequins or ribbon. If the group has bonded well, the host can ask if anyone is comfortable to 'show and tell' the group about their craftivism object and what they hope to do with it. If there are any pieces that you think are particularly great examples of effective craftivism, check first with the person to see if you can show and share the story behind it and its objectives with others, and make sure that others don't feel their work is less valued. If any trends have come out of the session, share some as a way of offering craftivism tips. If anyone has shared a story or comment with you that you think might help be a catalyst for further critical thinking for other people, ask them if they are happy to share it with the group or if you can share it on their behalf. For example, I delivered a workshop for one of the many Women's Institute groups in the UK and the trend of the night was summed up by Gill who said she had 'a realisation that doing small things is more productive than thinking big things'.

Community

The comradeship you get in groups of makers is well recognised. It's commonplace to read that crafting is cosy, diverting, and peaceful, but it's more complex than that. Complicated and sometimes confusing emotions, such as enchantment, hopelessness, frustration and ambition, can be brought to the surface during creative making in these settings. The opportunity to work with and through challenges is an important aspect of making's transformative and disruptive potential. Through these ups and downs, but driven by a bigger purpose, a culture of mutual concern and consideration can be fostered. The host should encourage and support people to work through their emotions, and strive to create the best message they can on their craftivism piece. Craftivism should not be seen as a production line, and the craftivists should not go for the obvious or easier answer but use this structured space and the supportive community created to step outside of their comfort zone and grow in their crafts(wo)manship.

I haven't been to an activism gathering quite like a craftivism workshop. While you should make your gatherings welcoming to all, like any event, often a particular tribe of people emerge. Our 'gentle protest' approach to craftivism in my experience creates a distinctive mix of people. Not only does it attract people who enjoy craft or other creative activities but its quiet nature also attracts shy and introverted people who are often too nervous or sensitive to go to an activism gathering. We attract people passionate about social change but who, like me, don't feel they fit into more extrovert and loud activism gatherings, or who feel they are burnt out and want a change. We attract women, transpeople and men. Men often benefit from the sessions because while they may never have done this type of craft before, they are open to listening and learning without preconceptions. All the groups create a melting pot of different thoughts, perspectives, ideas, experiences and varied political beliefs, which only enhance each individual's experience. I've never had anyone leave my workshops early, hate the workshop, or not been able to take part (so far!).

Making the same thing together and struggling together not only helps create a sense of community, it can also change power dynamics. We've had a politician learning craft techniques from an anarchist while together they discuss democracy, and grandmothers showing teenagers how to do a stitch called a French Knot in exchange for learning how to share their process on Facebook with their friends. An experienced campaigner has shared her success stories with a blogger who has never signed a petition in her life. People with different beliefs and political persuasions listen to each other's views calmly, partly through the reduced eye-contact needed to craft, and often find connections with each other because they have been helping each other with their craftivism action steps, creating a friendly space that naturally weakens feelings of judgement of 'the other'. Friendships are created through mutual learning and discovery. This non-hierarchical group creates fertile soil for bonding, trust and a sense of community.

Whether a gathering is with complete strangers or with people who meet every month there is often some mirroring that happens when people feel part of a community. If we see others working hard, thinking hard or discussing the project deeply, it encourages us to mirror these conscientious craftivists and get more out of the session ourselves. Rozsika Parker, psychotherapist, art historian, feminist and writer, describes a handmade personal product as a 'form of thought'[2] in her book *The Subversive Stitch: Embroidery and the Making of the Feminine*, writing:

> The process of creativity – the finding of form for thought – have a transformative impact on the sense of self. The embroiderer holds in her hands a coherent object which exists both outside in the world and inside her head. Winnicott's theory of mirroring helps us understand how the experience of embroidering affirms the self as a being with agency, acceptability and potency...The embroiderer sees a positive reflection of herself in her work and, importantly, in the reception of her work by others.[1]

Taking part in the same project as others, whether that's an object we each take home to keep, or a fabric patch that will be added to an installation, offers a sense of common purpose, bigger than ourselves, a sense of solidarity and a reminder that we are not alone in our fight to eradicate unloving practices in our world. Matthew Crawford, author of

The Case for Working with your Hands, writes that communal activities can evoke relationships between the skilled and apprentice, teacher and student as: 'a kind of philosophical friendship, the sort that is natural between teacher, students: a community of those who desire to know.'[2]

Craftivists Liv and Cirrus met at a craftivism mini banner workshop in Stockholm. Cirrus emailed me to say:

> During the workshop I was sitting next to another participant. We became friends through working on our projects together, which allowed time to share and learn from each other. After the workshop we stayed in touch and encouraged each other to complete our banners. Months later we went together to place our banners in non-intrusive locations around a walkway and entrance to a gallery in Stockholm. Liv stitched her message in Swedish and my work is in English. We have joked together that we don't think we would have had the confidence or discipline to finish our banner if it wasn't for our friendship.

One of the discoveries from the rapidly growing field of neuroscience is that mutual cooperation is associated with enhanced neuronal responses in areas of the brain. This suggests that social cooperation is intrinsically rewarding, which may explain why it's sometimes hard to get people to leave at the end of a workshop! Often people will ask if the host can share contact details of the group. For data protection reasons this is not possible but participants can share contact details with each other. People can be encouraged to stay in touch with each other and with the host, and to share their progress online to encourage each other to stay on their craftivism journey and inspire others to join it. Although virtual communities are different, they can continue conversations had at the physical meetings, continue to support us to grow in confidence as craftivists and remind us all of the experience of the gathering: we don't have to find a way to be a superhero but humbly to be part of something bigger and work in solidarity with others to improve our world.

Craftivists unite!

Crafting with others can be very empowering. For someone wavering in their craftivism or their activism it can be vitally helpful to gather a group or join up with a group, and do some craftivism together.

Making objects can serve as social lubricants for talk and engagement about difficult issues, provide the opportunity for new experiences of learning together and persevering through the difficulties, and the craftivism making can be a catalyst for future social action which may or may not involve craft as a tool.

One workshop is unlikely to change people permanently. We are all on different parts of our journey as craftivists and active citizens of our planet. But more often than not people leave a workshop feeling that they have been part of something special, with a head full of thoughts that they want to delve into on the way home about how they can be changemakers in all that they say, do and buy. The best gathering is one where people leave with their craftivism object (finished or unfinished), which will remind them of their crafterthoughts, and where they have gained a sense of community that is so often needed to encourage them in their future craftivism work. Our achievements through crafting communally should build confidence: if I can achieve this project, maybe I can achieve things in other parts of my life too.

7
Inner Activism

Yesterday I was clever, so I wanted to change the world.
Today I am wise so I am changing myself.

– Rumi

Was I being a hypocrite? My first craftivism projects were all outward facing. They were little pieces of street art to provoke thought and action in passers-by, or handmade objects as gifts for people in positions of authority to remind them to use their power and influence for good. I wasn't making anything for myself to remind me to be an active global citizen, to speak out when I see injustice, and to practise what I am preaching to others. I was focusing on others and putting myself at risk of doing craftivism that wasn't firmly rooted in my personal values. When an injustice needs people to sacrifice something in order to support the cause (buy less, change our habits or resist our own vices) we need to practise what we preach, show that the sacrifices are possible, and be role models for others. We need to do this before we ask others to change. Otherwise we are hypocrites.

Being the change we wish to see in the world doesn't come easily. We become what we do day by day. Unfortunately, vice comes more naturally than virtue: you just go into neutral and slide along with the way things are going. But virtue requires thought. You have to say, 'I need to take a decision to be this sort of craftivist now: gentle, humble, loving, kind, respectful, courageous.' They aren't simple rules to live by. We need to grow in maturity to know how to implement them in different environments with different people and in our ever-changing world. We need to work hard to make moral thinking and actions become second nature to us, as we may often be tempted towards self-preservation and status. Putting others before ourselves may never become 'first nature', but we can train ourselves in this habit so that when we see injustice we know what we can do to protest gently against oppression and harm. Character is formed by the thousands of little choices we make and those thousands of choices turn us into the people we want to be.

Our virtues and vices are not a private thing. If we want others to practise kindness then we need to reflect that. Practising kindness can be difficult, counter-cultural, even subversive at times. But we should remember to collaborate without compromise, critique without conflict, and be examples of global citizens who do not look down on other people but inspire and empower others to practise the characteristics of a good person.

Physical reminders

Go into a friend's home and you'll see how they have gathered little things around them that inspire, amuse or encourage them. We do it intuitively: we surround ourselves with objects that reflect a piece of us or who we want to be, that mirror our interests, our loved ones, and our beliefs and principles.

When discussing this chapter with my dad he told me a story I didn't know. We grew up in a white working-class area so my parents decided to have a large poster of Bob Marley on one of the living-room walls. They hoped that their children regularly seeing someone of a different race and whose music we enjoyed listening to would stop any racism or fear of the other. Next to Bob Marley was a poster of Babar the Elephant, from one of our favourite series of books. The poster, the books and other images we surrounded ourselves with influenced who we became: I didn't know the story behind our Bob Marley poster but I loved his friendly and thoughtful face on the poster.

Rarely do people want to have a poster of a harmful dictator or polluter up on the wall but often without realising the images we surround ourselves with can affect how we see our world. Are the Photoshopped images of thin models influencing the way you measure health, beauty or happiness? Is it helpful to have violent images on film or music posters or do they normalise or even glamorise conflict as a heroic way to solve a problem? When I was at university I worried about whether the extremely sexualised posters sold at poster fairs for students encouraged objectifying people rather than encouraging respectful relationships.

As a craftivist, what can we have clearly displayed to encourage us to keep striving to improve our world, to root our habits in our values, to remember to help others and to protest against injustice? We should focus on the vision of the world we want to live in, a world where all are cared for. Do you have quotes around your home, desk at work, or on your keychain that keep you hopeful and help to motivate you to go against the grain of the world's vices? Do you have images of role models who have made a positive difference in our world? Are you trying to be more environmentally friendly and leave sticky notes around for yourself to, for example, buy more ethical cleaning products?

What could we display to help us practise the values we want other people to practise? I have my changemaker portrait of Desmond Tutu on my desk to remind me to learn from Tutu about how to practise peace and reconciliation, and to forgive people. I have postcards of inspiring quotes and I also created a small statue of a zombie out of a little wooden drawing mannequin body, wrapping it up in white medical tape and drawing on a zombie face with a black marker pen. He reminds me not to walk through life on autopilot without questioning the world we live in. My magnifying glass pendant on my necklace is a catalyst for curiosity and looking more closely at issues. My stitched phone case reminds me to be an everyday activist: it's of the Dalai Lama and has a stitched speech bubble saying 'If you can help, do that; if you can't help, at least don't harm'. What would you make to glance at and root your actions in your values?

To support the Bystander Revolution organisation – which is an online space where people can find resources to stand up against bullying – I was asked to create a craftivism project to add to their list of 'small acts of kindness, courage and inclusion anyone can use to take the power out of bullying'. The project is to create fabric, hand embroidered small square sticky notes while reflecting on the issue of bullying and how to stop it. I also created some crafterthought questions to reflect on while making. You keep the final pieces to remind yourself to treat others how you would like to be treated, not to be bystanders in the face of bullying but to have the courage to help stop it, whether that's supporting the victim or showing love to the bully.* I made one for my desk saying 'Make someone feel valued', to remind me to look out for people being ignored, bullied or neglected, and to show them support or at least offer some kindness where I can.

The Creative Director of Bystander Revolution, Michael Wood, writes that: 'Transforming something as everyday and disposable as a sticky note into a hand-stitched, lasting message reminds us that with a little bit of

---

* See more examples of sticky notes and take part in the project by following the instructions and crafterthought questions at: www.craftivist-collective.com/bystander-revolution-challenge

effort and creativity, a few simple words can make an indelible impact.'

If the sticky note was made by someone else you might not think about how the message relates to bullying. But because you had to make it yourself and spent time reflecting on the 'crafterthought' questions when you were embroidering your sticky notes, your embroidered piece becomes a memory device, capturing your thoughts and feelings.

Memory device

Have you ever kept a book because you just loved reading it and keeping it on display reminds you of the story? I've watched the film *To Kill a Mockingbird* many times and I have the special edition DVD with an extra disc of special features on display to encourage me to think 'What would Atticus Finch (or Gregory Peck!) do?' when I see someone being treated badly. Seeing an object you have engaged deeply with can trigger a memory just as a sound, taste or touch can.

We can use the process of making to broaden our knowledge and understanding on an issue and to help us engage deeply and critically with it. If done well, your mind may well produce thoughts that spring up unannounced. They often disappear just as suddenly, but by thinking of the issue while making something, your object can become a memory device to capture and collect those thoughts. When you look at the object you've made you are more likely to remember the thoughts, epiphanies, connections and rollercoaster of emotions you had during the process from feeling overwhelmed or sad to feeling inspired and empowered.

Your object has 'thing-power': it is physical evidence that you can make things happen through patience, skill, discipline and commitment. As craftivists we should discover what the map of a moral world looks like, where the twists and turns are, and learn how to start changing our world, one step at a time. It's an exciting and ever-evolving challenge to follow a moral path through this world, where new technologies are changing how we live, and to see clearly the world with all its philosophical and ethical dilemmas. We need to continue to critique what we do, buy, say and think. My embroidered footprint object is a memory device, created as a craftivism project to remind me to think about the imprint I am leaving on the world, and it helps me to critique my daily steps and my own journey through life.

You can stitch a message on your canvas footprint on your own while you reflect on your daily steps, or do it in a group, but use the time to be mindful of and critical of your own habits before you ask other people to do the same. Place your footprint somewhere visible at home or at work where you can notice this symbol of life every day.

Craftivist Jessica wrote a blog post about her Craftivism Footprint:

> The footprint project is the perfect starting place for any would-be craftivist, for surely it is important that we have identified our own values and motivations for living in our world before we start looking to influence other people...I am proud to have the footprint as my first fully completed craftivist project, it looks beautiful in my recycled glass frame and will inspire me in my daily life and maybe to start my next craftivist project.

To make the project I made a stencil of a footprint using fabric paint on stiff canvas and then cut around the fabric and machine-sewed around the edges to stop the fabric fraying. You can then write in biro a personal message that links to the project aims. Then you do a simple backstitch over the top of your handwritten message.* It doesn't matter if it's not clear to other people what your message means as long as it has meaning for you. I stitched the message 'Where we journey matters. And how we journey matters too...' on to my footprint because my default attitude

---

* If you would like to make your own footprint, go to: www.craftivist-collective.com/craftivist-footprint

is to fixate on the goal and I need to remember that the way I reach that goal needs just as much care and commitment so that I'm not harming anyone on the way to a better world: that would be hypocritical! Other message suggestions are:

- How we live and walk on this planet affects not just us but future generations...
- 'Step with care and great tact, and remember that life's a great balancing act' – Dr Seuss
- 'What I stand on is what I stand for' – Wendell Berry
- 'If you are neutral in situations of injustice, you have chosen the side of the oppressor' – Desmond Tutu
- It's not so much the journey that's important, but the way we treat those we encounter and those around us, along the way.

My friend Barley Massey, who runs her own ethical craft shop Fabrications in London, taught me to think through whether to incorporate material that already has personal memories attached to enhance our footprint object. The backing fabric in the frame with my footprint was a dark red for a sense of urgency and depth, had a floral pattern to look as though my footprint was walking on nature and I used fabric from my grandmother to remind me of the unconditional love and support she gives me whether I succeed or fail at my goals. My footprint is in a frame on my bookshelf near my door so that I spot it on the way out of the house each day and it reminds me to think through my actions to make sure I'm living out my values. I don't read the message on my footprint each time I see it because I know it. It only takes a split second to spot your footprint but its symbol and 'form of thought' can start you on the right footing each day.

I remember in one Craftivism Footprint workshop a university student asked if she could stitch this message on her footprint: 'Drinking fair-trade artisan coffee and reading the *Guardian* isn't going to change the world'.

We had a giggle and she told me that it was too easy for her to tell herself that she was a good person without actually critiquing her actions or pushing herself to protest against injustices she saw. I thought it was a great idea and she said she would put it in her living room so that her housemates might find it useful too.

Your craftivism piece should be more than a self-affirmation message. It should challenge yourself lovingly to use your strengths, actions and opportunities to protest where you see injustice. Use the time stitching to take ownership of the message you are completing. You've committed your time, energy, heart and hard work into making something, so make something that embodies the values you want yourself and others to live by.

Personal development

The attentiveness you practise in your craftivism can help you practise slowing down in other parts of life and to savour overlooked occasions and actions. We must be mindful and put effort into even the smallest tasks. Experts say it takes ten weeks to change from old habits and form new ones. Your crafted object can encourage you to participate, extend yourself, go outside your comfort zone and break your routine, open yourself up to new experience and community.

I met Rin a few years ago. She told me she was scared to be an activist but watched my talks online, came to a few workshops and slowly started having a go at my projects. She tweeted this: 'I hope my craftivism piece helps change the world but more importantly it's changed me'. I asked her to expand on how her craftivism actions have helped her with her personal development:

'As a student, I engaged with traditional activism with youthful zeal. I wrote letters and signed petitions and went on marches and protest rallies. But over the years, life kind of took over and I lost the momentum and energy of those rather more uncomplicated days. The activism I had been so passionate about fell by the wayside. I suppose, being a natural perfectionist, I felt that if I didn't have time to commit myself fully to the big campaigns, what was the point of doing anything at all? Discovering the Craftivist Collective reminded me that everyone has a part to play...by striving to be the best version of myself – living ethically, thoughtfully, carefully and with real love for the planet and all its people – I can make a genuine difference. Every time I leave my house, one of the last things I see before I close the door is the 'stitched changemaker' card I made at a Craftivist Collective event, depicting J.K. Rowling (because I'm a writer) which hangs on the noticeboard in my hallway. Whenever I glance at it, I remember reflecting on the qualities threaded through the author's life as I stitched – her commitment to a project she believed in, her perseverance in the face of rejection, the way she has quietly and humbly used her fame for good. What an inspiration! If I were to sum up how craftivism has impacted my life, it would be with the Gandhi quote I've heard Sarah repeat many times: 'Be the change you wish to see in the world.' It's as simple and as challenging as that.'

Our craftivism objects won't change us by themselves...
I find the picture of the fruit tree helpful: if I plant a fruit tree I'll be lucky to get any fruit if I just leave it there. If I want the tree, or my craftivism object, to bear fruit I'm going to have to work at it. I'm going to have to help the tree bear fruit. Quick changes can be the blossom but to get the fruit we have to be gardeners and discover how to tend and prune, irrigate the field, how to keep birds and rodents away, look for mould, cut away ivy and repel other parasites that suck the life out of the

tree. We need to make sure the young trunk of the tree can stay firm in the face of high winds. Only then will fruit appear. Not easy going but if our tree isn't good from the root to the tip of the branches we have to question if our fruit will be healthy – the genuine article – or mouldy, even poisonous.

Through the process of our craftivism pieces – their planning, making and completion – we are taken on a journey that can make us more humane, more thoughtful, more able to see where the issues are, to think through them, take the hard moral choices and put them into effect in our craftivism work. It is, of course, not possible to be perfect in our craftivism or pure in our world if we want to be part of society rather than live in a cave away from it all. Most of us live in this messy world and are entangled in it. The essential minerals that go into all mobile phones are made in the Democratic Republic of Congo in cobalt mines with awful conditions for the workers and under a highly corrupt government. Should we give up having a phone when it's so helpful to mobilise and engage people in the craftivism movement? Weighing up the pros and cons, I have decided to have a mobile phone. Sadly that means I am part of a harmful system but as a customer I try to use my power to raise awareness of these injustices and campaign to stop them and keep looking for a more ethical alternative to swap to. Some people will see this as the wrong answer. We will continuously need to exercise our moral thinking every day, and weigh up the conflicting issues, but as my 'length of encouragement' ribbon says hanging off my door: 'Little by little, we travel far...'*

* I send this ribbon to everyone who orders something from www.craftivist-collective.com/ shop as a gift. Made in collaboration with Department Store for the Mind founder, Sophie Howarth.

Part III

Power in the Product

8
The Gift

Anger is the enemy of non-violence and pride is a monster that swallows it up.

— Mahatma Gandhi

I was annoyed. I had sent my local MP petition cards and online petitions about issues that I cared about and the only response was an email from a member of her staff telling me to stop contacting her. They said it was a waste of my time, their time and charity's money. I was shocked, I didn't expect that type of response. Our members of parliament (MPs) in the UK are supposed to listen to their constituents and represent their interests and concerns in Parliament. So shouldn't her staff at least have pretended to care, even if they disagreed with my protests? I didn't reply straight away; I didn't know how to. I was too angry to think straight. For days I thought about it on and off. Then when I had calmed down slightly I tried to put myself in her shoes and exercise a bit of 'intelligent empathy'.* Why would her office staff believe that this was the best response to send me? What would they have thought of me when receiving my petitions?

I was new to the area and had met my MP once, but she didn't know me. I was part of a group of eight other local residents at a charity coalition event near Parliament where we were asking our MP what they were going to do to tackle tax dodging by multinationals. I was too nervous to introduce myself and we had a few people in the group who knew her better and were confident to lead the conversation. I sat with the group and listened.

Looking back, the petitions I had sent my MP were either petition postcards or email templates I was receiving from charities I supported. All I had to do was sign them and press send on my emails or post them to her. Working for a large international development charity at the time, I read internal reports that had interviewed politicians and members of the business sector to find out what campaign tactics had an impact on them. It seemed that the people we were trying to influence doubted the commitment of people who signed these petitions because it was easy to sign your name against an issue without engaging in the issue more deeply. The huge majority of the petition-signers didn't seem to take further action so some politicians didn't see a big risk in not replying to their protest.

This struck a chord with me. When signing petition cards and e-petitions to my MP I would always add a little message on to the templates saying that I cared deeply about this issue and hoped that she would work hard to support the most vulnerable people in our society, but writing that didn't take much time either. I guess her team of staff

---

* Intelligent empathy is when you don't just try to put yourself in someone else's shoes, you also try to understand how they might have come to the decisions that they've made.

would have seen me as an 'armchair activist', just posting these quick transactional petitions to her and not doing anything else. I would have probably categorised myself as a slacktivist if I was an onlooker.

Maybe my MP and her team also doubted the level of my concern because I was sending her petitions on lots of issues from global warming to tax avoidance, human rights injustices to corporate greed. Did she see me as fickle? For me, these issues are all close to my heart and are linked to the growing inequality gap in society. After researching more about my MP and what her voting record was, I could see that she was new to her role, she had received lots of support from her political party nationally to help her win her seat, and she, so far, had always voted with the party line. Nearly all of the petitions I had signed were against what her political party was doing or believed in. It looked like we had very different ideologies and so maybe her team thought there was no point in talking with me since it looked like I would never vote for her or support her campaigns.

Also, as I looked at some of the petitions I had sent her, I realised the wording was very direct and impersonal, they never related to any local concerns and hardly ever included the words 'please' or 'thank you'. Most petitions said something along the lines of: 'Take action and get the government to do...' with not much room for discussion or nuance. If I was her I could imagine feeling exhausted by all of our demands, especially as they were mostly faceless requests that were not very polite.

I don't want to stop signing petitions, they can be useful to mobilise people around a campaign, gain public and media attention and pressure people in power to make a change. Each country works differently. In the UK, British citizens can submit and sign petitions for Parliament. If the petition meets the standards for acceptable petitions then over 10,000 signatures will receive an official response from the government. With over 100,000 signatures the issue will be considered for parliamentary debate. They can work. Maybe she didn't see me as a slacktivist but proactively wanted to deter me from signing petitions that included ones protesting against her political party?

As a constituent I didn't want to give up contacting my MP. I wanted to know more about how my MP was representing her constituents, including me. I wanted to see where I could make a positive difference within UK democracy, and working with or through our Members of Parliament still looked like one of many useful pathways to help break down structural injustices and replace them with laws that help create long-term social change. I decided that it would be useful to book an appointment to meet my MP face-to-face at one of her surgeries, state my commitment to these causes I had signed petitions for and find out the best way to help tackle them. We might agree on certain issues and she could tell me how I could support the campaign better. If we disagreed, I would ask how she came to that decision and change my mind if my argument was not as well informed. I didn't want her to see me as someone not willing to engage in dialogue and discussion. I wanted to show her I genuinely cared about being a responsible, loving citizen and working with people, even if our views are different. But how could I show this?

I thought about the email I had received from her staff, about how I could show her I was a friendly and kind person, not an aggressive activist (activists can have a bad reputation, sadly). I wanted her to know that I didn't just want to tell her what not to do, treat her like a robot, have my photo taken with her with a charity campaign prop for media attention and then leave. I also didn't want to be a pushover, and just let her fill the whole session talking at me, which had happened previously with another MP when I lived in a different constituency. I wanted to find out more about her passions, purpose and personality. I wanted us to treat each other like fellow human beings, show her my commitment to social change, have a conversation and see where we might be able to work together as critical friends not aggressive enemies.

This situation reminded me of a similar one I had experienced a few months before. I had a consultation appointment with a tattoo artist whose style of work I admired hugely. As he's in high demand, I waited six months for an appointment. I arrived excited. He was in a foul mood. He shouted at me to come back in an hour because his current customer arrived late and had put his whole schedule behind. I jumped. He made me feel very unwelcome and like a nuisance. I had not been shouted at for a long time. I wanted to cry. I wanted to collaborate with this skilled artist on a beautiful design in his style that would be a permanent piece of artwork on my skin. I didn't want to look at a tattoo that reminded me of someone who made me feel fearful, or worse, agree to a design I didn't like because I was too nervous to stand up to him. I went home upset but could understand he was stressed. I thought about how tattooing someone couldn't be rushed, and he probably felt very rushed. I decided to make him a card to give to him on my return because I was too nervous to tell this stranger that I love his work, want to work with him but he shouldn't have shouted at me. I'm not good with conflict, but I wanted our working relationship to be a healthy and respectful one. I superglued a Jelly Baby on to black card, drew an angry face on the sweet and made a badge in the shape of a speech bubble saying 'I'm angry, don't talk to me' and stuck it to the card. I hoped it would make him laugh and cheer him up. I wrote inside the card that I understood he was angry but that I love his work, had been looking forward to our consultation for the last six months, and I really wanted us to work well together so that we were both proud of the results of our collaboration and I wanted it to be a fun process for both of us. I said he could wear this badge the next time he was in a bad mood so he didn't make other people cry. I drew a smiley face at the bottom of the message. I collected my courage to go back to the shop and gave it to him with a smile. He read it in front of me and smiled back sheepishly. We then had a great talk and both got excited about the ideas we had for my tattoo. The card had helped break the ice, show my admiration for him and his work and say what I was too nervous to say in person.

Why do we love receiving gifts, even badly made ones? Gifts show us that the giver has been thinking about us, values us and has decided to spend time on us rather than doing anything else. There are so many things available to buy now that a handmade bespoke gift often feels more valuable. Maybe it's because it's homemade with imperfections that we love it more – we can connect to another person's vulnerability. Handmade objects can be really helpful ways for people to start honest conversations with others without that person feeling attacked or defensive. Writing a letter to your friend you've had a fight with to apologise and share your concerns allows your friend to read the letter in their own time, reread it, let it sink in, reflect on it and reply in their own time. Sending a card to someone who is grieving reminds them that you are thinking of them and will be there if they need anything but you will not push them to socialise if they want to be alone. Making a present for someone struggling with depression shows your love when you don't know what else to do. These gifts can break down barriers and show how much we care about people, especially if you are struggling to find the words. Maybe I could make my MP a gift to show her my respect for her in her difficult role and my commitment to be a good global citizen? It could also be an icebreaker to get to know her better.

I decided to hand-stitch a message on a handkerchief. I had a packet I had been given as a gift but didn't need them all (I already have two handkerchiefs I use). I was thinking about who uses them and how people use them: they've not just been used to blow noses. I knew they'd been used to show surrender in a battle, judges used them to place on their heads out of respect when they sentenced people to death, people offer them to someone who is crying. I liked that it was a soft, small and comforting object you could keep in your pocket. I thought it would be a fun metaphor for my politician to gently remind her not to 'blow it' but use her powerful position to make a positive difference in the world. I wanted to stitch an encouraging message for her that was also timeless and universal, so it wouldn't become irrelevant during her time as an MP. I picked a lilac-coloured handkerchief that had a faint pattern of small flowers all over it, the calmest and sweetest hanky out of the bunch. Surely she wouldn't be offended by this gift? I daydreamed that when she was tired or in a difficult situation at work she could hold the hanky in her pocket without people noticing and it would give her courage and energy to stand up against injustice. After discussing the wording with my family we decided on the words:

> Dear [her full name] MP,
> As my MP I am asking you to please use your powerful position to challenge injustices, change structures keeping people poor, and fight for a more just and fair world. I know being an MP is a tough, big job but please DON'T BLOW IT, this is your chance to make a positive difference :)
> Yours in hope
> Sarah (Corbett), [postcode]*

I wrote the message in my neatest, prettiest handwriting at the bottom of the hanky like a letter and then backstitched over the top. Normally I don't use capitals but in this case with the humorous wordplay to soften it I think it can work. It took me five hours on and off over a few days. While I was stitching I was thinking about the difficult job MPs have and the large amount of work her staff might have to do. I was thinking about what preconceptions they might have of me and how I needed to make sure I presented my gift for her in a humble and friendly way,

* I put my surname and postcode so that her office knew I was a local constituent.

showing that I was not demanding that she do something for me, but giving her a gift to encourage her in her new job.

I emailed her team asking for an appointment. I said I wanted to meet my MP because I am a new resident in the area, she's new to her role and I wanted to know her better and learn more about her aims in her role. They replied with an appointment time early on a Saturday morning at the local library. I dragged myself out of bed (I'm not a morning person!) with my hand-stitched gift in my pocket, my heart beating fast and met her with a nervous smile. She looked apprehensive at first and we shook hands and sat down at her desk with one of her team next to her. I said that I had sent her office some petitions I cared deeply about but that I wanted to meet her today just to get to know her a bit better and to give her a gift. I took out the hanky and gave it to her, blushing with embarrassment! She went from looking guarded to warm and appreciative. She opened it up, read the message and then turned it over and had a look at my stitching from the back. She said she had started doing a cross-stitch design for her friend's wedding present and that friend has her twenty-fifth wedding anniversary this year and the cross-stitch isn't finished yet! We had a little giggle about that and I said how long the hanky had taken me and I hoped it would encourage her in her role to prioritise the needs of the most vulnerable people in our area and the world as well as protect our planet from more harm. I told her that the time it took to make the present gave me time to think about the job of being an MP, the area we lived in and the global issues we are all connected to. I asked her why she decided to go into politics. She told me that she had previously worked for John Lewis Partnership before becoming an MP. I told her how much I admire their business model of being an employee-owned UK company. I briefly mentioned that I had met members of a small-scale worker's cooperative in Kenya whose business model was similar and so empowering for local residents as well as having life-changing positive impacts on the local community, such as providing finance to pay for school uniforms for local orphans and equipment to create 'vertical gardens' in areas becoming more drought-ridden because of climate change. I asked her what causes she was passionate about and she told me quietly about how FGM (Female Genital Mutilation) was affecting a lot of women in our constituency and she was working to support them and wanted to implement laws to stop this practice taking place. I encouraged her in this much-needed work and told her I was keen to help in any way that was appropriate. We discussed some of the issues I had sent petitions about and I made it clear that I was keen to learn why she decided to vote a particular way and she asked her colleague to send me more information about a particular bill she had voted on. I said that I would continue to send her the petitions I cared about from credible charities working on these issues and that I hoped her team would have the capacity to reply explaining their support or why they voted against it. I also agreed to be put on her local newsletter mailing list to keep up to date and to come along to any events I could support or wanted to know more about. We parted with smiles and handshakes.

I immediately wrote up as much of the meeting as I could in my notebook: what we discussed, what she said and what she was hesitant to say, what she seemed to be really passionate about and what she came across as quite passive towards. I wrote down my interpretation of her body language at key points and her interaction with me. I made a note of off-the-cuff comments she made on particular issues she might not have noticed but which were very telling. This would all help me when I met her again or was asked to contact my MP on a particular campaign issue to see if she would be in favour or against a bill. I also thought it would be useful to feed back some of this information we discussed with the charities who asked me to send the petitions to my MP. It might be useful information for them to help strengthen their campaign in a small way (often campaign organisations or groups have a list of particularly influential MPs to focus their attention on for specific campaigns). I encouraged groups and organisations who had not thought about working with her because they didn't share the same overall political ideologies, to get in touch with my MP's office staff to arrange a meeting. I reminded them not to judge a book by its cover but let them know that she was friendly, really cared about certain issues and could be a very useful ally to gain cross-party support on issues in Parliament. And cross-party support can be a very effective way of gaining more traction for a campaign.

I received an email from her team the following week thanking me for my hanky with a photo attached of it as a permanent fixture on the pinboard on her wall. Since that initial meeting we both refer to my hanky in all of our correspondence. Her team now know me as 'the hanky girl' (which is not what I was looking for but, hey, it helps them remember me) and reply to my emails. And we contact each other to ask for mutual support when needed and are more strategic in how we work together. For example, she was losing members of her local political party in the campaign she supported which asked the government to increase the aid budget to 0.7 per cent of GDP. To any MP it is a worry when you are losing local membership: you look bad to your party and you're in a weaker position for re-election. She cared about implementing an increase in foreign aid and so did I. We joined in a photo call alongside other constituents who supported the campaign for local media attention, which in turn helped her show her party members that she couldn't ignore the support for the aid bill even if she wanted to and I used the story to share with craftivists, other campaign organisations who were part of the coalition for this campaign and other supporters across the UK to help strengthen the campaign.

We still disagree; I can't claim to have changed her views or voting directly and I will never know how much impact my gift and our interactions have had, but it has helped us connect and build a mutually beneficial relationship. What the gift did do was to help me become a better lobbyist: I used the time it took to make the hanky to empathise with my MP, reflect on her situation and ambitions and think through how to interact with her in our initial meeting. Investing time in making this present gave me the courage to meet my MP in person rather than stay in bed. Handing over my hanky gave me a chance to meet her and get a feel for what makes her tick. I learnt so much from listening to her explain her voting decisions and I gained useful information to help me in particular campaign work, which I could share with charities. Without this small, delicate and imperfect handmade gift I'm not sure we would have worked together after the meeting or that I would have become as strategic in my lobbying to her. I believe that this one act of making her something touched her more deeply than any petition I have given her. The physical object still on her pinboard has been a tool for continuous and respectful communication.

Be a loving, critical friend

To make long-lasting change we need to be loving, critical friends rather than aggressive enemies and craftivism is a great tool to help with that shift. I have craftivism hanky kits people can use to help them connect to local influential people, build long-term relationships with them and communicate with them in a respectful and memorable way.* Some people hadn't met their local politician until making them a present gave them the courage to meet them. Craftivists around the world have made gifts for teachers, police officers, business people, journalists, senators and other people in positions of power as a tool to encourage them to use their power for good and to challenge them when they are abusing or wasting their power.

* For more information on the kits, see: www.craftivist-collective.com/dont-blow-it-hanky

Over the last seven years of making gifts for influential people I've learnt so much more since giving my first craftivism hanky to my MP. In this section (Part 3) we will look more at how gifts can have even more of an impact by looking at improving the aesthetics, the power of the language we use, how to have grace threaded through our gift, and how to use our gift as a catalyst for change.

9
Graceful Activism

You give but little when you give of your possessions. It is when you give of yourself that you truly give.

– Kahlil Gibran

Mr X Stitch, also known as 'the kingpin of contemporary cross-stitch', heard about my hanky gift and told me that he would struggle to make a gift for his local MP. They had met a few times and were both too stubborn to budge from their positions. He didn't like his MP and so had seen no point in working with him. I told him that giving a craftivism gift wasn't about agreeing with all of the gift-receiver's views or actions. It was a tool to help the craftivist treat this influential person the way they would like to be treated: to listen with an open heart, empathise with and understand where they are coming from (even if we don't agree with their thinking) and encouraging them to use their power and influence to help people and the planet rather than focus our attention on fighting to take their power away. A gift can help you start on the right foot with a new contact or restore an existing tense relationship. A few days later I got a text from Mr X Stitch saying, 'I was thinking, your craftivism is a very graceful form of activism.'

Culture of power

If we define power as the ability to get the job done, then grace in action can look illogical, even bonkers. We live in a culture where our default seems to be that the way to get stuff done is to do it ourselves: to gain power we think we need to take it away from others. Power is seen as a way to control people or change people's actions by force. Aggressive abuse is used to attempt to change situations and topple opponents. We often see it in politics and in our personal lives, too. How many of us resort to manipulation to try to get people to do what we want them to do? How many of us sink to abuse when others will not be the way we want them to be? I still see images in the media of graffiti, of activists throwing eggs at politicians and business leaders, and messages naming and shaming people, people shouting, belittling or ridiculing others, giant disrespectful effigies of people in positions of power being taken on marches. We live in a culture where we are regularly told 'all politicians are corrupt', 'police are pigs', chief executives are 'fat cats'. I can understand the anger towards these people but they are still people. These labels and actions create bigger divisions, making it harder to work together or even listen to each other. It fuels a culture of distrust, dehumanises people and splinters society into dangerous silos. Hate breeding hate. Exactly what we don't want.

What if we turned the ideas of power upside down, turned away from the desire to control others by force and encouraged those in power to try to always use their influence in the most loving way possible? Let's be subversive craftivists and not add to the cynicism we sadly often see in activism. Let's look at the bigger picture: instead of hating our enemies, let's show them love. Instead of brashly asserting and promoting ourselves and our agenda, let's quietly get on with the work of justice on behalf of others. Instead of trying to win every argument through sheer force of numbers or names on a petition or bullying an opponent, let's gently encourage them by sometimes being prepared to lose the argument. Instead of competing to take their power let's empower them to use their power well. Instead of fighting to punish people, let's fight to change the system and culture. Instead of creating battlefields, let's build bridges. Let's find our common values and connections, especially where there is the threat of conflict. Let's show belief and trust in the face of disbelief and mistrust. Let's admit we don't have all the answers, recognise our own flaws and help others quietly to do the best job they can without looking for praise. Let's aspire for a collective society, not an individualistic and competitive one. Let's strive to 'do no harm' and be honest with each other about how complex and difficult that can be within any organisation or group. We need to govern ourselves by a thoughtful conscience not by the status quo. Craftivists should be curious, creative and courageous: our graciousness might seem weak, passive or naive but it's far from it.

My definition of grace in this context

I am not referring to 'grace' as fashion-style or physical elegance. Instead, I use the word to focus on graceful attitude and actions: good manners, tact and politeness. But it's more than that too. Being gracious is about being kind, warm-hearted, humble and empathising with others. It's about putting the injustice issue before your own needs and seeing where you can support others to make long-term change. We should acknowledge our own flaws, which will help us offer forgiveness, and invest hope in the power-holders we want to influence. We should seek to see our part in the injustices we want to help fix.

The gifts we make to give to people in positions of power aren't about us, they're to help lift their spirits when things get tough and when they doubt their own ability to work for peace and justice. We don't have to give gifts to people in positions of power. It seems out of balance to do so. Our gift is not a reward or a cultural obligation and in many ways we might feel that they don't deserve kindness but that's why it can be so effective. Graceful activism is being genuine and sincere. We are practising what we want our world to be like: a place where we all care for each other and support each other to fulfil our potential and the potential of others, a world where we listen to each other's views and look at all information to see where we can work together. We start with good faith in each other (we may not end with that faith), are mindful of our judgements and preconceptions and we never give up on each other to show our humanity and do good work. We keep hope possible; we are not convinced by despair. It's our trademark as a gentle protester. It's fundamental not optional. We might be seen as sentimental fools. But our sentimentality is appealing. People like it. In an age of bad belief, cynicism and battles over power, graceful activism speaks of what's been lost and gives us hope. I believe generosity of spirit and grace are key to our being effective craftivists. Let's thread grace through our gifts so that they are beautiful on the inside as well as the outside.

Why give a gift?

So why are we focusing on giving gifts and not just sending a letter, chocolates or flowers? Craftivists focus on transformation, not just transaction. Gifts have the potential to transform the soul in ways that commodities simply cannot. Gifts can warm our heart, awaken our soul, inspire and empower us. Let's be gentle craftivists and harness that. Lewis Hyde, poet, cultural critic and author of the book *The Gift* writes: 'We do not deal with commodities when we wish to initiate or preserve ties of affection.'[1]

Commodity has value whereas a gift has worth. Unlike the sale of a commodity, the giving of a gift has the potential to move people emotionally and establish a relationship between the recipient and the giver, which can lead to long-term working relationships. We give gifts to people to remember their worth and encourage them: jewellery to show our love and support when we are not there, a book of poems to inspire a friend who loves to write. Milton Glaser, a celebrated graphic designer from New York, was equally good at arts and sciences. He remembers making a point to tell his chemistry teacher whom he hugely admired that although he loved his classes, he had decided to go to art college. His teacher took out a pack of Conté crayons from his desk and gave them to Glaser and said, 'Do good work.' Fifty years later, Glaser retold the story and said, 'To some degree, everything I do was supported by this idea that the only way I could pay him back was to do good work.' The gift of a pencil didn't require anything of Glaser, but the respect it showed from the teacher to his student gave Glaser the courage to follow his passion. Those pencils were a gift, not only a functional gift but also a gift that said 'I believe in you.'

Who to give your gift to

When you make your craftivism gift, you also make a commitment to initiate or continue a critical friendship with your receiver to help tackle injustices in the world together. Make sure you pick someone whom you want to work with and in an area where you believe you can have an impact. Humility, strategy and grace need to be threaded through this decision. Are you focusing on building a long-term relationship with someone of influence or is this part of a specific issue-led campaign that involves a 'target' for the duration of the campaign until it is won? Craftivism gifts are not useful for short-term urgent campaign actions because not only will you be rushing the making of your gift but it will look too transactional. However, it could be useful for issue-led campaigns that may take a year or more to implement. You don't have to see your gift-receiver every day or contact them every month, but after giving your gift you will want to keep injustice issues on their agenda by nudging them every few months or at key times relevant to the campaign, for example, when new laws are introduced or if the issue is a hot topic in the media. Ask professionals working in your area who they think would be the most appropriate gift-receiver for you to focus on.

Remember to connect with any charities or organisations that are also tackling the injustice you are addressing. They may have expert knowledge and resources that can support and inform you on the issue and how to tackle it, inspire you in your gift-making and help you feel part of a community of changemakers. There might be a campaign to stop fracking in your local area: the campaign might have a petition people can sign, events to attend and a skilled charity who are creating a proposed policy for the government to consider implementing. If one of the Ministers of the Department of Energy and Climate Change (DECC) is your local MP then you could really help the campaign by connecting with your MP and feeding back what you have learnt to the campaign managers. If someone else is already doing this in your area, why not look for another useful gift-receiver and ask the other campaigners to help decide who to target, perhaps a local journalist or a celebrity. Don't feel alone.

The safer and easier strategy would be to give a gift to someone who you like and want to thank and encourage to keep up the great work. I can understand that thought but remember that for the world to change we need to encourage those who might be creating harm to turn that harm into help. Don't simply focus on congratulating existing changemakers (you can do that too) but focus on what needs to be done and who can do something about it. We only have limited time and we need to invest it wisely. Be realistic on who you can reach. Your 'circle of influence' has your friends and family at its core, and it's these people who you have most influence with. Further from the centre of your circle are your colleagues, neighbours, maybe local faith groups or other local service centres like the local school, shops and library etc. If you don't know the prime minister personally and you are not living in their constituency then it is unlikely they will be within your circle of influence. It's fantastic if you can contact and get to know the CEO of a national or international company but if that's not possible why not focus on the owner of a local shop you can get to know and encourage to be as ethical and environmentally friendly as possible and a role model for other local shops? Shelley is a craftivist. She is embroidering a message of encouragement on a handkerchief for the owner of a local large craft shop:

> He has a lot of power in our area. My town is full of creative adults and children and it would be so great if he was a model of ethical business to inspire and influence other stores. I hope that it creates a friendship where I can encourage him to sell more ethical products, encourage the children to recycle their craft waste and maybe even consider only using renewable energy to run the store. But first of all I need to get to know him better. I go there all the time with my kids so that shouldn't be too difficult.

When members of the community I grew up in were trying to improve housing conditions in a tower block of apartments, they first focused their attention on the local housing officers but realised just in time that the people who they really needed to convince were the local housing manager and the elected councillor in charge of housing at the city council. Other powerful people to bear in mind are religious leaders, school teachers, board members, political councillors, journalists, newspaper editors, famous bloggers, YouTubers, Instagrammers and other people who have influence and who you could encourage to use that influence well.

The nature of giving

Throughout history gifts have been given to signify peace between tribes, countries, governments and royal families, and to keep relationships civil. Gifts between countries signify the close of war: the USA helped Japan to rebuild after the Second World War as the first step towards normalising relations. In contrast, after the war with Vietnam, the US congress refused all reconstructive aid to Vietnam, suggesting that the government didn't see the war as over.

We need to be aware of the flipside of giving a gift: it can imply wanting a gift in return. Gifts can also leave the recipient feeling obligated to us in some way, manipulated, or even humiliated. Gifts can sometimes establish or maintain hierarchies rather than break through them.

Giving gifts in anticipation of a repayment or out of duty takes away the spirit of our gift. Our gifts should be offered freely without a contract or agreement in return. Nevertheless, we should be aware that they are never truly free – that will always be a by-product of your gift – but we need to give up trying to control what that is or we risk losing our gift's positive potential. The more we try and control the reaction, the more we are showing bad faith in that person; faith that they won't offer thanks or connection, emotion or kindness back. This lack of confidence that we often show to people in positions of power has created a scarcity of trust and grace. This makes our gift even more needed in places of power where there is a high level of mistrust. You want your gift to warm the heart of your receiver, delight their senses and offer courage for their work.

What gift to give

Fortunately for us, the popular idea that handicrafts are associated with love means that it is a powerful tool to engage with people of political influence. For craftivists, it's tempting to make a gift that we like the look of and that our friends and peers would admire. But remember that the gift is about the receiver not about you or your peers. Let's stay graceful and humble and see our craftivism as a service, not a chance for celebrity. To do this we need to show creative restraint to make and give the best gift: it is easy to miss the mark. It's a discipline vital for any craftivist who truly wants to make an impact through their gift. There will naturally be a part of us embodied in our gifts – our wobbly stitches, for instance – but the aim of your gift is to encourage your receiver to work courageously with care for all those who will be affected by their decisions. You might want to make them a giant quilt to cover their office wall because you like making quilts and think it would look awesome, but is it going to antagonise them rather than bring them joy? Have you ever had that sinking feeling when you unwrap a gift and see that it's a colour you don't like or something you would never choose to wear yourself, like the infamous Christmas jumper made by a loving grandmother? The last thing we want is for our receiver to have that feeling. Just like refugees who might not want your handmade socks and would prefer the things they really need, making things that touch people's emotions and make them feel special is a true triumph. I discussed these difficulties with Rachael Matthews, textile artist and author of *The Mindfulness in Knitting*. She shared her thoughts on the risk of handcrafted gifts becoming weapons on an email with me, saying:

> The buzz of someone loving our gifts keeps us going. We imagine the gift being celebrated by receivers and others. With all this positive intention, how could the gift possibly go wrong? We can convince ourselves that a relationship is now sealed. But how is the sentiment returned? Saying 'I've made this for you so you must love me' is tricky. Our gifts should only ever be a clarification of what is true.

It is also important that our seemingly gentle gift isn't made for someone your gift-receiver is not, or for someone you want them to be.

This can cause tension instead of connection. Be mindful of what you are stitching into your gift, consciously or unconsciously. Does your gift contain a political preference they might not share, regional tastes they might not like or anything else that can weaken your graceful gift? Your gift is to show what you mean when you are struggling to say it: your faith in them, your commitment to being the change you wish to see in the world and helping them to do the same. Be clear, open and honest. And research your target to find a design, aesthetic and message that means something to them. (More on this in Chapters 10–12.)

During the making of your gift

Through the steps of deciding who to make your gift for, what the gift will look like (see Chapter 10: Compete with Beauty) and the message you will stitch (see Chapter 11: The Message) you will already have started the process of learning about the recipient of your gift, researching their role, the actions they take in their role, their interests, down to what colours they tend to wear, to help you figure out what type of gift is best for them. Now you can use the slow, gentle and meditative action of handicraft to empathise with them. Try and see the world from their point of view and make your connection with that person deeper. Not fully understanding their vision of their job or the world only gives us a new subject for thought while making. Let your gift-receiver help you expand your ways of seeing.

The root of altruism lies in empathy, the ability to read emotions in others. To lack a sense of another's need or despair is not caring or compassionate. Martin Hoffman, an American psychologist and professor emeritus of clinical and developmental psychology at New York University, argues that the roots of morality are to be found in empathy. Empathising with the victims of unfair structures, and thereby sharing some of their distress, moves people to act to help them.

Empathy builds on self-awareness and so don't forget to use some of your time to be mindful of yourself; the more open we are to our own emotions, the more skilled we are in reading the feelings of others. Remember that anger is almost always a secondary reaction so look for what's underneath your anger (are you hurt, jealous or something else?) and any anger you see in your gift-receiver. We always have choices about how we respond to emotions and the more ways we know how to respond to an emotion, the richer our life will be and the better craftivist we will be. Learn ways to handle anxiety, anger and sadness. Use the process of making your gift to help you prepare for meeting your gift-receiver and reflect on how you can support them in their work.

Psychologist Daniel Goleman, author of the book *Emotional Intelligence*, claims that: 'We catch feelings from one another as though they were some kind of social virus.'[2] While crafting, think about what it is that you want to spread. Is it anger, bitterness, hope, love or compassion? Addressing any preconceived judgements you have of your target and any presumptions you have about how they do their job will help with your emotions and preparation for giving your gift. Don't slip into over-simplifying. Imagine any barriers your recipient might have to implement best practice in their work: budget restraints, time limitations, consumer behaviour, colleagues who want to block improvements, other members of the public who are against the call for fairness and want to focus on individual benefits, etc. Use the time to ask yourself why they might be making the decisions they are: are they aware of the harm they are causing? Are they proactively supporting a policy or is it a by-product of another decision made by someone else? Are they supporting a law because their political party or company has strict guidelines for staff to do so? What power and influence do they have and what restrictions do they have in their role? What would help them implement a positive action? Is it support from customers or constituents or the potential for good publicity for the organisation on the issue that influences their actions?

Why not see if you can find any talks or interviews with them online and watch them while crafting to help you with your empathy? Are they friendly, guarded, defensive, funny? Are they talking about something they are passionate about, whether it's their work or a hobby? I am always keen to understand people who I disagree with on political issues. It helps me be a better citizen and craftivist. The film *Mitt* is an American documentary that chronicled the 2008 and 2012 presidential campaigns of Republican candidate Mitt Romney. It may be biased but it helped me understand how his upbringing, faith and political ideologies have shaped his politics as well as to see the demanding work politicians do during election campaigns. The films *Selma*, *Lincoln* and *Gandhi* also taught me about the emotional intelligence needed to work with people we disagree with. The time you have to make your gift is an opportunity to exercise empathy and think about how you can encourage your target to be responsible in their role. Goleman reminds us that:

> Failure to register another's feelings is a major deficit in emotional intelligence, and a tragic failing in what it means to be human. For all rapport, the root of caring stems from emotional attunement, from the capacity for empathy.[3]

Giving your gift

When do you give your gift? Giving a politician a gift in the middle of their election campaign might not be the best idea: they will be so busy trying to gather support that they won't have the headspace to reflect on it. They might not win the campaign and so the gift is then redundant. Whereas if you give them your gift at a quiet time of the political year you will have more of a chance to discuss their role, motivations, hopes of what they want to achieve and they might find your gift and discussion really useful to help them in their planning. Similarly, if you give a CEO of a business a gift during peak Christmas shopping season it might not receive the same attention as if you gave it during their planning season, which tends to happen in the second half of each financial year, i.e. six months after the end of the financial year (April).

Where are you going to give your gift? Can you find a quiet and safe place for your target to give them their gift, such as their office? That way they will not feel put on the spot or attacked, unlike at a public event when they may be surrounded by many people vying for their attention. If you can only meet them at an event, can you contact them, their personal assistant or another colleague in advance to let them know you will be there to give them a positive gift? That way they won't be nervous when they receive it and they may well make an extra effort to talk to you after the event. If you cannot meet them, find other friendly ways to attract them to your gift such as wrapping your post in a coloured envelope or package – a hopeful yellow might be more appropriate than an aggressive red (more in Chapter 10).

How are you going to give your gift? Our gift embodies our hope that the recipient uses their power to help the most vulnerable people in our society and protect our planet. It also shows them that we trust they can do a good job. Be careful not to give a gift that will have to be refused or declared as potential bribery. This can be a fuzzy area. For example, should a police officer accept an apple from a local shopkeeper? Is it extortion or connecting with a community they serve?

Meeting your target

Ideally you want to hand deliver your gift so there is time for a conversation. (See Chapter 11 if you cannot meet them and so will need to write a letter and carefully package your gift for them to receive.) Before you arrive, make time to be mindful of what you are bringing to the meeting, not just in the shape of your gift but also in your emotions. Most people can pick up on the emotional state you're in and so try to get in a hopeful, friendly and graceful mood. Don't arrive wearing politically charged clothing or props, or a large black hooded top that looks aggressive. Remember, this is your initial meeting and so you don't want the gift-receiver feeling unsafe or that you are there to manipulate them into thinking or acting in a particular way. Don't try and compete with their power, instead, acknowledge that they are in a powerful position and you respect that. The more respectful you can be, the more warmth they will feel towards you. And you don't need to ask for a meeting on neutral ground: it's human nature to want to put people at ease in their own setting, such as their office.

Arrive calmly and quietly. No fanfare, no photographer from the local newspaper or PR machine behind you. No one needs to know this meeting is happening. This is an intimate form of activism between you and your gift-receiver. Smile as soon as you meet your target and offer a handshake: emotions are contagious; we unconsciously mirror people we are interacting with through facial expressions, gestures, tones of voice and other non-verbal emotions. Most examples of contagion are subtle and part of a tacit exchange that happens in every encounter. We transmit and catch moods – both nourishing and toxic – from each other. For example, a small group of Buddhist monks during the war in Vietnam silently walked through a conflict area, causing the soldiers one-by-one to stop fighting and allow the monks to reach the other side bullet-free. Sadly the war continued, but this story shows we can have the power to pacify some situations. When two people interact, the direction of the mood transfer is from the one who is more forceful in expressing feelings to the one who is more passive. An emotionally healthy person who knows how to handle people is more likely to be effective. Those who smile at their boss although they dislike them, yet still keep their core values intact, have a high emotional intelligence. Stay mindful of the feeling in the room: some people are more susceptible to emotional contagion than others but starting your interaction on a positive footing is vital. If they are a loud and bubbly person then you will naturally interact differently to them than if they are softly spoken. Try and get an idea of how your gift-receiver is feeling and let that lead the way. Listen to their tone of voice, what they say, how they say it. Do you need to reassure them that you are not trying to trick them with your gift? Do you need to be clearer with them that you know they are very busy so you are grateful for their time? Is your body language aggressive or open? Psychologist Dr Frank Bernieri of the Oregon State University states that:

> How awkward or comfortable you feel with someone is at some level physical. You need to have compatible timing, to coordinate your movements, to feel comfortable. Synchrony reflects the depth of engagement between the partners; if you're highly engaged, your mood begins to mesh, whether positive or negative.[4]

Now to the art of conversation: ask strategic and open questions. This meeting is about getting a feel for what makes them tick, showing interest in their work, and seeing how you can support them to be responsible in their role, not telling them what you think about a certain issue. You can give them a quick explanation of what you have made them and why, but in an informal way. Let them read your message without feeling you have to fill in the silence. You could mention fun facts such as you used some fabric from your grandmother's stash or the felt you used is made from 100 per cent post-consumer plastic bottles. Activist and author Fran Peavey wrote in her book *Strategic Questioning*:

> How best can we be involved? We can start with deep and dynamic listening and questioning where the solutions are limited only by our imaginations. Our neighbors and co-workers have

important strategic information. So do we. When we listen deep into the heart where courage and intelligence lurk, strategies may be liberated into action.[5]

Ask them about their job. What does it entail? What do they love about it and what do they find difficult? Let them know that you are interested in the positive impact they can make through their job. One tip is to say their name a few times within your conversation: it naturally makes us feel valued and listened to. Can you make them laugh or smile? We're more likely to remember strangers who make us laugh. If you can have a positive tone, if you are compassionate and show empathy for them you are outstanding in emotional intelligence in what can be a difficult situation.

Try gently to steer the conversation, navigating it away from shallow pleasantries to deeper issues. Create a safe space for conversation and share some personal comments that might help you bond, such as the fact that you hoped they would like your gift and not see it as a waste, or that you picked a polka-dot pattern because they seem to wear lots of polka-dot patterned ties! Don't be disheartened if they are guarded and don't share a lot with you. They might not feel that they can be open with you, especially about private information concerning their organisation. People's emotions are rarely put into words. Some people may need time to gather their thoughts and emotions after such an unusual meeting before sharing their reaction (especially introverts). A key to intuiting another person's feelings is in the ability to read non-verbal signs: tone of voice, gesture, facial expression. One rule of thumb used in communication research is that 90 per cent or more of an emotional message is non-verbal. Such messages – anxiety in someone's tone of voice, irritation in the quickness of a gesture – are almost always taken in unconsciously. The skill that allows us to read the situation well or poorly is for the most part learnt tacitly. When a person's words disagree with what is conveyed by their tone of voice, gesture or other non-verbal channels, the emotional truth is how they say something rather than their words.

Before you leave, can you encourage them in their role and ask how you can help them reach their potential in their work? Are there any events you could attend? Could you get their email address to continue the conversation?

After the meeting, why not write them a note to say you hope they like the gift and you wish them all the best? This will hopefully open up a dialogue, and will mark the start of your journey as a gentle protester with your gift-receiver. Don't be tempted to make lots more gifts for them in the near future. It could dilute your impact rather than enhance it. They might question your motivation as being more about your love of making than your concern to help them.

Grace leads to grace

If our gifts and interactions come from a genuine concern, are delivered with a sincere heart and a desire for the best, then they are graceful. We may never know the full impact of our gift, or be able to measure it completely, but it's still worth continuing to have faith in your gift-receiver. Grace often produces grace in ourselves and others. Thread grace through your planning, making and interactions. To be truly graceful we need our gift to be graceful on the outside as well as on the inside, and that's where the next chapters come in.

10

Compete with Beauty

A thing of beauty is a joy forever: its loveliness increases; it will never pass into nothingness.

— John Keats

Bruce Mau the Canadian graphic designer, has a strategy to 'compete with beauty'[1] – to use beauty to vie for attention with business, society, money, social mobility and other areas of life. Craftivism uses beauty to compete for attention. Our beautiful gifts offer a reason for the gift-giver and receiver to meet. Our beautiful gifts can stir someone's heart and lead to a connection between both parties that more transactional activism tactics can't do. And if the gift exudes beauty in spirit as well as in its appearance it can make a lasting impression that will help you in your campaign. So how do we weave beauty through every part of our gift to help encourage decision-makers to make the choice to help and not harm our world? One element is its appearance.

We are all affected by aesthetics. What something looks like can determine how we feel, what we do and even how *we* look, often unconsciously. An art object can create feelings of pleasure, strength, beauty, comfort, compassion, security and camaraderie, as well as confusion, humiliation, fear or even rage. Aesthetics should be carefully designed into your craftivism gift. We need to design our gift with the receiver in mind, not with our own ideas of what is beautiful. We have a goal to reach, a function to fulfil: to engage a particular influential person and try to continue to encourage them, sometimes work with them, sometimes gently challenging them but always with the aim to help create long-term sustainable change. You want your gift-receiver to love their gift, take ownership of it, and ideally to want to have it on display to help remind them to make the decisions needed to tackle injustice.

We all instinctively know if something is visually appealing; knowing why it is appealing is harder. Nonetheless, we know how colours affect our emotions, we feel the impact size and symbols can have on our understanding of a gift, and we experience the feelings we get from seeing and feeling handmade imperfections. Design Critic Alice Rawsthorn writes in her book *Hello World: Where Design Meets Life*:

> But we cannot escape design, however much we might wish to. All we can do is to try to determine whether its impact on us will be positive or negative, and to do so successfully we need to understand it, the more thoroughly the better.[2]

Senses

As has been noted in previous chapters, engaging two or more of our senses can increase the connection we have with an object and its purpose. Our objects are already competing well for attention with online petitions and emails because they are physical as well as visually attractive. Using textiles to create soft, handmade sculptures can add a desire to touch and interact with your gift. 'I keep wanting to stroke it,' said a craftivist when I gave her a hand-embroidered fabric version of a sticky-note to play with. Try to make your gift soft and fragile so that the receiver will feel the urge to treat it with care and therefore engage more deeply with it. When designing your gift you want to reach as many of the senses as you can while staying within your brief (so that probably rules out taste!) of creating a long-lasting gift as a catalyst for connection, conversation and positive change.

Colour

It's no coincidence that we use phrases such as 'feeling blue' and 'seeing red': colour affects us emotionally, mentally and often physically. Colour affects everything from our mood to our productivity. From decades of research there are some generalities about the properties of colour we can learn to help us design our gifts. Some colours are connected to experiences and associations. For example, a particular hue of purple might remind you of a favourite relative's winter coat or a toy you grew up with. Others carry more universal meaning: yellow is generally a hopeful colour; orange gives off a feeling of vitality and success; red is stimulating, whether it represents adventure, passion, aggression or attention. I avoid red and black together in my craftivism because it can look aggressive rather than gentle. Grey is the opposite of red – neutral, passive, low-energy – but can be paired with a more powerful colour to create a new narrative. For example, if you use grey for the box to put your gift in, you are implying that you don't want to be manipulative; combining this colour with a purple ribbon adds a touch of luxury and helps your receiver feel valued. Why does purple remind us of royalty? Because purple doesn't appear in nature very much and so in the past it was difficult and expensive to make purple dye. However, too much purple can make your object feel artificial.

If you are unsure of the potential meanings of a colour then think about where it appears in nature: blue represents clarity, calmness and wisdom. It is the colour of the sky and ocean, both representing loyalty, dependability, honesty and trust. Paler versions of colour can create the same emotional response but toned down. For example, light blue is subtly wise and loyal but not too attention-grabbing, whereas royal blue exudes discipline. From the 1970s, green has become the symbolic colour for ecological activists all over the world: it is the colour of nature in many countries and of paradise in Islamic cultures, but ironically it can also symbolise poison because of the toxic substances needed to create green dye.

We all have our own preferences too and each of us have different associations with colours. Why not research images of your gift-receiver to see what colours they wear to help you create a combination they might find more attractive? Does your person love wearing pink or many colours at once? Do they stick to monochrome but repeatedly pair it with a splattering of red? Use colour to connect to your gift-receiver.

Symbols

Symbols are useful to engage different needs, desires, ideas, beliefs or fears. A raised fist represents protest, for example, while a coat of arms can represent authority. We can also use symbols to show fragility and vulnerability, which can attract people to your gift. Instructive symbols intend to regulate our behaviour or tell us to perform a particular task, and can be used to replace words if you are struggling to fit your message on your gift. That's why I used a handkerchief and stitched a message framed around the wordplay 'don't blow it'.

To engage a powerful person and to create intimacy with them, you want to focus on attracting them to your gift using symbols they connect with. For example, if they love gardening, can you design flowers and leaves on your gift? Or use floral fabric to represent flourishing, positive progress and rooting their professional actions in their values? If they love music, can you find fabric with musical notes on or stitch a line of music on your gift with the musical notes showing a hopeful tune, maybe even with lyrics relevant to your cause? Use symbols sparingly in your gift so that the receiver does not feel they are being pushed in one direction. Subtlety is key.

Originality

We live in a world surrounded by mass-produced items. It's much easier, quicker and often even cheaper to buy a gift rather than create one, which is why most gifts are bought rather than made. You can compete with mass-produced objects for attention by creating something not only beautiful but which also clearly took a long time – naturally giving your gift more special value. Personalisation will make your gift-receiver feel special: it harks back to value placed on bespoke objects where only the wealthy in history could afford them. We all want to feel seen and heard and so try to make your gift as tailored to your gift-receiver as possible to show that you've really thought about them, want them to enjoy their gift, and you are offering kindness to *them*.

You want your gift to connect to their heart just as much or even more so than their head, and one way to do this is through imperfection and intentional flaws. In a time when standardisation is the norm, we often yearn for idiosyncrasies. Symmetry has the power to calm us because we are used to seeing it in nature (sunflowers, beehives, pine cones and so on) but nature always has little flaws, imperfections and irregular natural details to remind us they are natural and fragile. 'Wabi-sabi' is the name given to the Japanese aesthetics and worldview centred on imperfection and transience. Leonard Koren, an American artist, aesthetics expert and writer describes this aesthetic of beauty as 'imperfect, impermanent and incomplete'.[3] Characteristics of wabi-sabi that we can learn from include asymmetry, roughness or irregularity, simplicity, modesty and appreciation of the innocent integrity of the object and processes involved. For example, frayed edges of fabric can move us into associating them with antiques, heirlooms and keepsakes, forging a stronger emotional rapport with the user. These imperfections create a space for 'intimate activism' between the gift-giver and receiver: by offering your imperfect but handmade gift you are putting yourself in a vulnerable position, hoping they will accept your wobbly object and cherish it. You are giving them power, very different to other forms of activism that compete for power.

Integrity

Robert Grudin, the American philosopher, wrote in his book *Design and Truth*:

> Good design enables honest and effective engagement with the world. If good design tells the truth, poor design tells a lie, a lie usually related, in one way or another, to the getting or abusing of power.[4]

BP's green and yellow sunflower-inspired logo does not have integrity. BP adopted that emblem and dropped its old name, British Petroleum, in 2001 at a time when ecological protests against the oil industry were growing and it wished to present itself as a responsible company that cared about the environment. Whenever BP have been involved in ecological disasters, such as the 2010 explosion in the Gulf of Mexico, its sunflower logo has been ridiculed as insincere and inappropriate, understandably so.

Similarly, if your gift is made with the intention of manipulating the recipient, he or she will be able to tell. We all can. Size is often an indication of whether your gift has integrity or not: aim for small and beautiful not big and brash. You want the person to treasure your gift without it being imposing or too intimidating to display. A 'quiet gift' will help the recipient make their own decisions to do the right thing, not force them into action.

We need to keep in mind the integrity of the resources we use to make our gift. If we want to encourage a local but world-famous fashion blogger to use their power to ask their followers to only buy ethically made clothes that will last, then we want to make sure our object doesn't fall apart or have a message that will become out of date. We need to design environmental responsibly into our design and design obsolescence out of our gift.

Spirit

We can more often than not tell the difference between a gift someone has made with love but which might have lots of mistakes, and someone who has rushed a 'gift' but has made fewer mistakes. We can tell where people have taken short cuts and where people have really thought through every detail, hoping to please the person the gift is for. In the past I've arrived at a politician's office with a 'gift' that wasn't truly a gift. Once it was a giant engagement ring borrowed from a campaign organisation to offer to my MP in exchange for acceptance of a strong climate change deal. It was a great visual image for a photograph to be used in local media for the campaign but it wasn't a gift. It was a prop for the photograph we needed for the media we wanted. And it felt wrong to say it was a gift.

Trust your instincts

We should use the knowledge we have to help us design something that is both useful and beautiful, but don't forget to trust your gut instinct too. I made my hanky for my MP before I read about the impact colour can have, but luckily my instinct was right and the pale purple handkerchief did resonate with her (she does wear purple often). Design decisions combine intuition and thought.

The survival of the beautiful

'The survival of the beautiful'[5] is what American philosopher David

Rothenberg calls the underlying principle of a phenomenon Charles Darwin called 'sexual selection' in his 1871 book *The Descent of Man*. Darwin sought to explain why the male of certain species appear to defy the law of natural selection by retaining some features that served no practical function, such as a peacock's tail whose sole purpose, Darwin argued, was to be so beautiful that it would arouse the sexual interest of females of the species, thereby enabling the male to breed and the species to thrive.[6] It could be argued that the same can be said in contemporary society: if the traditional form of an object is exceptionally pleasing to look at or to touch, it is likely to survive because we will continue to crave it, even though a more convenient alternative is readily available. For example, beautifully bound books are still sold even though it's quicker, cheaper and easier to download an ebook. Handmade gifts represent a close bond with someone else. Even if they are bleached by the sun on a pinboard or have stains that won't come out, they are difficult to part with. Try and make your gift survive through its beauty.

MP staff drinks: round one

I took seven MP staff members for drinks in the House of Commons bar to find out from them if this craftivism method had any impact on the politicians they worked for. I'd invited people from the three major parties (at the time), Conservative, Labour and Liberal Democrat. I had recently finished delivering a national craftivism project in collaboration with Save the Children's 'Race Against Hunger' campaign. The campaign asked politicians to put hunger at the top of the agenda at the G8 in the summer of 2013. It was an important year because the G8 was hosted in the UK by the UK prime minister that year. The project was to rally the UK craft community over six months to show that we cared about this issue deeply and were joining the movement to encourage UK politicians and world leaders attending to be part of the solution to tackle hunger and not be part of the problem.

I asked craftivists to craft three jigsaw pieces. One was to go towards creating a touring art installation to galvanise support for the campaign from the UK public. The second piece was for the craftivist to keep as a physical reminder to do their bit to tackle hunger personally. The third jigsaw piece with a stitched message was to give to the craftivist's MP to encourage them to ask our prime minister to work with other world leaders to tackle world hunger. With over 900 jigsaws we created a powerful installation at the People's History Museum, Manchester that toured the country throughout 2013 being displayed at schools and cathedrals, shopping centres, craft fairs and beyond. Within a few months our #imapiece hashtag was tweeted over 2,000 times, reaching over 7 million people, 180 blogs were written by makers about their involvement, reaching over 19 million readers. The project was covered by thirteen magazines and newspapers, reaching 3.4 million readers in print. Over one hundred politicians were contacted by craftivists across the country, calling on them to support the campaign and to write to the prime minister, asking him to implement Save the Children's suggestions to help tackle world hunger.

After the project had ended I asked these seven people who all worked for politicians what the strengths and weaknesses were of giving their politicians the jigsaw gifts. Did the gifts have any impact at all on their decision-making? How could we have improved the project? Here is what they said about the aesthetics of the project (their response to the messaging is discussed in Chapter 11).

Yes, the jigsaw gifts were novel, unusual and extremely memorable, said all seven. They genuinely loved the gifts and all mentioned particular jigsaw pieces that had resonated with them personally. They don't often receive gifts in the post or in person and so when they do it can really brighten up the day of the MP and their staff. If the jigsaws came in the post in a brightly coloured envelope with a handwritten letter, they stood out next to other correspondence. They would show other colleagues the gift and handwritten letters. One staff member said, 'I made a point of showing my boss [the MP] the jigsaw gift to cheer him up after a long day of replying to complaints and demands. It cheered up the whole office as well as got the team talking about the issue and what we could realistically do to tackle it.'

I found it fascinating to learn that one of the motivations for displaying our jigsaw pieces in a politician's office (either in their constituency or Parliament office) was to show off to other politicians and politicians' staff. 'We are quite a competitive bunch,' said one staff member. 'We often display gifts from constituents to show colleagues, journalists and other visitors how popular our MP is.' The gifts help them decorate their often quite bland-looking offices without being so big that people might question if they swayed their MP to particular decisions. I hope some visitors asked the MP or office staff what they did do to be a piece of the solution to world hunger at the G8! Staff said that the fact that each jigsaw piece was unique and not branded with a charity logo or charity name made them believe that the constituent really did care personally about the issue and weren't just 'charity robots', doing what charities told them to do.

All staff agreed that they would prioritise appointment requests from craftivists who asked to meet their MP to give them their jigsaw gift. Who doesn't want to receive a gift? Politicians' surgery times are often on a weekend, we have to make them bearable for them, especially when most of the time people come with complaints, demands or unrealistic requests, such as 'stop the war'. The fact that nearly all of the craftivists who met their politician hadn't met them before and were pretty nervous had an impact on the politicians and staff: 'Their nervousness, lack of activism experience and the fact that they hadn't met us before suggested that they really cared about the issue. We can't tell if people really care by the petition cards we receive that just include a signature.' Staff also said that it was very useful that the constituents themselves were not wearing a charity branded T-shirt. 'We need to show media, our local party members and constituents that people care about an issue. By wearing charity T-shirts in photo shoots it can dilute the impact by just looking like an advert for a charity.'

Gift with beauty

A gift, made with care and a sensitive aesthetic, does have an effect on the person of influence and on their staff. If we want our world to be a more beautiful and harmonious place for all then let's compete for attention with beauty, not with ugly aggression. But the message needs to be just as attractive or it could cancel out the impact of the beauty...

11
The Message

Handle them carefully, for words have more power than atom bombs.

— Pearl Strachan Hurd

You could make the most beautiful gift possible for your target audience: hopeful colours, tiny intricate stitches, subtle hints of a pattern on the delicate fabric and all wrapped up beautifully in a box with a bow. But if your message says 'PAY YOUR TAXES NOW!' you are at risk of breaking any potential ties you might have been able to make. Let's be honest, who wants to be told what to do? No one. Don't use your gift to impress others, or to assault someone. Try your hardest to make the message connect deeply with your gift-receiver to help fulfil the potential they have in the powerful position they are in.

Not only is 'PAY YOUR TAXES NOW!' aggressive in its language, capital letters read as shouting causing some people to stop listening (especially introverts and hypersensitive people). Our message and the way we design the lettering is vital for our gift to be received warmly. Encourage and support people to do what is in the best interests of a healthy society. Offer your gift to help them act kindly and courageously, rather than trying to teach them a lesson. Empathise. Your voice will come through in your gift regardless and you want the message to resonate with the receiver of your gift; let it speak to them personally as well as politically.

Finding the right words

A craftivism gift with no words is open to misinterpretation. I could make a small, green, fabric baby's-hand-shaped design for my MP but without the stitched message 'We do not inherit the earth from our ancestors. We borrow it from our children', how would it be clear its function was to encourage the politician to campaign to tackle climate change for the sake of future generations? People could see it as a hand of a green monster! Words avoid miscommunication, make clear what the gift's function is, and show our belief in the statement we have crafted as well.

In my experience, having the gift-receiver's name stitched into the object itself helps create value for your gift for that person, especially if you address them respectfully. I also recommend you sign off your message with your name, such as 'Yours in hope, [name]'. That way your gift could be a catalyst for conversation with others who notice the gift if they ask 'Who is [name]?' I would also refer to where you want them to use their power and influence: 'Dear Mr Smith, I encourage you to use your power and influence as [name of their role] to make kind and life-saving decisions through your business.' That way the gift-receiver knows that they can't use personal philanthropy as an excuse to ignore the impact their decision-making in their business has.

Your message should be encouraging in its tone so that your receiver will want to display it with pride. An important part of positive psychology research focuses on encouraging people to believe that they can produce the desired results and prevent detrimental ones by their actions, otherwise they have little incentive to act or to persevere in the face of difficulties. Your gift should encourage realistic optimism. A diminished sense of personal effectiveness negatively impacts motivation and competence and so positivity is vital. Again, use intelligent empathy to understand what your recipient would appreciate. You wouldn't want to hang something on your wall that is negative or demonising – neither does your recipient. You want your message to acknowledge that it might not be easy to make a positive change, but it is possible. You're looking to open up a dialogue with the person you're sending your gift to and to show your support for them. Provoke thought and action through your gift for the receiver, don't preach at them: stitching a question into your gift or an open statement that ends with an ellipsis (row of dots '...') to hint that you want them to fill in the rest of the statement can be useful. Wouldn't it be great if they ended up treasuring your gift both physically and philosophically?

Try to make your content universal with a timeless message. The more specific your message, the more time-bound it is and the more transactional it can feel for the gift-receiver and therefore less like a gift. You want your gift to be a moral compass, to help the gift-receiver visualise their positive impact and stay on the right track long-term. You want to inspire them, empower them, give them hope that people believe in them and not to demonise them. Find a relevant message you can keep referring to with your gift-receiver. Show that you, the gift-maker, are an individual driven by hope and that a compassionate vision of the world is behind the gift. Have they mentioned anywhere who their role models are? Can you include a quote from these role models on your gift? Do they remind you of anyone because of their personality or background?

You could include a quote from a famous and respected person and say that they reminded you of them because of their ambition, their artistic flair or similar journey. For example, if a local business owner has become very popular and is setting up more stores but you think they could be more ethical through the management of their staff, energy consumption or waste disposal, why not stitch a relevant quote from the Dalai Lama: 'Open our arms to change but don't let go of your values'.

These messages could open doors to lots of different conversations and show your gift-receiver that you are trying to understand their situation. Familiar quotes can help your message be memorable, as can familiar phrases, rhymes and poems, but make sure the message isn't so well known that it sounds cheesy and leads to no impact.

I wouldn't encourage you to focus on humorous language – you don't want to make fun of unjust structures that are causing pain and suffering – but puns, alliteration and wordplays can lighten your message and make your gift memorable without turning into bad taste. Some words and phrases are loaded with meaning: for example, it's more engaging for people to hear 'fair play' rather than just 'fair'. Fair is a word that could be challenged and has too many different interpretations. 'Fair play' makes us think of a game where both teams need to be treated fairly for the sport to work: you would not have one well-equipped team of twenty players playing against a team of five people who are barefoot. Does the company or organisation your gift-receiver works for have a slogan you can co-opt to get your message across? For example, the supermarket chain Tesco has the strapline 'Every Little Helps'. It would be easy to stitch 'Every Little Hurts', which has an immediate emotive response, but remember that a positive message has more longevity than a negative one. Instead, why not try: 'Please don't blow your opportunity to support life-changing decisions through Tesco's business practices. As you know, every little helps...'

The power of our craftivism gifts lies in its use as a tool for conversation and connection, so we want to make sure our message isn't patronising but excites and intrigues the recipient, and encourages them to think about what this gift means, how it is speaking to them and how they can use it to support them in their difficult work.

Milton Glaser, the celebrated graphic designer I mentioned in Chapter 9, provokes thought and action rather than preaches it. His messages linger in people's minds because the viewer has to interpret them – they aren't spoon-fed the message. His posters are intelligent, and that's why they jump out from the noise around them: the message respects its viewers and believes we can decipher it without help. His most famous image is 'I ♥ NY'. It's unusual, simple, and forces our brains to interpret the sign. The heart famously represents love and the posters were used all over New York by the mayoral office. It wasn't too difficult to work out that the message said 'I love New York'. Not only do we interpret the message, we also enjoy the achievement of deciphering it. We are more engaged in the message and therefore more likely to remember it.

Fonts and layout

'Helvetica, Times New Roman and Comic Sans walk into a bar. The barman turns to Comic Sans and says "Sorry, we don't serve your type in here."'[1]

We are all type consumers and have an emotional response to fonts. Each font, by its design and layout, has a personality that influences our interpretation of the words we are reading. Fonts trigger our imagination, evoke emotions, prompt memories and link to all of our senses. They can tell you if the message is serious, light-hearted, academic or childish. Done well, type becomes invisible because it fits the message perfectly; done badly it can distract you from the message or cause you to mistrust it or even misunderstand the message. Think what font or fonts you are going to use to fit your message.

Soft curls on lettering can create intimacy and quiet contemplation because the font isn't easy to read and so you have to get close, focus on what you are reading, and let it sink in. Round shapes seem safe and friendly whereas jagged shapes feel dangerous or aggressive. Capital letters can feel LOUD. A spaced-out word encourages you to read it s l o w l y. Thick fonts feel heavy and loud; thinner fonts create delicacy. Words sloping down with gentle curves can create sadness in your message. Tight curves in an upward slope can look more playful, whereas angles sloping forward can create anger and agitation. If a font looks wobbly and rustic it can imply the object is handmade, even if it's not. The fonts that look like Roman inscriptions can give your piece an almost philosophical air of gravitas and longevity. Fonts can take on associations: when 'Gotham' font was used to spell out 'Hope' and 'Change' in Barak Obama's 2008 presidential campaign it became the typeface of inspiration and optimism.

I recommend that as gentle protesters offering a gift we focus on fonts that portray a personality of humility, respect and grace, and do not compete for power or attention. I often encourage people to write their message in their own handwriting and then stitch over the top of it with a backstitch. Not only is the simple stitch a repetitive action to help with meditation on the message but our writing is unique, individual and personal, which can create intimacy. Try and make the writing neat and tidy, so it's readable, perhaps softening the curves if your writing is particularly pointy, but not so neat that no personality comes out of it. Your personal typeface is likely to be unfamiliar for your gift-receiver, which will naturally cause them to slow down their reading and pay more attention to the shapes spelling out a message.

Letter or card to complement and add explanation to your object

For your gift to have more meaning, I recommend you attach a letter to it, especially if you cannot meet your gift-receiver in person or are nervous to speak to them directly about the issues you care about. A letter not only lets you explain yourself clearly without getting tongue-tied, it's also great for the receiver because they can read it in their own time without the gift-giver watching them and expecting an immediate response.

Writing a thoughtful and attractive letter to your gift-receiver is often slower and more painstaking than an email. In the age of emails, tweets and texts, the personal touch of letter writing is incalculable. My grandmother insists she can tell from our handwriting how we are feeling just as much as she can from our words. She believes our letters reveal our motivations and deepen her understanding of us. I'm not sure I agree with her but I respect her thinking. I love sending letters to family and friends and I've been told that they love receiving them. 'Emails are a poke but letters are a caress'[2] writes Simon Garfield, author of *To the Letter: A Journey Through a Vanishing World*. A note passed by hand: you can hear it, see it, feel it much more than a WhatsApp notification.

A friend who is a political advisor to a shadow cabinet minister helped me create a template letter for craftivists to use to hand over with their jigsaw piece gift as part of the Save the Children craftivism project. The letter needed to do four things: explain what the campaign was about, show how committed the craftivist was to the issue as a constituent, show the MP the influence that this craftivist had that could impact on the campaign, and request that the MP would reply to the letter to explain how they would be a piece of the solution to world hunger. You could adapt the template below for your own letter to go with your gift and cause. For your letter to be as effective as it can possibly can be, personalise it as much as you can. Remember to write from your heart!

[insert address and date]

Dear [insert MP name],

My name is [insert name] and I live at [insert address, including postcode] in your constituency. I'm contacting you because [insert information about how you're involved with the Craftivist Collective and your thoughts about world hunger].

I'm passionate about Save the Children's #raceagainsthunger campaign because [include your thoughts about why you are motivated about this campaign].

As part of the project I've joined hundreds of craft-lovers across the UK who care deeply about world hunger; we want to use our hobbies to make the world a better place, make time to think about the issues alone and talk about them in groups whilst stitching, and do positive campaigning to encourage MPs like yourself to be the change they wish to see in the world. You can see what we've been up to at www.imapiece.craftivist-collective. com, where you can see our tweets, instagrams, images and other conversations with each other. [insert a link here if you have shared your involvement in the project with people online or offline or taken part in the project in a group].

I've spent hours of my time stitching a jigsaw piece which forms part of an art installation in March in Manchester that will then move across the country in 2013 for other people to see, which demonstrates how together we can all be part of the solution. My piece reads [insert information about your piece]. I've also stitched a jigsaw piece I'm going to keep to remind myself to strive to be the best global citizen I can be through what I do, say, buy and vote on. My jigsaw piece is on display in my [insert where you've put your piece] because [explain why] and says [insert message and reason why you chose this message for your jigsaw to keep].

I've stitched a third piece, which I'd like to give to you to encourage you to be part of the solution to world hunger. [insert as appropriate: Please can I book an appointment to meet you and give it to you? or Please find this piece enclosed]. It took me [how many hours] to make and it might not be perfect but I hope you can keep it to remind you that I'm here supporting you to do the moral and right thing. In order to demonstrate your support I ask that you at least write to the prime minister, asking him to use the hunger summit in June to invest in life-saving interventions to prevent malnutrition in children. Please let me know his response.

I'd love to know your thoughts and your staff's thoughts on the issue, and what other steps you might be taking to tackle this issue. And don't forget the wonderful words of John Ruskin:

'What we think, or what we know, or what we believe is in the end of little consequence; the only consequence is what we do'

[insert as appropriate:

I hope to hear from you soon with a date and time to meet and I hope you like my jigsaw.
Or
I look forward to your response and I hope you like my jigsaw.]

Yours sincerely,

[insert your name]

[insert your contact details, including postcode, email and telephone number]

MP staff drinks: round two

After the feedback from the seven staff members of politicians on the strengths and weaknesses of the aesthetics of our jigsaw pieces I asked them about our messaging. They all agreed that they hadn't received letters like ours before: some of them were very long, most were handwritten and they all ended with a tangible request rather than started with it. The staff were moved by the positivity of the letters but also saw the content as a challenge for them to prove how they were part of the solution. The group said it was moving to read 'I'd love to know your thoughts and your staff's thoughts' as they are hardly ever mentioned in correspondence. Because the letters were often so very different and the question was a broad one, it was difficult for the staff to do what they normally do: cut and paste an answer as a reply to a petition card. They felt they had to delve deeper and refer to other parts of the letter to show their appreciation and commitment to represent constituents as an MP. They found it useful to learn more about their local craftivist to work out how they could support each other in the issue and potentially other issues they could support each other on. MPs are often interested if the craftivist has links to groups within the constituency – perhaps the craftivist is also a governor of the local secondary school or is a member of a large local church congregation – this is all useful information for the MP's local office staff to hear because they are always looking for contacts within the constituency to work with on different issues. Because of the universal and timeless message, many of our jigsaw pieces are still hung up in politicians' offices, reminding them of this campaign and their commitment to it, even after the campaign had officially ended. It also keeps the door open for the craftivist to discuss other injustices with their MP and see where they could work together to address them.

The message and the medium

A time-limited cliché of a message will not last, whereas a universal, thought-provoking message can have value over more than one campaign.

Your message should fit your medium, and the medium should fit the message on your craftivism object. Our gift should have beauty in its form, and thoughtfulness in its message. It's these seemingly small considerations that can decide the impact of your gift.

12
Catalyst not Conclusion

Talent wins games, but teamwork and intelligence wins championships.

— Michael Jordan

One of the largest retail companies in the UK wouldn't budge. For three years, the UK-based charity ShareAction had been asking the company to become a Living Wage* employer. The chief executive at the time refused. Shareholder activists asked again at the 2014 Annual General Meeting (AGM). He said again that they would not pay the UK Living Wage.

Nearly 3,000 employers in the UK have become accredited as Living

---

* Living wage is an hourly wage rate calculated by independent experts to provide enough for someone to live with dignity and support a family. Currently it is £9.40 in London and £8.25 for the rest of the UK, but it gets adjusted annually to account for cost of living changes.

Wage employers, including nearly a third of the FTSE 100, the largest publicly listed companies in the UK. These include big names like Nestlé, ITV, SSE, Pearson, GSK, and Burberry. But at the time (2015), no high-street retailer had signed up. Taxpayers are subsidising employers for their low pay because by not paying people enough to get by, the government needs to provide benefits to top up their salaries. If retailers paid the Living Wage, the UK government would save £11 billion.* Moving off low pay and on to the living wage allows people to work one job instead of multiple jobs and to spend time with their families. More than 5 million people in the UK earn less than the Living Wage.

The company in question is a national institution and has a presence on every high street, providing high-quality and affordable products from knickers to natural yoghurt and more, and most people in the UK grew up with the company having a presence in their lives. It is seen as a company with solid values. A company to trust. Low- and high-cost brands alike look to this company as a business leader in the retail area. ShareAction wanted this well-known company, which employs 80,000 people across the UK, to lead the way. If it became a Living Wage Employer it would have ripple effects within the retail sector. But the chief executive wouldn't budge.

I received a message from the CEO of ShareAction, Catherine Howarth. They didn't want to give up. Catherine had read my *A Little Book of Craftivism* and asked for my help.

We have tried many approaches to engage the company in discussion but we haven't managed to gain traction. Your process is unusual but I think it just might work.

* www.citizensuk.org/subsidy_report

I was given five weeks to plan and deliver a campaign before the company's 2015 AGM. My goal was to get a meeting agreed between the company and ShareAction to discuss the possibilities of becoming a Living Wage Employer. I wanted to create a craftivism project that would initiate a new relationship with the company as well as repair the tense and weak relationships with the CEO. ShareAction, Citizens UK and Living Wage Foundation would then take it from there to keep the campaign moving. Could our craftivism campaign be the nudge that could get the living wage ball rolling?

Strategy and delivery

I had never done shareholder activism before but it fitted our gentle protest approach perfectly. The CEO had been blocking any chance of a meeting for the past three years and so I decided to focus on engaging all fourteen board members who would be attending the AGM, not just the CEO. Maybe some of them would support the living wage and influence the CEO to agree to have a meeting. My hanky had helped grow a respectful relationship with my MP and so instead of trying to come up with a new craftivism idea I decided to build on that one (no need to reinvent the wheel each time you do a new campaign, craftivists!). We needed to show that becoming a Living Wage Employer made business sense as well as being the right thing to do. We also added the five chief investment officers of the largest investing companies in the company to our list of gift-receivers, hoping that they would support the campaign. The company would find it much more difficult to ignore their requests than ours. We also targeted five of the celebrity models that had been photographed for the company's recent advertising campaign as their involvement could help our campaign gain more media attention.

I bought twenty-four handkerchiefs from the company to show that we were not boycotting them. When recruiting craftivists for this project, I contacted experienced and keen craftivists in the Craftivist Collective from across the UK. Plus I thought it might be more effective to choose craftivists who were part of the company's core demographic of loyal customers. We had two male craftivists and twenty-two female craftivists who fitted their loyal demographic of customers. Many of this group were quiet people who didn't want to attract attention. I didn't want to risk anyone being loud and brash at the AGM or slipping into traditional negative activism campaigning. This campaign had to be different. I wanted board members to see we were a group of concerned customers who happened to also be shareholder activists and we wanted to encourage them to do the best job they could in their roles, not bully them into an action.

I matched up twenty-four craftivists with each of the twenty-four hanky-receivers, taking into consideration any interests or similarities I thought these pairs might have in common. For example, I matched one craftivist, Alex Noble, a fashion designer, with a fashion designer who modelled for the company, and a craftivist who has just become a new mum I paired with a board member who has small children. I then posted the hankies out to the craftivists, choosing the colours and patterns that I thought would best fit the gift-receiver. I also included 'crafterthought' questions for craftivists to reflect on while they stitched:

1. What challenges do you think your designated hanky-receiver would face trying to implement the living wage?
2. How could you support them in facing those pressures?
3. How would you feel if you were a staff member working full time for this company but couldn't afford to pay for basic necessities to live comfortably?

I persuaded each craftivist to research more about their board member to help them create the most emotionally engaging bespoke gift they could, in the hope that their designated person would cherish and be inspired by their gift. I encouraged the craftivists to research everything

– such as what clothes they wore – watch any talks they have online, read any articles they had written or been interviewed for, find out their hobbies, previous work experience and if they were trustees of any other organisation etc. I emphasised that it was really important to try to get to know them and what makes them tick from their public presence online.

The hanky's message had to be just as beautiful, thoughtful and graceful as the design was. I asked the craftivists to use the template below for their message but encouraged them to tweak it to suit their board member and themselves. It was intentionally timeless and universal so that it didn't seem transactional. It deliberately did not mention the Living Wage for this reason. We wanted the board members and others to take ownership of the decision to pay the living wage since they are the ones who will have to enforce it. I encouraged the craftivists to stitch part of the message in their own handwriting to keep the gift personal and intimate but they had creative control over how to design the rest of the layout and in what craft style, such as cross stitch, appliqué or other forms of needlework. The template message was:

Dear [full name of board member including title],

Please don't blow your opportunity to support life-changing decisions through [said company]...

[an inspiring quote the hanky-receiver could relate to, stitched in a bigger, prettier font with any other embellishments they wanted to make like images/symbols etc.]

Yours sincerely, [the maker's name]

I gave a list of inspiring and relevant quotes to the craftivists as examples of the positive tone, length of quote and style to go for but they could suggest other quotes to use. Caroline, who made a hanky for a senior independent director, said:

> My recipient is Sikh and so I found a quote with the help of my Sikh friend: 'By the karma of good actions, some come to serve the Perfect Guru' by Sri Guru Granth Sahib Ji for my hanky. I want to inspire him to understand that the true quality of a retail brand will be shown by how they treat all their staff.

Craftivist Louise was an economics student and stitched a hanky for the chief financial officer, using the words of Anita Roddick, founder of The Body Shop, 'Being good is good for business'. Craftivist Gemma made a hanky for a non-executive board member with the message: 'Kindness is always fashionable and always welcome'. The words were cross-stitched on a square patch of fabric from a piece of clothing that her grandmother had bought from the company decades ago and then stitched as a patch onto her handkerchief. One board member was the trustee of a national garden so his craftivist stitched flowers on his hanky. Another was on the board of an opera company so his hanky had musical notes and a quote from a musician. Each of the twenty-four hankies were completely different but all positive, encouraging and beautiful. It took five hours on average to make each of the bespoke, hand-stitched hankies and I encouraged the craftivists to use the time making the handkerchiefs to reflect on the Living Wage, the job of their gift-receiver, to put themselves in their shoes and to think through what would connect them to this hanky gift if they were the receiver. Craftivist Gemma commented:

> I thought about the person I was stitching it for. I wondered how her life looked and the daily changes she faced as a woman in business. At first, I concentrated on the differences between us

but by the end thought about our similarities and the changes that all people face in modern life.*

To explain our gifts to our gift-receivers and the link to the Living Wage campaign I asked the craftivists to write a letter to be given with their hanky alongside a double-sided information sheet on the Living Wage created by ShareAction that could be folded into their envelopes. They were all placed in gift boxes wrapped in different-coloured ribbons, tags with the board members' and others' names on, and with our cards or letters inside.

As part of the campaign, I also encouraged craftivists across the UK to set up a 'stitch-in' – my gentle craftivism version of a protest 'sit-in' demonstration (more on stitch-ins in Chapter 14) – outside one of the company's stores in their area. I asked craftivists to invite no more than twelve people who looked like the company's customers and to set up a colourful, friendly and inviting picnic near the entrance to the store. Craftivists were encouraged to wear colourful clothing they had bought from the store (or looked like they were from the store!) and bring jam sandwiches and tea to offer to those whom they spoke to. The 'stitch-ins' were non-violent, non-threatening and their purpose was to intrigue passers-by and to encourage customers and staff to ask what we were doing, as well as to show the staff that we valued and loved them and wanted to support them by campaigning for them to receive a Living Wage. It was a positive campaign to encourage the company to do the right thing and lead the way for the sector; it was not bullying or demonising them. Craftivists took photographs to share on social media with a positive message encouraging the company to implement the Living Wage.

* www.craftivist-collective.com/Gemma-Morrison-My-Craftivism

These events helped us gain local and national media attention in print, online and on the radio before the AGM. We were covered in *TimeOut London*, on Brighton Radio, and in the *Observer* magazine, among others, which gave us exposure. However, we learnt that many magazines and blogs would not cover our story because the company was an existing or potential advertiser – this was useful to know for future campaigns.

A petition was set up online, which gained 79,000 signatures before the AGM. ShareAction was simultaneously mobilising an Investor Collaborative for the living wage, made up of institutional shareholders with billions of pounds in British companies, including asset managers, pension funds, charity and faith investors. These large shareholders have written in 2015 to all of the FTSE 100, including the company we were targeting, in support of the living wage.

We also wanted to gain support from the 1,000 shareholders attending the AGM and raise awareness of the campaign with the journalists who were attending. Our small budget couldn't stretch to making 1,000 craftivism hanky kits to hand out to shareholders at the entrance but we managed to stretch to 250 kits. Each kit contained information on this campaign and how they could support it as shareholders, as well as needle and thread, one of the small white hankies we used at the 'stitch-ins' that were ethically printed in a local independent London shop saying 'Please don't blow your chance to pay the Living Wage' plus instructions and 'crafterthought' questions to reflect on while stitching.

The day of the AGM 2015

Fourteen craftivists attended the AGM,* wearing their smartest and friendliest clothing made by the company (or in the style of the company's clothing). We designated two craftivists to document the day on social

---

* One for each board member.

media and two craftivists to take notes. We arrived at 9.30 a.m. to hand out the kits to shareholders and greeted them with a simple, 'Enjoy the AGM', and handed over a kit to them with a smile. The 250 gift packs went very quickly. The company and their security staff did not seem to mind us handing out these gifts quietly and in a welcoming manner. It was a good start to the day.

Then we had some conflict. A staff member came over to take our fourteen handkerchief gifts off us. She said she would deliver them to the board. We wanted to hand them over ourselves at the end of the AGM. The staff member said this would not be possible. We managed to negotiate and agree that she could have half of them and we would hand over the other half at the end of the AGM. We hadn't planned for that disruption to our plan and were saddened, but then lined up to register our attendance. Some of us had bought a share in the company before the event so we lined up in the shareholder queue. Some of us had received proxy votes from ShareAction so were in a different queue. We had prepared two questions to ask so two of us went to submit them while the others went to the room to see if they could find fourteen seats together near the front. The staff collecting the questions told us that they had heard about our campaign and were interested to see the gifts. Many of the staff told us that they had been following our campaign and were very much aware of our activities and media coverage. Some staff were very friendly; some were more defensive or wary of us. We reassured them that we love the company and just wanted to help it fulfil its potential as a good company leading the way.

The room was a large conference hall with 1,000 shareholders and many journalists, heads of departments and others. There were large cameras on stands to film the AGM for people to watch live online. It was packed out. At the front was an extremely long table with fourteen chairs in a row facing the audience. The board members all walked in and sat down. They seemed so distant on the stage. The chairman of the board started his introduction. And guess what? He mentioned our campaign: 'This campaign was a test case for how these campaigns should be run.'

It is very rare, even unheard of at AGMs that a campaign would be mentioned in an introduction or at any stage of the meeting. We were surprised but glad that it looked as though he respected our campaign. But we couldn't tell if that meant we might get the meeting we wanted.

After a summary of the company's year and future plans it was time for questions. Caroline, who had made a hanky for a board member and is a trustee of ShareAction, calmly and clearly asked the board to update the shareholders on what deliberations had been made on the UK Living Wage since this was raised at the AGM 2014. The CEO reminded us of their competitive rewards for their staff, implying that these should be enough, and said that he believed that the company treated its workers fairly, but otherwise didn't answer Caroline's question.

Then I was ushered to the stand. On the way up, I spotted our group of craftivists and gave them a smile. They knew what to do. With a deep breath, my heart racing, I looked at my small piece of paper with my question on it. It said at the top: 'Say slowly. Long pauses. This is important'.

'Good morning. I'm Sarah Corbett and I'm a shareholder. I've spent the last few weeks working with fellow craftivists around the country on a project that we hope will be life-changing. We are super-excited about this AGM and giving each of you our handcrafted bespoke gifts to encourage you to make positive life-changing decisions in your roles as board members. Our gifts to you have taken in total over a hundred hours to stitch. Over the last few weeks we've had lots of fun stitching, chatting and engaging customers, staff and passers-by at your stores. What we've learnt is that people love your company but they expect a lot from you. They were very surprised you do not pay the Living Wage and are keen that you do become a Living Wage Employer in the near future. So here they are, our gifts [at this point, all the craftivists stood and held them up above their heads for all to see]. We hope you treasure their timeless messages. It would mean a lot to us if you made the time to meet the makers of your gifts at the end of the AGM today, please, and agree to a meeting with ShareAction to discuss the Living Wage in more detail. Thank you.'

The audience clapped. This was a nice surprise, especially as other questions did not receive applause. The chairman thanked us for his beautiful hanky made by craftivist Fran. He must have been one of the seven who received their hanky early from a staff member. What seemed like a crack in our plan had actually been a benefit! He said to the whole audience that she had clearly researched his work, passions and values and wrote him a thoughtful letter. His handkerchief featured a quote by the Dalai Lama reading: 'Open our arms to change, but don't let go of your values.' He went on to say, 'It's a campaign that is thoughtfully done and heartfelt. We feel every bit as heartfelt about our employees. Do meet us at the side of the stage here at the end to drop off your gifts.'

A staff member from campaign organisation 'Labour Behind the Label' asked the company to pay their non-UK staff a Living Wage and guarantee their health and safety in the factories. A retired economist shareholder spoke of the benefits of the Living Wage to employers and shareholders and asked if the company was working towards this accreditation. In total, there were four questions on the Living Wage. This showed that the Living Wage was an issue for many people and the fact that they were not taken off the question list for being too similar suggested that the board might be interested in discussing the subject further. Other questions included how the company would address the lack of shape in the new women's clothes, the decrease in quality of the men's trousers and why the company wasn't growing their number of stores as much as two large budget stores. It was a fascinating day to be part of and it helped us craftivists understand the demands on the board and staff from shareholders.

Throughout the AGM we shared the event with our followers on social media. We received encouraging tweets from groups and individuals, including some from the influential Women's Institute (many of whom fit the company's core customer demographic) and from popular journalist, author and TV presenter Lucy Siegle. One of our tweets had seventy retweets that day including from author and journalist Owen Jones, who had nearly half a million followers on Twitter at that time.

When the AGM officially finished, our group of fourteen craftivists walked calmly but swiftly to the side of the stage. I briefed the craftivists beforehand to carefully listen to their board member's tone of voice and watch their body language as well as listen to their responses to our questions, and then to email me immediately after their brief meeting with all of this information to help us figure out who could be a useful ally and who might proactively try to block our goal. I had a private chat with my hanky-receiver who told me quietly about her stance on the Living Wage and said she would do what she could before she left her position on the board in nine months' time. Quietly, with a smile and a giggle, I told her that our gifts are only the start not the end of this discussion and we are a stubborn bunch and so would be in touch to hear about their progress and would continue to offer our help to implement the Living Wage where it might be useful. She gave me her email address and asked me to keep her updated. She also told me that the board were all looking at the seven gifts and letters given out before the start of the AGM, debating who had the best hanky and were keen to see the other seven. She said they were all talking about the campaign and Living Wage before they walked onto the stage and we should be proud of what we had achieved so far.

After the meeting she tweeted: 'So impressed with the clever campaign thank u' to her 149,000 followers and included two images that represented the campaign. It might not seem like a lot, but any public response by a board member is really promising and it is unusual for them to share it. A non-executive director told her gift-maker that she would 'treasure' her hand-stitched handkerchief. Some board members were less open, less warm and did not offer praise. One board member seemed very guarded and not keen to discuss the Living Wage but this was all useful intelligence for the campaign and we wouldn't have gained these insights without meeting them.

I managed to speak to the chairman, who seemed genuinely moved by his hanky. I told him that Fran sadly had to cancel at the last minute from her home in Brighton because of a wave of terrible migraines she is susceptible to. But she had really wanted to hand deliver her gift to him. I thanked him for his kind words and asked if we could have a meeting to discuss the Living Wage further. He said that in many areas it was the fault of house prices causing people to struggle to live sustainably, not their wages, and that his company gave one of the best rewards packages to their staff. I reminded him of the research that shows a Living Wage would reduce absenteeism, improve recruitment, retention and morale of staff. I respectfully said that their discount package is better than most but a discount on a skirt does not help people pay their living costs. He went on to say that our work was 'an approach that appeals to us all'. He said he would not be speaking to us if we had been shouting outside with placards. 'The way you've done this is remarkable,' he said. 'It got more conversation than any campaign outside.'

Before the chairman was moved on by his team, he told me to 'send Fran my love' with a big smile and then quickly corrected himself and said in a more professional, authoritative way, 'I mean regards, regards.' A member of staff told me that a meeting would be set up with the Director of Sustainable Business to discuss this issue more.

I headed straight to the ShareAction headquarters in Bermondsey, London to work with their Communications Officer to write and send off a press release of our results of the day to the press.

Post AGM

Work wasn't over for our twenty-four craftivists. I had warned them in advance that our hankies were the catalyst, not the conclusion, and we might be needed again to help with the campaign. Our meeting with the Head of Sustainability didn't happen until January 2016 (eight months after the AGM). Not a good sign. So before then we handmade Christmas cards for our board members and the other hanky-receivers to remind them that 'all we want for Christmas is for the company to pay the Living Wage' and be a shining light for the rest of the retail sector to practise their values. We said that we hoped one of their New Year's resolutions would be to help implement the living wage. We included our disappointment that we hadn't yet met with the Head of Sustainability, but that we hoped they still liked their hankies and that this card encouraged them to use their power to help move this issue forward.

It was disheartening for craftivists not to receive replies from their gift-receivers but I had to remind us all that our receivers may feel they can't give anything away or be seen to be against the company's current strategy and so we had to just hope that our cards encouraged them and showed them that we still believe they can do great things. This was difficult to do, but we had to stay hopeful and persevere.

When the meeting did arrive we went in a strong position. July 2015's government budget announcement of a 'national living wage' added a further spotlight to, and awareness in the public of, the real Living Wage and the problems in the retail sector. We were reassured that the company recognised the business benefits of treating people fairly and they told us they had been considering the Living Wage at the highest level. We were also told that their new CEO (who was already on the board so had received one of our hankies) would officially start his post in April 2016 and hoped to make real progress on this.

The meeting with the Head of Sustainability included representatives of ShareAction, Citizens UK, the Living Wage Foundation and myself, representing the Craftivist Collective. We also had a representative attend from one of the top five investor organisations that had the most shares in the company we were targeting. Representing the company, the Head of Sustainability said that the director of HR couldn't make it because of last-minute changes to her schedule. This was a bad sign. In our meeting, we heard repeatedly from him that his company was determined to be a leader in being a great place to work and he was open to the fact that the Living Wage may be a key element in this goal. That was a better sign. We made it clear that with nearly a third of the FTSE 100 and nearly 3,000 employers accredited as paying the Living Wage, the Living Wage now formed an important part of what made the best employers. However, despite the repeated message that people are at the heart of the business, we wanted to see clear evidence that the company was investigating what it would look like for them to adopt the Living Wage. We asked that the HR director be at our next meeting since she was the person to implement the Living Wage, not the head of sustainability. We answered his questions and pushed for another meeting with HR. We told the head of sustainability that our craftivists would be sending another card to our hanky-receivers (this time on the theme of Valentine's Day, asking them to show their love for their employees and implement the Living Wage) and the online petition had risen to 83,000 petitioners, who we would have to update with the progress of this meeting and the campaign.

In April 2016 we asked UK craftivists to send the new CEO a card congratulating him on his new role and encouraging him to implement the Living Wage. I suggested images and messages asking him to be our hero, knight in shining armour, a shining star for his employees and the rest of the sector, focusing on encouraging him not bullying him. The new CEO had risen up the ranks from the shop floor, which is a huge achievement for anyone and a possible benefit for our campaign, which affects the people working where the new CEO had come from.

Soon after, we heard from the chair of trustees of ShareAction who had seen the company's chairman at an event. He and his wife had said that our handkerchiefs had a profound impact on the board and the Living Wage wouldn't have been on their agenda without our gentle protest. He eagerly introduced the trustee to the new CEO who was also there. The CEO said that he was very grateful for our campaign and was keen to write to each of the craftivists to thank them, which he did. Again this was unprecedented and gave us hope. However, we still knew to be cautious.

At the end of April 2016, the company announced to the media that they were going to pay above the current Living Wage rates. This was great news: 50,000 employees had their pay increased! But they didn't say they were committed to accreditation, which means they could fall below paying the independent Living Wage in future years. Soon after the announcement a meeting was arranged between our coalition, the head of sustainability and the director of HR to explain the detail of their move towards a Living Wage. In this meeting the company was much more open with us. We pushed for accreditation to guarantee that the company would, year-on-year, implement the new Living Wage calculation. They explained that they would give the Living Wage but it would not be possible to become accredited because of the limits and paperwork each year. We did not agree. This would be the next step in the campaign.

Extra allies

The board members were friendly but keeping their cards close to their chest. We needed to find someone on the inside of the company who could share more on the best approach to campaign for a Living Wage accreditation and tell us what the barriers were. I researched who was on the company's sustainability committee. I asked a few contacts I had who worked in sustainability if they knew any of the committee members. One friend did. I'll call him Joe and the committee member Mr Ally.

I asked Joe that if he saw Mr Ally, could he casually mention that he had seen the announcement for the Living Wage online and wondered if the company would be accredited Living Wage Employers and if not, what was stopping them. I told Joe to update me with any information if possible. Joe did better than that, he emailed Mr Ally and copied me in to the email conversation, endorsing my work and encouraging us to meet. Joe told me:

> If your campaign wasn't so positive I wouldn't have told [Mr Ally] about it and introduced you over email and tell you both to meet up. He's still secretly an old-school hippy so you will get on.

Mr Ally started the meeting by asking me about the campaign strategy, delivery and what evidence I had that we had had an impact on the board. He went from looking sceptical to impressed and went on to tell me that he met with the CEO every week as a consultant and committee chair, and so he wanted to be in the loop on what we had done so far and where we thought the company could improve. He was keen to update the committee he chaired with our campaign. He told us which of the top three board members to focus on who were in charge of the Living Wage implementation and were warm to full accreditation, and which board members were less supportive of the Living Wage. I trusted him and so I suggested different ideas for what we could do at the AGM in 2016 to push for accreditation and he was very helpful in saying what might cause tension and what would go down well with them.

AGM 2016

I encouraged twelve craftivists to join me at the next AGM in July 2016 (two less than the 2015 AGM since one board member had recently left and one had become CEO). The aim was to inspire and empower board members to take the final step needed to become a Living Wage Employer: accreditation. We were keen to show them that we were not going to give up on this campaign. Giving another stitched gift that had taken hours might dilute or conflict with their first hanky. I didn't want them to see it as a gimmick or even a bribe. What could we offer to complement their hanky? Again a symbol that had seemed to work for people in the past was a jigsaw piece. Accreditation was the last jigsaw piece needed for the Living-Wage puzzle and the board members were the ones who could demand that it be implemented. Our handmade cards focused on the board members completing the puzzle so that we could celebrate the company's achievement. To go with each card I also made key rings in the colours and patterns to match each individual handkerchief and placed them in small silver boxes wrapped in ribbon. Ribbon that was created as a collaboration between the Craftivist Collective and Department Store for the Mind. The ribbon said repeatedly 'Little by little we travel far...' which I thought fitted our narrative.

We received a much warmer welcome than the previous year. And to our surprise, the board members spoke to us for much longer periods of time and were more open and friendly. Some of the board members even sought us out to come and talk to us. When we showed the board members empathy by saying that we understood the difficulties they had in their roles, most replied with a big breath saying that they were very grateful to us for saying that. Their guard came down so we could have some respectful discussions about the challenges they felt they faced by agreeing to be accredited. One board member told us that after the AGM 2015 she took her hanky home to show her two small children who then wanted to know what the Living Wage was and she had to explain it to them. One board member donated her handkerchief to the company's archives to be added to other objects that 'represent key moments in the company's history'. The wife of the chair of the board commended us on a very shrewd campaign and the chairman quietly told me that our campaign put the Living Wage firmly at the top of the agenda in the following three meetings. Meeting the board members in person again strengthened our relationship with them, showed our commitment and we gained valuable insight on who we believed supported accreditation and who came across as opposed to it; listening to the arguments for and against helped strengthen our campaign.

As with most campaigns like this, the process is slow but we are making progress and our hankies had a big part to play as catalyst. We made clear progress: the campaign set the bar higher at the company, encouraging them to be leaders in their sector for other companies to follow, 50,000 employees have had their pay increased, and our craftivism gifts were an important catalyst for these changes. Like most campaigns, this one is messy, complicated and we have to be wise. We need to be cautious that the ethos behind the Living Wage is taken on board: it's about paying people fairly.

Opening doors

Our craftivism hankies definitely opened the doors to have a meeting with the company but there is so much more to craftivism than handkerchiefs. We could have aggressively or smugly thrown our hand-embroidered hankies at the recipients. As craftivists we need to be appropriately crafty in many ways. Five important elements to complement your handmade gifts and to help strengthen them as catalysts for change are:

1. Ownership: Our messaging and interactions with our recipient should focus on how we can help and encourage *them* to implement the changes we believe they should. They are the ones that have to enforce the changes, you can't. If our recipient takes ownership of the suggestion, the changes are more likely to happen and happen quicker. We congratulated the board members at the 2016 AGM for paying the Living Wage and made it clear that we couldn't wait

to congratulate them when they became accredited Living Wage Employers.

2. Empathy: If we can understand the challenges our recipient might face in implementing our changes, how busy they might be in their role (and personal life) with competing issues to address, then we will hopefully come up with effective and attractive ways that we can offer to help them with delivering the campaign they have taken ownership of. At the AGM craftivists made a point of saying clearly to their board member that they understood the pressures they were under in their role and that gaining accreditation as a Living Wage Employer can take time and isn't easy but we believed in them. This small statement and acknowledgement created allies with most of the board.

3. Allies: We need allies in companies or governments if we hope that long-term changes will be made. We spent time nurturing warm contacts and time looking for other allies when we were faced with blockers.

4. Commitment: We show our commitment not just in making the gift but in the less fun parts of the campaign. The head of sustainability asked me at the AGM 2016 whom I was going to target next year. I made it very clear to him that his company was our only target for now and we were not going to give up. Not only did it show him our determination, but it showed that our priority was accreditation and not our love of sewing or fame.

5. Ripples: There may be hidden or unplanned effects of a campaign. At the second AGM we heard from board members, their colleagues and even partners about how our hankies had had impact on them personally, from creating conversations at home with their families about the Living Wage to the wife of a board member wanting to join our collective!

I asked Catherine Howarth, chief executive of ShareAction, if she was happy with our craftivism campaign. Her feedback was:

> Craftivism was magic for us. Not only did it bring soul and beauty to our efforts to create social change through shareholder activism, but it turned out to deliver the most fantastic results. The board of the company were powerfully influenced, particularly the chairman. Thanks to the impact we made at 2015's AGM, it was just a few short months before the company confirmed major pay rises for the lowest paid at the company.

At the time of writing, we are still working with ShareAction and the other coalition members and allies to help the company become accredited Living Wage Employers. Important and positive changes have taken place, but as so often, the journey is not yet over.

PART IV

Power in the Public Sphere

13
Intriguing Craftivism

Evil flourishes when good people do nothing.
— *Edmund Burke*

Fifty years ago the writer and philosopher Hannah Arendt witnessed the end of the trial of Adolf Eichmann, one of the major figures in the organisation and delivery of the Holocaust. Covering the trial, Arendt coined the phrase 'the banality of evil' to conceptualise how these monstrous acts could have happened. This doesn't mean that evil has become ordinary or that Nazi soldiers had committed an unexceptional crime. But rather, Arendt argued, that Eichmann and many of his cohorts had acted without intention, failing to think about the crimes they were committing and the effect their job 'duties' would have. The acts were not banal but what had become 'banal' was the non-thinking. By calling a crime against humanity 'banal' she was pointing to the way in which the crime had become, for many of the criminals, accepted, routinised, and implemented without moral disgust, political indignation, or resistance. Their crimes were committed in a daily way, systematically, without being adequately named and opposed. Arendt also wrote: 'The sad truth is the most evil is done by people who never make up their minds to be good or evil.'[1]

As craftivists we need to act thoughtfully, not banally through life. Awareness of injustice is only the start. Knowledge is power but only if we use it well and often. It is too easy for us to follow 'rules' in our workplace or in our peer group that undermine our principles. Our harmful actions may not be crimes, but we should be aware of how our actions and behaviours can support harmful systems and how our lack of action against injustice can be harmful. For example, we know that we can harness energy from the sun, wind and water. We have the inventions, systems and equipment needed to live in a greener, cleaner and safer world. We are the first generation to know, understand and appreciate the scale and complexities of the problems we collectively face. Yet half the world overeats whilst the other half is malnourished and 10 per cent of the world's adults control 85 per cent of the world's wealth. We need paradigm changes: we need more electric vehicles and fewer gas-guzzling ones. We need slow-fashion brands, not just 'eco' ranges added to a fast-fashion brand. We need a redistribution of wealth, not just more philanthropic giving. Laws are needed but we also need to change some of our individual behaviour and collective culture.

We need to think about our own actions and our own involvement in injustice: our 'inner activism' (Chapter 7). But we also need to help each other when we see 'non-thinking' happening in our environments, when we see failure to think about the impact actions and words have on other people and situations. Major shifts in collective and individual consciousness are required to solve many entrenched injustices in our world and these shifts need lots of little-and-often actions just as much as big gestures.

What was once called 'the banality of evil' we might now call 'normalisation'. Our world is changing constantly and forcing us to live differently. Ten years ago, the varieties of social media didn't exist and now they are part of our everyday life. Let's help make social responsibility part of all of our daily lives too, threading it through all that people do and say. Let's not just wait for atrocities to happen before we campaign against them. We need to gently nudge ourselves and others if we see something questionable or we see a harmful presumption being made. We need to name and oppose the status quo where it is stopping our world from fulfilling its potential for being a wonderful place for all. As Desmond Tutu rightly says: 'If you are neutral in situations of injustice, you have chosen the side of the oppressor.'

Culture jamming

As craftivists we should look for opportunities to attract attention to social injustices, especially where there is wrongdoing that has been normalised and is not being challenged. We can use imagery and messages in the public sphere, advertisements and articles in media outlets, in fact, any resources we can share with others are important as tools for disruption. Many charities and activist groups shine a spotlight on injustice to gain attention, educate, create conversations and mobilise support. As craftivists, our work should complement the work of other changemakers to ensure that evil doesn't flourish in areas when it seems that the majority of good people are doing nothing or not enough on these injustice issues.

Craftivism objects can have more impact as lots of little gentle nudges rather than large one-off events or actions. They can be tools to help people question social norms, engage people quietly and respectfully, not shine a light of shame or embarrassment on them. We can inspire and empower others to act against injustices, and encourage them to ask questions of our society and of their own place in it. Our objects can point people towards more information to help them on their journey as active and intentional global citizens, but in a way that people can engage with in their own time. I believe the current activism toolkit is lacking in these everyday tools and we can help create those tools using small intriguing crafted objects.

We can become 'culture jammers', disrupting media culture and its mainstream cultural institutions and corporate advertising. Culture jamming includes street parties and protests, flash mobs, events such as 'Buy Nothing Day', 'subvertisements' or altering common symbols such as McDonald's golden arches or Nike's swoosh to engage people to think more about their eating habits or fashion choices. The jammer often goes for shock value but we can use our more gentle approach to culture jammers by creating quietly intriguing and delicate artefacts as tools for collective and individual consciousness shifts.

A suitable place

For your craftivism to have most impact you need to think about the physical environment it will be in. Think about the environment's history, its current state, the way it is used and by whom. Use the environment to enhance your activism message and impact and not to distract from it.

Look for where there are injustices happening but also where people might not be connecting their actions to those injustices. This is where your objects can have the most impact. For example, a shopping mall could be an effective site if you are protesting against the unethical side of business. Are you going to place a craftivism object somewhere that is under threat of demolition or next to the office of those in control of the demolition? Will you leave it in a place steeped in history that is linked to your chosen issue, such as next to a famous library to remind people of the importance of free education for everyone? Perhaps instead of your local area, choose the financial district, fashion district or technology district where people in those sectors of work often have their offices. There are many options!

It will be tempting to leave your objects in areas where your friends will see them, accredit the object to you and praise you. It is also tempting to put your object where street art and creative marketing are welcomed and celebrated. But the point of your object is to intrigue people. In my experience, putting up pieces in such creative areas leads to them either not being noticed amongst the other pieces of street art placed nearby or your piece will be taken by someone quickly because they think it might be worth something. Whereas, if you leave your object in an area where you don't see street art, often passers-by in that area notice it more and are usually too surprised to take it down because they aren't used to seeing street art in that area! I placed a stitched mask on an outdoor statue in a wealthy area of west London and it stayed up much longer than a similar object I hung in a trendy part of east London where street art is abundant. The east London piece was taken away within two days.

A suitable audience

Every interaction with the public has potential for deeper engagement in an injustice issue, which can lead to social change. Find somewhere where your target audience will be and decide how your object can question the banality of evil through its imagery, message and location. Do you want to focus on reaching out to decision-makers directly, a company's core customers or a politician's constituents? Is it a group of bloggers at an annual conference you know they will be at, or the general public who walk through an area every day, not realising it is linked to an injustice? If you are looking to engage people online (more in Chapter 16) then you might want to prioritise creating an intriguing image of your piece in an area relevant to the issue and share it online with the audiences you think would benefit from the image. For example, to address the housing problem in many large cities around the world you might want to leave a craftivism object outside a row of empty social houses that tenants were evicted from that is being replaced with more expensive and much smaller private homes that local residents cannot afford. Not many people might come across your object in person but online this provocative photograph might encourage more conversation about the importance of having a home and community and whether the current housing market is helping or hindering that.

A suitable time

When you display your object is important too. Will it be a month before an important law will be voted on so that you can help galvanise support for or against it? Or a day after a company announces they are going to stop paying maternity leave for their staff? Think about the kind of object you could use as a tool to shine a spotlight on their unethical practices and encourage change. Try and plan a time to display your object that builds on your message: it could be a UN-named day such as World Food Day, the birthday of a celebrated activist, the anniversary of an incident you want to make sure never happens again (for example, the Rana Plaza factory collapse in Bangladesh on 24 April 2013), a popular secular or religious date such as Valentine's Day where you could ask people to show their love for someone other than their partner or crush. You can create things to leave leading up to that date or launch your campaign on that day using your objects as a form of guerrilla marketing to create a buzz.

Legal or illegal?

Be aware of any laws so that you are not going against them. If you are placing anything on private property, the owner can stop it or confiscate it as it is illegal. Any interference with private property can be seen as trespassing, which could result in criminal or civil action being taken against you. Your craftivism should not cause damage and you should not use it to obstruct people from moving around the area – both actions are illegal. If the police find you leaving objects around public property, they could argue that you are littering, which is also a crime. So do please keep all these factors in mind when deciding where to put your craftivist object.

Placing your object should take a few seconds and shouldn't attract too much attention. Sometimes it can take longer. For example, I decided to weave yarn made from remnants of cotton T-shirts (that would have ended up in a landfill) into a window grid of an empty derelict building near my home to create a large cross-stitch design, which I knew would take over an hour. It was near a busy road and fashion district with lots of shops and market stalls. I thought lots of people would come across my design. I planned to create the design at 5 a.m. as I had heard from a street artist friend that this was the time that the police swap shifts and so wouldn't be patrolling. Doing it at this time would also avoid busy crowds or drunken groups, yet as I was placing it in summer, it was light enough that it was safe. Don't work late at night when you might be unsafe and consider inviting a friend to help and show mutual support. A street-cleaning van stopped and two large men shouted, 'Oi, what are you doing?' I showed them my design on paper and the yarn with a nervous smile. I told them that my design wasn't permanent and if they didn't like it I could cut it all down now but that I wanted people to think about putting people before financial profit and I thought my design in that location might create thought and conversation on this important issue. There was an awkward pause and then one of the men said to me, 'Nah, you're all right. But just don't put any of those vinyl stickers up.' He pointed at them on a nearby lamppost. 'They are a b***** to clean off.'

Aesthetics

As craftivists, one of our roles is to ask uncomfortable questions of the general public which need to be addressed if we want to change our society. We want to attract people to engage with these challenging questions with an open heart and open mind, to intrigue them with some small and beautiful objects that are hung or placed off eye level – below not above eye level works best to show humility. Our gentle pieces of craftivism should not beg for attention but quietly invite engagement through their attractiveness. That way people can feel excited and proud that they have spotted your object and are then curious to see what this little pretty thing is and what it says. The aesthetics of your object will have a strong impact when it is next to grey concrete landscapes such as large buildings or scaffolding, much more so than when it is next to cute colourful shops or parks. Your soft and colourful object could be seen as gently protesting against the harsh and grey environment.

When making objects to display in public I often use shiny sequins because they sparkle and shimmer in natural light, quietly attracting people's attention (I use copper-coloured sequins to look like gold coins if my message is about money). Other embellishments like buttons and ribbons that have symbols on them can enhance and add to your message as well as make it more memorable for visual learners. For example, if you are concerned about the violence in your area don't fight violence with violence but show your worries and vulnerabilities in your work by purposefully using non-threatening colours (such as yellows and pastels) and kitsch patterns; show the fragility in your object by leaving frayed edges on the fabric; include human imperfections in your stitches and hang it below eye level to show humility. You could add a ribbon that depicts children holding hands to show your concern for children in the area. Colour, patterns of fabric, fonts, symbols all deepen the image of our message through their engagement with our senses, but be careful not to clutter your piece with too many messages or too much visual stimulation (see too Chapter 10). Put yourself in the shoes of the people you want to engage: what might be a gentle nudge to help them realise that people in the area are concerned?

You want your object to be alive, to move minds, shift thoughts, challenge assumptions and direct people towards change. Our intriguing craftivism pieces should be more implicit than explicit in their content. You want your object to linger in people's consciousness.

Message

The message (see too Chapter 11) for your intriguing objects can be the most difficult part of making them. Creating effective messages is demanding. It may be easier to come up with negative messages, but positive ones are more likely to encourage change in the viewers. Similarly, objects that are left as 'random acts of kindness' with affirmation messages such as 'you are wonderful' are lovely, but they are not protesting against injustice: if a bully sees it will that challenge them to rethink their harmful actions or will it encourage them to carry on as they are? You want to gently encourage people to question and improve on their actions and our collective culture without devaluing them – there is always room for improvement! If your message is a statement *at* the viewer it does not require a response. It will be less memorable for people because it does not encourage interaction, thought or action. Remember that craftivism is always about action. Your craftivism objects should be pretty to draw people in, create a safe, respectful space for exploration, and engage your audience with a perceptive message to question the status quo and their involvement in social injustice.

Spend some time creating a few variations of your message on the theme that you care about to reach a particular audience in a particular context. Trying to work out the right message teaches us to enjoy problem-solving. This part of your craftivism doesn't come easily to most people. Our instinct is to warn people of the worst thing that could happen, say something positive so as not to upset them, or project our views on to other people. We need to start from the response we hope viewers will have and then work out how to achieve that through our message. Ask yourself what your worst response would be if you read your message on a handmade object found in public and try to mitigate this. I often call a family member or a friend who understands the audience I hope to connect with and talk through the best language and wording to use to reach them. Keep an eye out for slogans and messages you like and make a note of them for future craftivism projects. You can also search the internet quotations by typing in a theme and then 'quote' for inspiration.

Think about the format of your message. Turning your statement into a question mark can prompt your viewer to engage more deeply in the message. I also often use ellipses – (dots) '…' – on the end of my messages to create more intrigue and thought from the viewer: ellipses imply that there is more to be said on this issue or that you want the viewer to carry on the statement, e.g., 'There is enough on this planet for everyone's need but not everyone's greed…' Try not to use exclamation marks or capital letters: you risk appearing like you are shouting and preaching at people, not gently conversing with them (introverted people are especially sensitive to this). Don't pick messages that your audience may have heard so many times that the words no longer intrigue them. Try not to oversimplify a message. Stitching 'Make tea not war' might be something that people like but you want people to think and act on your message, not just agree with it or be confused on what war you are talking about and how to fix it! The more simplistic the message the less engaging it can be because there is no space for ambiguity (but not so ambiguous that it risks misinterpretation) or thought or interpretation. If it's too vague (which war is the statement talking about? War is a difficult thing to stop!) then people don't know what to do with your statement even if they agree with it.

You want to be realistically optimistic about the effect you will have. When creating craftivism street art it is better to focus on something bite-sized for your public craftivism and engage in more complex issues through gift giving or other activism tactics. Your message could be a fact, quote or riddle that encourages the onlooker to think about what the answer is or how to tackle the issue. Rhymes can be powerful because they stay in people's minds. Good quotations can be great too. I love creating messages that you often have to read a few times to understand what it's saying. Think about your audience: if you are trying to engage people of a particular faith, can you respectfully quote a religious book or religious leader they care about? If you are engaging bankers, can you find a quote from a highly respected financier discussing ethical practices in business?

Make your work intelligent and ask for intelligence back from your audience. You want your work to connect with people, and be relevant to them. Let yourself be moved emotionally, and hope that others open up too because that is where life can change.

I was concerned about gangs hanging around in a small public basketball pitch near an office I worked at. You could see people were intimidated by them. Many of the gang members wore large T-shirts with images from violent films like Al Pacino in the film *Scarface* or musicians from music often described as 'gangster rap' such as the murdered rapper B.I.G. on them. I was worried that they might see violence and intimidation as the only power they had or could have or that they felt peer pressure to gain power from people by scaring them, carrying weapons or joining gangs. One morning I hung a small message in the bottom corner of the basketball pitch where they hung out. The message was a quote I found from Martin Scorsese: 'It seems to me that any sensible person must see that violence does not change the world and if it does, then only temporarily.'

I stitched the name 'Martin Scorsese' on the object after the quote because I thought that they might not listen to me or Mother Teresa on violence, but maybe this quote from a director they might admire would have impact. I also thought they might not expect this message coming from a director known for making violent films. Without stitching Scorsese's name, the message could also look judgemental and preachy. Did the message stay up and engage the audience? I didn't wait around to find out: it was too risky. But I hope it encouraged them to see that someone cares about them and wants them to be the best versions of themselves.

We're on a journey

Your object is a catalyst for change not the conclusion; an invitation not a closed concept. Activism is about more than awareness-raising, it's about asking for action. You want people to be so intrigued by your object that they reflect more and investigate more about the issue you have spotlighted and see where they can tackle it as a consumer, constituent or citizen.

The last thing you want is to shock someone with a sad fact and then not offer ways they can get involved to tackle the issue. You want people to be curious, not feel overwhelmed or worse, disempowered. You could add a pin badge from a campaign organisation that your issue links to as a way of encouraging people to join that group or find out more information on their website. You could stitch a social media account or a hashtag for an online conversation, such as #whomademyclothes. That way you can keep your message intriguing, interactive and frame it as part of a wider campaign and discussion.

I have labels that craftivists around the world stitch onto their objects that say 'Made with courage and care, Craftivist Collective'. It shows that, for the maker, the object was a courageous act not an act of showing off. They worked carefully to make this object useful for people. It is also a useful tool to inspire people to google the name for more information on craftivism and on the issue. I encourage craftivists to blog the story of their progress online, including photographs of their object in situ as well as a short essay about their motives, strategy, hopes, crafterthoughts and more information around the issue they are passionate about. I recommend craftivists include links to online sources and organisations campaigning on their issue. The blog can also be shared on their social media. This way you are inviting the viewer to see the craftivist's journey and discovery as their own, and also letting them choose when to engage with the issue in their own time.

Street craftivism

One of the most popular craftivism projects I have created are 'mini banners'.* These banners are flying solidarity's flag for those suffering as a result of the world's injustices or they're questioning our culture to see how we can improve it for all. They are made to turn heads and influence change with the hope that people walking down the street will spot, out of the corner of their eye, a colourful cross-stitched mini banner waving in the wind. Because the text is small the passer-by has to decide whether or not to go up closer to read the message. If they are curious and open-minded then they are more likely to approach the object and that's when I hope the message provokes thought and action in them. I hung one banner off eye level on railings down Denmark Street in London, a street famous for its music shops and music venues. It said: 'When the power of love overpowers the love of power, the world will know peace' – Jimi Hendrix.

It's an intriguing message because it doesn't tell you what to do and you have to read it a few times for it to sink in. It can also encourage you to relate the content to your life as well as to that area. And it is from one of the world's greatest guitarists, Jimi Hendrix!

This project can be made alone in public or private anywhere as well as in a group. These are the type of questions I recommend you think critically about while stitching a mini banner so that you create your own crafterthoughts:

1. How can your banner's appearance, message and location appeal to your chosen audience in the best way possible?

* www.craftivist-collective.com/mini-banner

2. Is your work encouraging positive change or pointing fingers? Let compassion and understanding be your guide, never contempt or pride.
3. How can you strive to be part of the solution to the issue you're addressing? What can you buy, think, say or do differently?

You could turn these banners into masks to wrap around a statue using string or Velcro. I placed a protest mask on a statue in an area where there is no street art and where the statue's head was accessible and visible (not on a high podium where you wouldn't see the message!) and so it really stood out. I also asked a vintage shop if I could put a mask on a mannequin in their shop window in an area where lots of fashion students and fashion lovers live, work and shop. The mask said: 'There is no point to a globalisation that reduces the price of a child's shoes, but costs the parent their job...' I could have tried to gather the courage to put it in an unethical chain store window but I was too scared. Although it might have been seen by more people, it would have been taken down quickly by staff or they may have stopped me before I could put it up. The vintage shop kept the mask up for a few months and the owner allowed my friend to take some professional photographs that have been shared online and in books and magazines. The reach your objects will achieve – whether offline or shared through social media – is an important thing to consider when thinking through your strategy.

Hundreds of craftivists have used this mini-banner project to great effect around the world at any time of year. Each September over the last three years craftivists around the world have made mini banners to question the ugly side of the fashion industry during London Fashion Week.

Altering existing objects

You could alter an object that is already well recognised and connects to many individual memories and cultural history. I altered the look of one Barbie to address gender inequality. I used to regularly catch a train from Clapham Junction to an office in Waterloo. Clapham Junction is the busiest train station in Europe. On my way home I would often pass a group of teenage boys and girls hanging out on the steps at the back entrance of the station. They were not causing any bother at all, just socialising. I kept noticing that the lads would be quite loud and boisterous and the girls often said nothing or just giggled. The boys would have their arms around the girls and it made me think: did the boys feel they had to be confident and lead the conversations and did the girls feel they had to 'sit pretty' and not speak up? Maybe I was reading that into the situation but I did want to address the gender inequality I thought I was seeing with a 'gentle protest' approach.

Gender equality is not only a fundamental human right but a necessary foundation for a peaceful, prosperous and sustainable world. That's what the United Nations Sustainable Development Goals says on gender. Gender is one of the seventeen goals the UN prioritises. While our world has achieved much progress towards gender equality and women's empowerment under the Millennium Development Goals (such as equal access to primary education for girls and boys), women and girls continue to suffer discrimination and violence.

I decided to create a striking image of a battered and bruised Barbie with tape over her eyes and mouth. She held a small placard with a message written on it to provoke this group and passers-by to think about and discuss the impact gender inequality has on all of our lives. I placed it near the group but not too close, and below eye level to intrigue people. Two lads came up and asked me what I was doing. I showed them and read out the handwritten message on the placard I had picked to encourage thought and conversation: 'You can tell the condition of a nation by looking at the state of its women' – Jawaharlia Nehru (1889–1964) first Prime Minister of independent India.

I asked them if they felt they had to be confident and a 'protector' of their girlfriends, maybe pay for everything for them, or if they could just be themselves around girls and treat each other equally. We had a chat about the pressures they sometimes feel to be 'the men' and that they thought that girls probably did feel pressure to look pretty for them. I asked if they were okay with me leaving my Barbie for others to see. The response was, 'Yeah, we will look after it.' The photograph has not only been published in numerous books and magazines but also been shared over the years on blogs and social media creating more discussions on gender equality. Students at The New School for International Affairs and Media, in New York City, have taken part in this project as part of their course for a few years. One of the students, Emilie Romero, used the project to advocate for freedom from child marriage. Her placard said: 'Women are the only oppressed group in our society that live in intimate association with their oppressor.'* Powerful stuff. She wrote a blog post for the Craftivist Collective website saying:

> By taping the Barbie's mouth shut, it symbolises how many US women feel about having their health rights taken away, silenced and abused...I decided to make this activity more about process than product; therefore my camera was used more as a decoy to draw people in to engage in the messages being seen. After people had witnessed the 'Barbie Effect', I pretended to do camera interviews, which got people engaged in conversations about female advocacy. In the end, Craftivist Collective inspired me to do more, and it really showed me how easy and fun advocacy can be.

Shopdropping

Another form of culture jamming that craftivists can harness is

---

* I learnt later that this was a quote from Evelyn Cunningham, a reporter during the civil rights movement in the sixties, whose obituary can be found here: www.nytimes.com/2010/04/30/nyregion/30evelyn.html

'shopdropping', also known as reverse shoplifting. Shopdropping subverts commercial space for artistic and political use. My 'mini fashion statements'* are an example of shopdropping. I use pocket-sized scrolls as powerful and poignant little reminders of the role we can all play as consumers and collectively as culture creators. Also, if anyone who works in fashion found one, I would hope it also challenged them to think about their role of complicity in the fashion sector. They're designed to be placed in clothes pockets for people to find, open and make us think more about how the clothes we buy are made, and how we might be able to help tackle problems such as poor conditions for workers or the use of materials that are damaging to the environment. The hope is that these intriguing objects will lead to an appreciation and celebration for things that are made with love and care. Fashion is for everyone. That means it should answer to everyone. The contemporary consumer votes with their money and with 'likes' on social media. Our social-media-friendly scrolls could have an impact both on customers and with ripples within social media to influence fashion companies.

To make these mini fashion statements, carefully write in your most attractive handwriting one of the three messages below on a small strip of thick paper about 4cm wide and, when it is rolled up – I use a biro to wrap the scroll around – it should be about 1cm tall (ideally a high-quality, textured and recycled piece of thick paper to give it extra value). The process of writing the scrolls creates a quiet space for some contemplative thought on the words you write and what they mean. I also created an embossing stamp of the Craftivist Collective logo (without the words, just the scissors and thread image) to make a mark in the top and outside of the scroll, adding texture, creative detail and hopefully value without adding any more resources. This anonymous scroll can create

* www.craftivist-collective.com/mini-fashion-statement

more intrigue and shows humility rather than a motive for fame.

The three short messages to pick from are:

1. If clothes could talk…
   What tales might they tell? Stories of how they were made with love, joy and care? Or sadness, tragedy and heartbreak?
   What would your clothes say to you?
   @Fash_Rev

2. 'Clothes maketh the person' – that's quite a responsibility, isn't it?
   If we are what we wear then shouldn't we try to make sure that our clothes are made by garment workers who get paid well & treated with dignity & the planet is not harmed during the making of our clothes?
   @Fash_Rev

3. Beauty is not just in the eye of the beholder…
   It is woven into the very fabric of the cloth. Our clothes can never be truly beautiful if they hide the ugliness of worker exploitation.
   Join the #FashionRevolution & find out if your values are threaded through your clothes x
   @Fash_Rev

The paper is then rolled into a scroll and tied together with pretty and delicate coloured ribbon in a bow. I choose colours that link to luxury such as purple and mint green to make these objects seem more expensive. On the outside of the scroll the message 'please open me :) x' is written in lowercase letters and in the craftivists' own neat, curly handwriting to stir up interest from the person who finds it, with the smiley face and 'x' kiss evaporating any worries people have of finding these notes, and 'please' showing that they have the power, not the maker. I worked with expert wordsmiths at the sustainability agency Futerra to come up with three intriguing messages for the craftivist to pick from to write on the scrolls. Giving three choices of messages to share gives the craftivist ownership and decision-making in the project but also makes sure that the three expertly written messages are not altered, which can dilute the impact. I was keen to get the balance of each message just right to protest against the ugly side of fashion but not to be judgemental of the reader. Each message ended with '@Fash_Rev' to encourage people to join the Fashion Revolution global movement, which believes in a fashion industry that values people, the environment, creativity and profits in equal measure and has a mission to bring everyone together to help make this happen. The reader could find @Fash_Rev on social media, share an image of their scroll and tag @Fash_Rev or put '@Fash_Rev' into an internet search engine which will direct the reader to the website for more information.

This project could engage any member of the public, especially people who love the beauty and creativity that comes from fashion, who love expressing themselves through what they wear but might forget about the ugly side of the fashion industry. I first delivered the project during Stockholm Fashion Week 2015: a good time and opportunity to promote a more sustainable world (and for me to see if the project worked!). It can be done by individuals and groups around the world at any time of year but can be particularly powerful around, for example, the anniversary of the Rana Plaza factory disaster when on 24 April 2013 over 1,100 garment workers in Bangladesh lost their lives, or the anniversaries of other tragedies that we shouldn't forget but should make sure don't happen again.

One response to this project written on the 'crafterthought' board in my 'Gentle Protest' exhibition in Stockholm, August 2015 from an anonymous participant said: 'I find your work attractive, sensible and ingenious. It also raises fundamental questions about possible ways to change the world.'

Another attendee commented: 'You have opened my eyes and made me think about my clothes in a new way.'

The power of curiosity

It's easy to deny our own agency or say that what is happening isn't all bad, thereby letting ourselves and others off the hook of needing to change our own behaviour and actions. In denial can be a very attractive place to be, but overcoming denial and despair – our own and that of others – is fundamental to local, national, societal and cultural transformation. As craftivists we should disturb the status quo where there are harmful systems and structures in place, and we should encourage people to act more intentionally and ethically where they can. However, we also need to accept that we should not, and cannot, force people to act or think differently. For long-term change to happen, people need to take ownership of their thoughts and decisions and that starts with people deciding for themselves how to act. Our craftivism objects can help to be catalysts and tools of encouragement for people but they should never be aggressive. Changing hearts and minds is often a slow process and needs to be approached gently even when we want urgent action to stop harm happening to people.

Curiosity may have killed the cat but it won't kill human beings. In the case of concentration camps, curiosity and asking important questions could potentially have saved lives. We need to see our craftivism object as an attractive invitation away from a banal way of living and towards a more thoughtful, intentional and mindful way of life as a citizen, consumer and constituent. Our craftivism objects, if created strategically, can invite the discoverer both to be surprised by what they find and to wonder about the world we live in and how we all shape it, intentionally or unintentionally.

14
Pretty Protests

I attract a crowd, not because I'm an extrovert or I'm over the top or I'm oozing with charisma. It's because I care.

— *Gary Vaynerchuk*

I will never forget the day I made an old lady cry. It was years ago. Before I became a craftivist. It wasn't on purpose. I was in my hometown of Liverpool and its first Primark store was just about to open. It was the talk of the town: all these pretty clothes and so cheap! I knew people who were against this fast-fashion brand but I couldn't find any groups who were going to demonstrate against its unethical practices at the opening. Surely there was going to be a demonstration to show the true cost of these cheap clothes: sweatshops, undignified labour practices, unlivable wages, abuse of garment workers and fast fashion filling our landfills? I rallied a group of friends to set up a demonstration on its opening day. I didn't want to do it. My gut feeling is to walk over to the other side of the road if I see a demonstration because I don't want to be shouted at, judged, told what to do or what to think. I felt that although we couldn't close down this very large store with one demonstration, people should be aware of the ugly side of these pretty clothes. People should be encouraged to question their role in the fashion industry. A public protest could help be a catalyst for those thoughts and conversations we should be having.

I had never set up a demonstration before. I found ten friends to join the protest, some musicians who were used to performing and some experienced activists, but I struggled to attract most of my friends. They did not identify as activists and were too nervous or shy to join in. We made placards with facts on them about the pay, number of hours worked and the treatment the garment workers received while making these clothes. We all wore ethically made red T-shirts with protest slogans on. I made leaflets with facts on them about the bad practices and the effects 'fast fashion' and their poorly made clothes have on our environment. I researched how to do a lawful demonstration on www.liberty-human-rights.org.uk, I had a phone conversation with one of Liberty's free advisors and I printed off their document on legal protesting to put in my back pocket to show to the police if they questioned our right to protest. We made sure we were not in the way of the entrance of the store or making too much noise so that we could not be moved on for antisocial behaviour. I made sure our leaflets didn't touch the floor so that we couldn't be moved on by the police for littering.

I hated it. It felt like most people looked at us disapprovingly and some people told us to leave. Staff came out to tell us that Primark was part of the Ethical Trading Initiative (ETI) so that there was no need for us to be there. We tried to say respectfully that the ETI is a voluntary group with no binding regulations that Primark have to put into action and we showed them evidence of Primark's immoral practices but they brushed us off. And then I made an old lady cry.

She looked about eighty years old, very small and frail. She walked up to me from the shop with her large Primark bag full of purchases. She asked me quietly with a wobbly voice if the information was true on our placards. I said that sadly it was and we should challenge Primark to change their ways as well as shopping in more ethical shops. 'Cheap clothes come with a big cost,' I said. She whispered to me that it was one of the only places she could afford to shop for her, her children and grandchildren. Her eyes started filling up; mine started filling up too. I was so focused on getting our message out there in the public domain that I hadn't thought about the different ways people might respond to our protest and the different reasons people might have for shopping in Primark. This woman who was so respectful to me clearly felt terrible when she learnt about Primark's record of treating their garment workers badly, and she also seemed embarrassed that she had been 'caught out' supporting them. I felt ashamed that I had been so thoughtless. I took out a small piece of card from my pocket I had ordered from the charity 'Labour Behind The Label' and gave it to her, explaining that when she no longer needed her receipt she could place her receipt into the card, fold it over and give back her receipt to Primark staff. The card said that as a customer she wanted them to clean up their practices. I explained that this small act could help have the message discussed higher up in the company and the more customers who would do that, the more impact it would have. I reminded her that she had power as a customer and smiled apologetically. She smiled back with eyes still shiny from her tears. We both agreed it was awful how some companies acted and she went away with the cards inside her Primark carrier bag.

Our resistance to Primark at its opening day had some positive results. We gave out all of the leaflets we had. The local newspaper and radio station mentioned our protest. Over 400 signatures were collected for our petition that we handed over to the Primark store manager at the end of that day. We took a photograph of the handover to attach to our press release and we sent a copy to local MPs to ask the government to do more to stop human rights abuses in the retail sector. But I wasn't sure that the type of demonstration we did was as effective as it could have been. I didn't feel that we reached out to the people queuing up to go into Primark or passers-by in a way that allowed both 'sides' to listen to each other and converse. The protest felt like a battle, not an activity that inspired action from the public. Our protest felt counter-productive because instead of engaging people – staff, customers and passers-by – on the issue and seeing where we could all tackle the ugly side of the fashion industry together, I was worried that we had created a bigger gap rather than a bridge and a movement for change. And I couldn't stop thinking about the old lady who had cried when she learnt about Primark's unethical practices. I wanted to empower people, not to make them feel useless or shamed when confronted with the facts. Surely there must be another way to protest publicly about injustice, a way that is attractive, kind and hopeful for all involved? How can we create pretty protests that help people open up to our message not close off?

Goals of a craftivism gentle protest

The goal of any protest is to raise awareness and knowledge of an issue, and to show how we can all help to solve the injustice. It's also about galvanising support for your campaign to show your target company, government or other influential decision-makers on this issue that a large proportion of people demand the end of one practice and its replacement with a more ethical one.

As craftivists we should always be thinking strategically about how to have the biggest impact possible. This means looking at where others are protesting against the same issue and where they may not be. Where can you fill a gap if your issue isn't currently being seen, discussed or acknowledged or where more pressure needs to be added? What influential audiences should you focus on? Think where your act of craftivism and the presence of craftivists could help strengthen a movement for cultural shift.

I believe there are four key ways craftivism can create 'pretty protests'.

1. Intimate protest
    When volunteering for charities, I used sometimes to hide in the toilet when I was supposed to be asking people to sign petitions. I didn't like interrupting people walking to work or hanging out with friends. I didn't like pressuring people to sign a petition and it often felt like a very shallow transaction on both parts. As an introvert, it was extremely tiring too, but I kept doing it because sometimes I would have thoughtful conversations with people and I would learn so much about different views on what I was campaigning about. These moments are rare but long one-to-one conversations I had with strangers have stayed with me, and hopefully with them too.

    I remember one man at a festival I was campaigning at, where I was asking people to sign petition cards. He told me that campaigning was pointless. So we respectfully discussed his point of view, looked at where campaigns had been won and lost throughout history and why. We shared our worries and hopes with each other and by the end of the chat this lovely man (and sober, no less!) signed my climate justice petition and asked if he could give me a hug to thank me for challenging his cynicism. We both left the conversation with revitalised energy to keep trying to improve the world.

    It was these types of intimate conversations that I missed when I was told to focus on getting as many signatures as possible. But it's these conversations that can deepen engagement with your audience on your campaign, last longer in people's minds and often create new conversations with their friends and family. I believe that craftivism can help create more of these one-to-one intimate conversations to strengthen and add to our activism toolkit.

197

As I've said in Chapter 6, craft materials and activities can be a social lubricant: when stitching alone on public transport, in parks or cafes, people often ask what you are doing. In my experience, stitching a small craftivism object that has provocative words on the theme of social change can intrigue strangers often more than if words were not included. To harness this curiosity, once you notice they are watching you, smile and go back to stitching. This technique offers a friendly ground for open discussion with no pressure attached. If people ask you what you are making, quietly show them, read them the message, explain what you are going to do with the object and ask them for their advice on where to put it to have the most impact. By ending with a question you are initiating a conversation on the issue you are questioning or protesting about. Don't force a discussion and if it looks like people are busy or tired then acknowledge that by apologising if you are taking up their time. This leaves the power with the other person. Crafting creates a respectful safe barrier between you and the other person because it helps break eye contact to stop the conversation from being too aggressive or intense and the craft materials in your hands keep you a safe distance away from each other so that you are not invading each other's personal space.

I have spoken to lots of people one-to-one in this way over the years: bankers, teachers, retired couples, single mothers, students, all sorts. I have learnt a lot from listening to them and discussing what solutions we can take to alleviate injustices in the world. Sometimes we disagreed, but we listened to each other's point of view and mostly ended with a smile and good wishes. As a craftivist, this intimate protest is a very useful research tool to help you see how to engage people in your campaign in a way that will resonate with them. Key themes that you need to address might come out, whether it's people not feeling they have the facts to support the campaign or that they don't know what they can do personally to tackle it. A counterargument that you did not expect but found held a lot of weight with people might be repeated by different people at different times. You can feed all of this information back to other campaigners and organisations working on this issue to help strengthen the larger campaign and see how you can tackle these concerns in your own work. Scottish Craftivist Jess comments: 'I made my first piece on the tube and at work and a few people asked me what I was doing already! Yay for craftivism!!! Jess x'

You don't need to strike up conversations with strangers at first. You can start with practising on your friends and family. Craftivist Rachel wrote me a letter saying: 'Thanks for all the inspiration to do this, I've really enjoyed it and found it easier to talk to my friends about these issues when they see me sewing away 😊 '

2. #Popupcraftivist

Building on 'intimate protest', you can harness the power of social media to create a space for small groups of people to do craftivism in places you wouldn't expect to see a protest. Like a pop-up shop, you could pop up temporarily as a craftivist. Choose a friendly venue, such as a cafe, safe park area or somewhere else not in the way of others but not hidden. Share where you will be on social media and have a pile of craftivism resources with you to entice people to come over and start crafting with you. I do this with a suitcase I got from a relative. The suitcase can add intrigue and beauty to your protest. On the outside lid of the case I recommend writing #popupcraftivist so people can find you easily, and it will inspire curiosity from others as well as letting people know where you are. Why not cover the inside of the lid with a cross-stitched quote on fabric to make it clear that your protest is friendly? The quote from cultural anthropologist Margaret Mead on the inside of my suitcase gets many positive responses from people with many of them asking to take a photograph of it to share with others: 'Never doubt that a small group of thoughtful, committed citizens can change the world. Indeed, it is the only thing that ever has.'

It can be scary putting yourself out there, so why not pop up somewhere you know first? I asked the arts festival Greenbelt if I could pop up at their festival and they agreed. It is a small festival, I knew lots of people there and so felt safe and supported. I set up my suitcase in one of the cafes under a canopy where I wouldn't be distracting people from a performance. I asked my sister to join me. Inviting a friend not only helps you feel supported but makes it more likely that people will come and talk to you because people are herd animals: we like to make connections with others and we are strongly influenced by what those around us are doing. For example, if we see an empty restaurant and a busy one, most of us would choose the busy restaurant to have a meal in. We were stitching a craftivism footprint each, one of the best craftivism objects since it doesn't include lots of elements we might lose in the mud and the project is easier for beginners than other projects. Within minutes, a group of five people in their twenties asked what we were doing. I showed them a final version of what we were making and asked if they would like to make one with us. They joined us and we stayed for over an hour and talked about the different ways we can protest against injustice and how we can all work towards creating a more beautiful, kind and fair world, one stitch at a time. Other people came and left with their footprints and extra thread all wrapped up in little resealable bags I gave out so they could finish off their craftivism project elsewhere at the festival or at home.

Think about setting up at a place people know. At the Secret Garden Party festival I found a perfect spot on the top of a small but high man-made hill. It had on it a giant fox statue made out of wicker approximately ten metres high. I wore my fox hood (a gift I was given the year before, as you do! ;p) and decided it would be fun to ask people to join us under the 'crafty fox' (we renamed it!) since it was so easy to see from most parts of the festival. This time we had around twenty people in the sun, including a family of nine spanning three generations. I had three volunteers with me at the festival who joined me in handing out resources, explaining the project and showing people what to do. Craftivist Sophia attended:

> I stitched the message 'a journey of a thousand miles starts with just one step' on the fabric footprint shape Sarah gave me. It's not an everyday experience for many people, and that in itself makes it an ideal thing to have at a festival. It also provides a great balance point to all the shouty noisy madness which often typifies festivals these days. People soon drifted over to join us, drawn to the calm friendly atmosphere. Festivals really need the moments of calm, personal connectedness that sitting and stitching provides. It was a breath of air and a moment that will always stay with me.

Festivals, parks and cafes can be great places for intimate protests. People aren't rushing as much so there is time for discussion and reflection. It doesn't always work however: I tried the same formula at one festival that was for younger people but they were too energetic and didn't want to do something slow and meditative. It didn't help that some were taking illegal drugs whilst stitching. Some areas and times will work better than others and that's fine. I've popped up in Union Square in Manhattan the day after I was giving a lecture at Parsons New School, New York. An older German gentleman on holiday sat nearby having his lunch. He didn't join me in stitching but we did have a great conversation about the importance of education, critical thinking and how to live more ethically. Then my cousin's friend who was new to New York heard about this little session and came to join in. She didn't know anyone in NYC and so thought this would be fun. Then four other people turned up. We all chatted and I took some photos to share on social media and for my German friend to show his son, a schoolteacher, to see if his school might do something similar. With your travelling suitcase you never know where you might be invited and where there are opportunities to encourage critical thinking and social change.

3. Craftivism circles in public

'Craftivism circles' in public have multiple uses. Their priority is to craft and discuss social injustice with other craftivists to help form and strengthen a movement for change. Through their public nature they can also engage passers-by. Wherever you are in the world, if you want to set up a craftivism circle, pick a safe place but try not to pick a venue where only like-minded people meet: you want a diverse group of people to feel welcome and also a diverse group of people interested in what you are doing in order to create spaces for 'intimate protest' with craftivists and non-craftivists.

I used to meet people in the Royal Festival Hall public area on the London Southbank to craft together. It was central so most people could get to it after work without too much difficultly and the venue was very welcoming towards groups meeting there. It was a space always full of diverse crowds, which is a great opportunity to raise consciousness of issues with people who may not have engaged in them before. You didn't have to buy anything from their cafe to sit there, it had disabled access, and we gathered a group of chairs to sit in a circle together. Not only was it a great way to meet new craftivists in a safe, welcoming space, but our presence intrigued passers-by and other venue attendees, creating a catalyst for conversation. Our group gatherings tended to be quiet whether it was two people or twenty people and gave us a chance to discuss issues in depth with each other and for others to see that craftivism groups exist and people are trying to encourage change on particular issues. We made sure we were not interrupting other people's meet-ups near us. Often the noise from our area would go in waves from thoughtful chats to silence and sometimes one-to-one conversations. That only intrigued passers-by more, seeing us all head-down, focusing on stitching our messages. After we had met there a few times, Nikki, a Learning and Participation Assistant at the Southbank Centre came over to us to welcome us and tell us that she and her colleagues loved having us there. She even joined our group and is now a committed and experienced craftivist, often helping to lead workshops and events. Craftivist Nikki comments:

> As an organisation we were used to seeing all sorts of groups making use of the space. What struck me was the diversity of the group. I loved finding out that there were lots of people there for the first time, and that new people and passers-by were welcome to join in. I liked the fact that it wasn't immediately evident who the 'leaders' of this group were and who was brand new. The inclusivity of the group was refreshing and I felt part of it straight away. Six years on, I am proud to call myself a craftivist. Craftivism continually challenges me to think about my daily choices and offers a constructive and hopeful way to engage with complex, often otherwise overwhelming issues.

4. Stitch-ins
The above public protests are more subtle than other forms of protest but can still have considerable impact. However, sometimes

we still need to protest directly against particular powers and I believe we can sometimes do this through what I call a 'stitch-in'. Taking the idea from 'sit-ins', a form of direct action that involves one or more people occupying an area that directly links to their protest and sometimes refusing to leave until their demands are met, I hoped to create a more gentle and pretty protest approach. We can also learn from the history of craft groups crafting in public, from the women who knitted liberty caps in between executions during the French Revolution to the women who knitted themselves into webs during anti-nuclear protests at Greenham Common in the 1980s. Their presence, calmness, colour and wit showed them to be strong, committed campaigners, engaged the public and press, and added weight to their campaigns, shining a light on practices they believed should be changed.

The first stitch-in I coordinated was in support of the campaign 'Fair Fares Now' led by the campaign organisation Better Transport and the voluntary activist group Climate Rush. The campaign was for cheaper, fairer and simpler train fares. Some train fares were more expensive than flying to the same location! This wasn't just bad for those struggling to afford to travel to work but the cost of train fares was not helping us decrease the carbon emissions that increase global warming. Our goal was to strengthen the campaign and encourage the UK government to put laws in place to make sure that companies couldn't hike up the costs so much that people couldn't afford to get to work, and the price rises also made it more attractive to go on short-haul flights. There was an important annual transport meeting chaired by the Minister of Transport coming up. This was a good opportunity to show the minister and the other attendees that the public wanted change. I asked people across the country to stitch a piece of fabric in the shape of a train carriage with a message on the importance of tackling climate change and the issues of over-expensive transport costs that I could then sew together into a giant row of bunting to display at the entrance of the meeting and other useful events and venues in the future to keep up the pressure.

I thought we could stitch our fabric train carriages inside train stations since we wanted to engage that audience and it would create a striking photograph to attract media to this campaign. Our protests were during the summer months and were purposefully small and attractive. Using the same approach as our stitch-ins in Chapter 12, we made the protests look like a picnic but we held them inside train stations. Craftivists were encouraged to dress as if they were going to a fancy picnic in the park and to bring a picnic blanket to sit on. We limited most picnics to twelve people or fewer so as not to intimidate people or get in the way of travellers but so that we would still be visible to all. We brought flasks of tea, scones, sandwiches or cupcakes to eat and to offer to those who made conversation with us. I encouraged people to practise active listening when interacting with the public and to create a place for exchanging ideas and raising consciousness of the climate change issue and of the inequality in the world. Our focus was on intriguing and attracting engagement not enforcing our views on people.

The stitch-ins not only created conversations offline with travellers who signed our petitions during the sessions but local and national media covered these unusual and visual events. We also gathered evidence of the concern on this issue from travellers to hand in to the transport minister at the annual meeting. When we displayed the bunting (which ended up as eighty metres wrapped around the railings leading up of the entrance of the meeting!) and told the minister what we had been doing across the country from the North East of Scotland to the South West of England, he seemed shocked and had a long conversation with us about the meeting and his position on our campaign. The members of the meeting thought we were going to give them the bunting but we said that it was going to Better Transport to display in other venues to continue to galvanise support. This seemed to turn their smiles into concern.

For every stitch-in that is directly related to a specific campaign you need to plan how best to connect with the people who have the most power to fix or improve the situation, and which members of the public those people will listen to the most. Will your stitch-in be on public or private property? That will inform you how to deliver your protest within the law. Think about whether it would be better to have your stitch-in outside the venue or in the venue's cafe, if they have one, or elsewhere. Don't forget to do your research and find out if delivering a stitch-in is actually a useful action to take. I spoke on the phone to one student craftivist who wanted advice on doing a stitch-in inside her university's library to demand disabled access. I asked her why the university had refused access. She hadn't checked. This new craftivist then came back to me with her findings: the university were putting disabled access into the old building within the next few months but had forgotten to announce it to the public. No stitch-in was needed but I encouraged the student to help the library share the information with students so that they were up to date with the progress.

Mindful of our presence when protesting

Be mindful of the presence you are creating that will help or harm your goal of challenging injustice in the world and promoting an alternative. On 20 December 1956 a federal ruling took effect and led to the United States Supreme Court decision that segregated buses were unconstitutional. This was just over a year after the Montgomery bus boycott had been spearheaded by Rosa Parks refusing to give up her seat on the bus for a white passenger and subsequently being arrested. On

19 December 1956, Martin Luther King shared widely his list of guidelines for those who would be using the bus again. Although this list is after a protest win I still read and reread it to help me think through what our own craftivism guidelines should be for any 'pretty protest' we do and how to be mindful of the people we hope to engage effectively with our protest. It shows us how to be emotionally intelligent in our actions and to remember to be aware of how our presence is understood by others. I hope as craftivists we can be as thoughtful, loving and empathetic as Martin Luther King Jnr and members of the Civil Rights Movement.[1]

December 19, 1956

INTEGRATED BUS SUGGESTIONS

This is a historic week because segregation on buses has now been declared unconstitutional. Within a few days the Supreme Court Mandate will reach Montgomery and you will be reboarding integrated buses. This places upon us all a tremendous responsibility of maintaining, in face of what could be some unpleasantness, a calm and loving dignity befitting good citizens and members of our Race. If there is violence in word or deed it must not be our people who commit it.

For your help and convenience the following suggestions are made. Will you read, study and memorise them so that our non-violent determination may not be endangered. First, some general suggestions:

1   Not all white people are opposed to integrated buses. Accept goodwill on the part of many.
2   The whole bus is now for the use of all people. Take a vacant seat.
3   Pray for guidance and commit yourself to complete non-violence in word and action as you enter the bus.
4   Demonstrate the calm dignity of our Montgomery people in your actions.

5 In all things observe ordinary rules of courtesy and good behavior.

6 Remember that this is not a victory for Negroes alone, but for all Montgomery and the South. Do not boast! Do not brag!

7 Be quiet but friendly; proud, but not arrogant; joyous, but not boisterous.

8 Be loving enough to absorb evil and understanding enough to turn an enemy into a friend.

Now for some specific suggestions:

1 The bus driver is in charge of the bus and has been instructed to obey the law. Assume that he will cooperate in helping you occupy any vacant seat.

2 Do not deliberately sit by a white person, unless there is no other seat.

3 In sitting down by a person, white or colored, say 'May I' or 'Pardon me' as you sit. This is a common courtesy.

4 If cursed, do not curse back. If pushed, do not push back. If struck, do not strike back, but evidence love and goodwill at all times.

5 In case of an incident, talk as little as possible, and always in a quiet tone. Do not get up from your seat! Report all serious incidents to the bus driver.

6 For the first few days try to get on the bus with a friend in whose non-violence you have confidence. You can uphold one another by a glance or a prayer.

7 If another person is being molested, do not arise to go to his defense, but pray for the oppressor and use moral and spiritual force to carry on the struggle for justice.

8 According to your own ability and personality, do not be afraid to experiment with new and creative techniques for achieving reconciliation and social change.

9   If you feel you cannot take it, walk for another week or two. We
    have confidence in our people.
GOD BLESS YOU ALL.

Guidelines for pretty protests

1. Welcome people who are nervous of protesting into a safe and
    attractive space, especially people who might be part of what your
    target company see as their core audience.
2. Bigger is not always better: don't demand attention or show off;
    invite attention. Attract people positively through small and
    beautiful objects and actions.
3. Focus on engagement: let the passer-by initiate conversation and
    take time discussing issues with them.
4. Create intimacy: engage people through one-to-one conversations
    using humility and emotional intelligence. Encourage people to
    be the best they can be as employees, consumers and citizens, not
    judging or demonising them and offer suggestions about how they
    can do this.
5. Offer vulnerability not violence: be open to change our own minds
    through listening to people we disagree with as well as encouraging
    others to question their thoughts and actions by asking them
    strategic and open questions.
6. Creativity creates curiosity: continue building intrigue and
    discussion through online images and messages, helping people
    learn more about the issue and how they can tackle injustice.
7. Be a conduit for a better society, a role model of a thoughtful and
    proactive global citizen.

Alison, the blogger at www.anotherlittlecraftycreation.wordpress.com,
took part in one of our craftivism projects and on her blog she wrote:

Campaigning for worthy causes doesn't have to be about shouting in the streets (something I would never feel confident to do) but hopefully enough little voices can have the same impact.

Practising pretty protest

If I was going to deliver a protest outside Primark again I would do it differently. The message would be more intriguing, focusing on how we all need to slow down and take time to think about what we are doing and buying. Companies like Primark should produce fewer new clothes so that they can be more careful on their production process and we as consumers should enjoy the shopping process slowly; seeing what clothes we need and what will last, not giving in to quick impulses but buying clothes we will cherish. Craftivists could occupy a small but visually stimulating area visible near the store where we could make 'cake pops'* to look like snails and other craftivists could give them out with informative flyers. We would encourage friendly conversation about the importance of slow fashion to not only help tackle the ugly hidden sides of the fashion industry, but also for us to appreciate our clothes more. We would share images of these crafted snails and intriguing messages before, during and after the opening of Primark, encouraging people to find out more about Primark's production processes to help them make informed consumer choices. The old lady would then not be in tears but encouraged and empowered to be part of the change she wishes to see in the world.

* A 'cake pop' is a small round piece of cake coated with icing or chocolate and fixed on the end of a stick so as to resemble a lollipop.

15

Wearing your Convictions

Courage is what it takes to stand up and speak; courage is also
what it takes to sit down and listen.

— Winston Churchill

We need a new normal. But most of us don't want to be the one to rock the
boat. We want to fit in, feel safe, we don't want to separate ourselves from
people. We join a queue, we find ourselves as part of a standing ovation
for a play we didn't think was that good. Social proof is a psychological
phenomenon where people assume that the actions of others are the correct
behaviour for a given situation, regardless of whether it is or not. Social
proof leads not only to public compliance but also private belief. In a recent
study, social-psychologist Dr Sander van der Linden[1] uses the social proof
theory to illustrate that people are more likely to reduce their consumption
of bottled water when simple information on the negative impacts of

bottled water is preceded by 'social proof' that others have already started to behave pro-environmentally as well as stop buying the bottles. We often need to see new cultures in others before we have the confidence to join them. Therefore to create a new normal we need social proof.

What's this got to do with what we wear? Perhaps more than any other cultural object, fashion is a visible measure of what's going on in society at a given time. Fashion is widely inclusive because everyone wears clothes. Four hundred years ago, society's fashion biases prompted Shakespeare to include a speech from Polonius to his son Laertes in the play *Hamlet*:

Costly thy habit as thy purse can buy,
but not expressed in fancy rich not gaudy;
For the apparel oft proclaims the man.

Rightly or wrongly, we constantly make assumptions about who people are, what they do, what convictions they hold, and how they live, all based on the way they dress. For those of us who can afford to choose the clothes we wear, fashion can be used to express our identity, reveal who we are or who we want to be. I believe we should use the way we dress to protest against harmful actions and cultures in the world and use it as a tool to help put in place an alternative future and a new normal through social proof.

Standing in not standing out

Uncertainty is one of three major factors that encourages the use of social proof. When we are unsure what is helpful for society and what is harmful we are more likely to look for and incorporate the opinions of others into our decisions.

Subcultures show us that a group of people don't agree or accept certain norms in society. Throughout the history of fashion, many protesters have worn different 'uniforms' to show their political convictions as individuals and groups and to create an alternative society. Hippies grew out their hair and wore loose-fitting clothing with imagery of flowers or the peace sign. Before and during the Vietnam War revolutionary figures like Fidel Castro and Che Guevara became heroes for many people who then appropriated military surplus clothing, which they wore to anti-war protests. In the 1970s, punk fashion was a reaction to popular culture's elaborate and materialistic looks by wearing ripped or dirty-looking clothing, often unkempt short hair, accessories referencing S&M and body modifications. The 'Riot Grrrl' fashion of the 1990s was openly girly and sexually aggressive with singer-songwriter Kathleen Hanna wearing 'slutty' outfits as a protest against their perceived sluttiness. The Izikhothane, a South African subculture of young men in townships, rebelled against the norm in their area by showing off in flamboyant and well-tailored suits. Dr Christine Checinska calls them 'elegant anarchists'.[2] These different fashions show diversity in belief and lifestyle choices, and are breaks from conformity. They can be visible forms of everyday activism either protesting against limitations on personal identity or protesting against harmful systems that hurt people, our planet or both. By standing out from the crowd they provoke alternative opinions to the mainstream, encourage questions and uncertainty instead of accepted social norms. For some, wearing these clothes is membership to a group that shares their point of view.

If a protest march is covered in the media politicians and businesses are then more likely to feel the pressure to respond and so protestors try to be as eye-catching as possible. Extraordinary costumes are worn. Giant puppets can be attached to frames around individuals. Other props like banners, placards and megaphones are used to help a protest to stand out. There are also protests where people wear a group uniform to promote solidarity within the group and form a unified mass, sometimes called a 'black bloc'. Often anarchists in these 'black blocs' wear black clothing, scarves, sunglasses, ski masks, motorcycle helmets with padding or other face-concealing items during marches to conceal their identities and hamper criminal prosecution by making it difficult to distinguish between participants and to protect them from pepper-spray. The stylised mask of Guy Fawkes based on the illustration by David Lloyd has become a well-known symbol of the online hacktivists group Anonymous and was used by members of the Occupy movement and other anti-political and anti-establishment protests around the world. Joining these groups can create a strong bond, an identity and a sense of belonging. However, such clothing also risks becoming a form of armour and a sign of division, rather than working to unite people to create a new normal.

Many women in the suffrage movement were concerned and aware of being separated from the mainstream because of what they wore. Suffragettes knew that combining fashion, feminism and politics would have impact. Cally Blackman, lecturer at Central St Martins, University of the Arts, London, wrote of the Suffragettes in the book *A Portrait of Fashion*, co-authored by Aileen Ribeiro:

> They sought to effect change not by challenging contemporary fashion and ideas of femininity, but by conforming to them. Haunted by the stereotypical image of the 'strong-minded woman' in masculine clothes, pebble-thick glasses and galoshes created by cartoonists, they chose instead to present a fashionable, feminine image.[3]

They took care to 'appeal to the eye', particularly to the media. In 1908, the newspaper *Votes for Women* declared: 'The suffragette of today is dainty and precise in their dress.' Five years later, sellers of the *Suffragette* newspaper were requested by leaders within the movement to 'dress themselves in their smartest clothes'. Women would embellish their clothes with small pieces of jewellery picked out in semi-precious, coloured stones or enamel to fit the colours of the suffragettes: purple for loyalty and dignity, white for purity, green for hope. The suffragettes' colour scheme, devised in 1908 by Emmeline Pethick-Lawrence, co-editor of *Votes for Women*, was an early triumph for fashion branding. Members were encouraged to wear the colours 'as a duty and a privilege'. Mainstream shops Selfridges and Liberty sold tricolour-striped ribbons for hats, belts, rosettes and badges as well as coloured garments, underwear, handbags, shoes, slippers and toilet soap. Women could express their own identity and continue to wear fashion comfortable to them while also being part of a movement for change. The strategy worked! The membership grew and it became fashionable to identify with the struggle to get the vote for women.

As craftivists we could create another subculture with our own fashion style but we would risk separating ourselves from the mainstream and from others who might not like our chosen aesthetic style even if they care about the issue. It's tempting to create a distinct group to feel a sense of belonging with others similar to ourselves, to feel safe and supported, and as a way to distance ourselves from harmful parts of society and to show our anger at harmful social norms, but we risk creating tension with others and coming across as judgemental of them not just their actions, which can stop people from engaging in the issue. I encourage craftivists around the world to wear their small craftivism objects on top of their own clothes everyday, not just at political demonstrations. Our members are eclectic in style, age, creed, colour and sexuality, yet by wearing the craftivist objects they make, they show that they're part of a movement for change without having to cover up their own authenticity. Whether you dress in gothic clothing, skater gear or a twinset and pearls, you are all welcome to do craftivism as you are and wherever you are. You can be yourself.

Solidarity

When a person perceives themselves as similar to the people around them, they are more likely to adopt the behaviour of those people. Campaign organisations often create objects for people to wear to encourage as many audiences as possible to support the campaign. The objects can increase public awareness of the issue, increase public recognition of a campaign brand and gain media attention. All this helps increase the popularity of the cause. British archaeologist Ian Hodder writes:

> Objects are powerful within both everyday life and within pedagogy, they motivate learning and they become significant beyond their material physical selves. They enable human needs to externalise felt convictions; the need to articulate tacit emotions; to visualise relationships, to picture abstract entities; to make the intangible tangible and therefore graspable.[4]

A red ribbon in a small loop is known by many to be a symbol of solidarity with people living with HIV/AIDS, especially on 1 December, World Aids Day. Badges against the South African apartheid regime were not only worn by people in South Africa but also by people all over the world. In 2012, Quebec students protested against a proposal by the government to raise university tuition fees. Alongside widespread strikes and demonstrations, students created a small red square as a symbol of their campaign for people who supported their campaign to wear. Seeing thousands of red squares on people's clothes was a striking image.

The white band was the symbol of the Make Poverty History campaign in 2005 with 8 million people in the UK wearing it as a wristband, armband, headband or lapel badge. Alongside marches, Live 8 concerts and other events throughout 2005 leading up to the G8 meeting in Scotland, the campaign gained global attention and support. At the time Douglas Alexander (Labour MP) was Minister of State for Trade with special provision to attend the cabinet meetings. I asked him what impact people wearing the white bands had on world leaders at the G8 that he worked closely with. His response was:

The white bands were a very visible and distinctive symbol of people's support for Make Poverty History, and that support was vital to the progress that was made at the G8 Summit in Gleneagles in tackling extreme poverty.[5]

I sell badges saying 'I'm a Craftivist' in a warm yellow colour, made ethically in the UK. Some people buy them to identity as a craftivist. One customer left feedback on an online shop saying 'I will wear mine with pride'. Other craftivists use them to connect to people: 'I have worn mine to work the past few days in the hopes of sparking conversation.'

It's so easy to forget about the 'silent majority' when the media often focuses on extreme views and actions. Seeing strangers far and wide from all different cultural and subculture groups passionate about changing a harmful system and wearing the same object to stand up for the world they want can be incredibly empowering and give us the strength to take action against injustice and help us not to feel alone doing so. Another example is the use of the safety pin by UK residents as a symbol to fight racism in the wake of the Brexit vote 2016. A Twitter user proposed that people wear a simple safety pin to show that they are 'a safe person to sit next to on a bus, walk next to on a street, even have a conversation with'. Within three days the symbol began trending on many social media platforms. People shared photographs online of them wearing theirs and adding the hashtag #safetypin. It's a sad time when we need a symbol to identify ourselves as non-racist but it was a way for the silent majority to show support to those who feel unsafe and to show solidarity with other non-racists. I wore a large nappy safety pin and joined the campaign. It created smiles with people who were also wearing a safety pin, conversations with people confused why so many people were wearing them, and safe spaces for BAME* community

* BAME is an acronym for black, Asian and minority ethnic.

members to share their bad experiences and worries. It showed viewers that racism should not be accepted as the norm.

Subtle commitment

Wearing something to show support can help us deepen our conviction and commitment to a cause. By deciding to wear a badge, bracelet, ribbon, etc., you are encouraging yourself to live by those convictions and you are making yourself accountable to others. However, we should also be mindful not to see wearing our convictions as the only protest action to take.

Fashion designer Katherine Hamnett is known for her iconic over-sized white T-shirts emblazoned with large protest statements. Over the years, Hamnett has been very open about her growing scepticism over whether her T-shirts have accomplished any permanent political change, or worse, whether they have been used as a 'substitute for action'. Katherine Hamnett designed one T-shirt that said on the front in large letters 'Choose Life'. It was directed at drug abuse and suicide but is now used by some members of the pro-life movement who protest against abortion. This was not Hamnett's plan.

As craftivists we should be cautious when making wearable protest objects. We should take care not to promote messages that are too vague, aggressive or could be misinterpreted. Craftivists need to see these objects as living things that call us to see and act against injustice not to replace other forms of activism. Stay within the gentle protest approach of provoking with positivity, not preaching at people or patronising them, but also try not to oversimplify complex issues.

Not all of our wearable objects have to be visible to the public. You could make something that is not visible to others but that keeps you focused on practising your principles. Some people in South Africa wore small pin badges against the apartheid system on the inside of their jackets to be in solidarity with others but to avoid persecution or arrest.

In collaboration with Sophie Howarth of Department Store for the Mind we made five varieties of messages on small woven labels for people to purchase, that we call 'Gentle Nudges'. We encouraged people to sew them into their clothes (whether visible to the public or privately placed) as little reminders to live a positive life:

1. Solidarity not sympathy
2. Good intentions are just the start
3. Tough mind, tender heart
4. Listen to people you disagree with
5. Use head, hand and heart

When we use that item of clothing we can read the woven label and reflect on what it means for our day-to-day life. I put 'solidarity not sympathy' on one of my gloves, 'tough mind, tender heart' on the inside of a jacket and 'listen to people you disagree with' more visibly on a T-shirt pocket for others to see. How can you use objects to help you practise your principles privately or publicly?

Speaking with not speaking at

One of the arts of our gentle protest approach is intriguing people with our handmade wearable objects rather than preaching at them. We don't have to shout out about our views or speak *at* people. We can wear them as part of our daily outfits and wait for opportunities to speak *with* people about how to practise their principles where and when these conversations naturally crop up. We often forget how effective this can be, embedding social injustice into everyday conversations and practising the new normal we want through what we wear as well as what we do and say and think.

Try to keep your message hopeful, positive, timeless, and use it to invite discussion not to force it on people. Be careful to research clothing brands. Some brands claim to be making a positive impact on the world but when you look into their practices they leave much to be desired. Research your items, ask the staff questions and think critically about what you choose to wear and to promote to others.

Like the suffrage movement you could use jewellery to help attract conversation. I have a long necklace with a magnifying glass pendant on the end. People often compliment me on it and I tend to respond saying: 'Thanks, I got it in a little independent letter-writing shop and I use it to remind me to stay curious about our world and look at the detail of the things I buy to see if they are made ethically or not.'

If you reply with a short comment and a smile, you might be planting a thought in that person that could grow into action. Either way, it's worth having those thoughts verbalised to someone as a way of showing to ourselves and to others that we care about our planet and the way we treat people.

Another way you could make a positive impact is by mending your existing clothes or those of friends. Through his project 'The Visible Mending Programme', my friend Tom van Deijnen is helping to grow a trend

> to highlight that the art and craftsmanship of clothes repair is particularly relevant in a world where more and more people voice their dissatisfaction with fashion's throwaway culture. By exploring the story behind garment and repair, the Programme reinforces the relationship between the wearer and garment, leading to people wearing their existing clothes for longer, with the beautiful darn worn as a badge of honour.[6]

The more we see visible mending on people's clothes, the more normal it becomes to mend our own clothes. 'Make do and mend' was a slogan during the Second World War but sadly is now unusual. The visibility of the mending (normally in a contrasting colour) makes the object more intriguing and invites discussion.

If we do our work with emotional sensitivity we can inspire, empower and encourage others to think about who made their clothes, the impact they have on the planet, and the harms of our current culture of consumption that we should protest against, while also celebrating ethical companies alternative to the mainstream social norm. Be careful not to sound arrogant or judgemental, nor to show off or force your message on people. Social proof can speed up when you follow cues from people that you perceive to be more knowledgeable than you or people that you respect, and so it is important we practise what we preach. We need to make sure we have done some research to discuss what we are promoting. We never know if our comment and actions will stick with people.

A Heart For Your Sleeve*

In December 2015 the UN climate talks (sometimes referred to as COP21) were being hosted in Paris for world leaders to work together to lower our global carbon emissions. It was an important meeting to create a strong and binding global agreement to lessen the permanent damage global warming is having on our planet, on people now and of future generations. I worked with The Climate Coalition, a UK campaigning organisation, in the lead up to this conference to galvanise UK public support, awareness and media coverage.

The Climate Coalition is the UK's largest group of people dedicated to action on climate change. With 11 million supporters through a network of over 100 organisations from environmental and development charities to unions, faith groups, community and women's groups, they were a great organisation to work with to gather as much widespread involvement as possible in our project. They launched the UK-wide

* Join in this project with more information here: www.craftivist-collective.com/fortheloveof

campaign 'For The Love Of' on Valentine's Day 2015 and as part of that campaign I created a timeless craftivism project called 'A Heart for Your Sleeve' that is still used today. Here is my thinking behind the project to help you in the creation of any social-proof craftivism projects:

1. Objectives

   Everything we love has been or will be affected by global warming and we need to lessen its impact with the help of a strong and binding COP21 agreement. I wanted to attract the craft community to support the campaign, and I wanted to reach this audience through social media and craft-related platforms. The message had to be timeless to give the objects longevity, and the craft activity had to be slow and repetitive to show the maker's commitment and allow them time to engage deeply on the issue. There had to be room for personalisation of the object, so that craftivists could connect with it, take ownership of it, share their voice and feel part of 'For the Love Of' campaign. And of course I needed the kits to be as ethically made as possible.

   I wanted a visible sign that people could wear that would intrigue others, and encourage conversation off- and online, especially in places you wouldn't expect to hear a discussion about COP21. Also, the visible sign needed to be encouraging: asking world leaders for help, not demonising them. That meant I wanted an object that was big enough for people to notice, but not too imposing or attention seeking. It needed to be intriguing and subversively charming rather than confrontational.

2. Design

   I came up with a heart-shaped badge with a white curved banner across it in the style of old-school sailor tattoos. Instead of a red, I chose green, both because it's recognisably a symbol of the environmental movement and because it's more unusual to see a green heart than a red one.

The fabric for the front of the heart would be donated from craftivists and supporters. Any shade of green and small patterns would be allowed as long as they didn't distract from the colour green and white banner message. The fabric was then turned into pre-cut, ironed, green cotton hearts, of different shades and patterns, fused together with 'Bondaweb' so that the fabric didn't fray in a craftivist's hands and wasn't too flimsy to hold its shape while stitching. The backing fabric of the heart would be green felt made from post-consumer plastic bottles to give it strength and stiffness with the option for people to stuff their heart if they wanted.

The white banner would also be made in felt made from post-consumer plastic bottles and the message would be written in biro in the craftivist's own friendly style on the white banner and stitched over the top in backstitch, giving the craftivist time to reflect on climate justice whilst their hands were busy. The message would be something that the craftivist loves – something tangible and concrete, so bluebells, bumblebees or their Aunt Betty, not something general like reading, dancing or swimming. A kit was made with all the instructions, objectives of the project, message suggestions, top tips for doing effective craftivism, 'crafterthought questions' to reflect on while stitching, and all needed resources (except scissors).

3. Making activity

The hearts could be stitched alone or in a group or as part of a stitch-in or pop-up event. Each heart should take at least thirty minutes to make, with the repetitive hand movements comforting the stitchers as they thought critically about environmental issues. To help them reflect while they worked on their hearts, I created a list of crafterthought questions:

- How can I strive to be part of the solutions to global warming? How do my everyday actions, like the things I buy, say and do affect it?
- What challenges face political and business leaders trying to tackle this problem? How can I support them in their work and challenge them as critical friends rather than aggressive enemies?
- How can I encourage others to focus on what they love about the world we live in while also joining the movement for climate justice?

4. Sharing to show support

   Once the heart badges had been made, I asked people to wear theirs anywhere on their sleeve to create intrigue and to invite conversations on climate justice. I also encouraged people to share their progress and final piece on social media with friends, family and fellow craftivists, explaining the project and tagging Craftivist Collective on Facebook, Instagram or Twitter (@craftivists) with #fortheloveof hashtag so people could follow and I could share the work to inspire others to join in. If the craftivist had a blog, I encouraged them to write about the project, process and their crafterthoughts.

'A Heart For Your Sleeve' was a successful campaign in a number of ways, capturing the imagination of craftivists, crafters and the members of general public alike. Workshops were set up at craft markets, craft events and with craft groups, and hearts were shared on social media platforms and on blogs. I wrote a 'Good Read' article for the September 2015 *Mollie Makes* magazine that reaches 40,000 readers worldwide, and reached the target demographic we were focusing on. Kits were ordered from across the world – it's a project that people can continue to join in with during the on-going discussions around climate justice anywhere in the world

Surprisingly I was commissioned to create a green heart for the Executive Secretary of the UN Framework Convention of Climate Change (UNFCCC) Christiana Figueres, a Costa Rican diplomat who would be chairing the global climate change negotiating process: a huge and difficult job. The commission was from someone very high up in the environmental sector in the UK who was going to meet Figueres at a closed conference in the City of London before the Paris convention and wanted to hand deliver it as a gift to encourage her in her difficult task at Paris. The person who commissioned me knows how passionate Christiana is about fighting climate change, how tirelessly she works and how challenging her important role is. In the light of the failed COP15 in Copenhagen, I wanted to show our encouragement and support to Ms Figueres. Knowing that she had two adult daughters whom she often referred to in talks, I wrote 'Our Children', referring not just to her children but also to the children of the world, and stitched a row of children underneath like paper cut-outs. The person who commissioned me had heard from a contact that Figueres had a poem on her fridge door that she loved: 'You Guys' by William Ayot. I picked these lines from the poem and stitched them on the back: 'this is your time for being what your people need you to be' and ended with a 'x' kiss. Christiana Figueres wore her heart on her sleeve during her keynote speech to businesses in the City of London. Images of her giving her speech were circulated worldwide on social media where you could see my handmade badge on her sleeve. I shared the image on social media to encourage more people to take part in the project and Figueres replied to my tweet with:

@Craftivists Honored to wear and heartfelt
thanks for special message on the back!*

---

* Direct link here: www.twitter.com/CFigueres/status/660430361139265536

Come as you are

Be true to your character, don't feel you have to become someone you are not in order to be a craftivist. Activism needs to be seen as a normal part of life, in the mainstream and available to all people, regardless of what they look like. Activism should not be seen as weird and on the margins, an abnormal activity that only certain types of people do. Issues of injustice should be addressed daily and the more they are visibly challenged, the more social proof (widespread support) increases and power-holders from politicians to your peers take notice. Some politicians and business people may see which way the wind is blowing and act accordingly regardless of their own convictions, others may point to the visible support for change to back up their concerns and give them the helpful backing to change policy. The wearing of an object that highlights injustice and shows a personal passion for particular change might sound small but it can help shape our world.

The wearing of a particular uniform can help us feel part of a like-minded group but it can also be fraught with danger: if every environmentalist has to wear hemp clothing then those who don't will feel excluded. People should rightly wear what they are happy with. The more we see caring about the environment and other people as something that the majority not minority do, the harder it is to ignore. We need to change activism from being seen as a hobby to being seen as a part of being fully human. Wearing our convictions is a question of integrity, being true to ourselves, and it can encourage thought and ethical action in others who see that we are acting out our principles daily. Everyone to a lesser or greater extent communicates something through what they wear – the issue is what we communicate.

16
Reaching Out

Each one of us can make a difference. Together we can make change.

– Barbara Mikulski

I sometimes hide that I'm an activist. Not because I'm embarrassed or not committed but because it can stop people from talking to me. At parties when people ask 'what do you do?' and I reply 'I'm an activist' with a smile on my face, I can see their barriers go up. My barriers sometimes go up too when I meet activists: I worry they will want to have heated discussions all night about politics rather than dance to Beyoncé, or they will remind me of all the suffering going on in the world at the same time as I'm having my gin and tonic or they will guilt trip me into coming to their next protest. But most activists I know like a giggle as much as the next person. It's a stereotype we need to change if we want more and different kinds of people to become activists. So I started saying 'I run a social enterprise', even though at the time I was still an Activism Manager for Oxfam GB while also running the Craftivist Collective. For the same reason, when I tried online dating I put 'a social entrepreneur' in the 'occupation' category

It helped. I met a guy online whom I seemed to have lots in common with: we both enjoyed Icelandic music, wandering around hidden parts of London, going to artsy things and his job was making stuff too (he's a special effects artist for films, if you're interested). We chatted online for a bit. It was just before Christmas and so we decided to meet up in the New Year. After sending each other a few text messages over Christmas, I got a text saying, 'So what do you actually do in your job?' I was walking to meet a friend so I quickly replied that I mobilise and train people to become effective activists. It seemed to fit both of my job roles. I got a reply a few days later. 'It was nice talking to you but I don't think we are a good fit. I hope you have a great New Year.' I was not impressed. After a few days of mulling it over and trying to put myself in his shoes, I replied:

> If you think I am an activist who uses violence, bullying or shouting at people to protest against injustices, I'm not, I promise. My social enterprise is a reaction against that. It's about using handicrafts to create a kind, quiet and beautiful form of activism called 'craftivism' and it's mostly for people who don't want to take part in aggressive forms of activism. But if you don't agree that we should try to improve our world to make it an even more wonderful place than it is then yes, I agree, sadly we are not well suited and shouldn't meet. All the best. Sarah

We went on our first date on New Year's Day and had a happy six months together. We are still friends and he continues to encourage me in my craftivism work as well as regularly telling people to have a go at my gentle protest approach.

The power of non-activists

When people who don't call themselves activists start to speak up it can create a tipping point. A political party's loyal supporters joining a campaign against one of their policies can have more impact than thousands of people speaking against it who would always vote for another political party. Cross-party support is gold dust. Also, a diverse audience of support, especially from people not directly affected by the issue, helps increase the chance of media and political attention for the protest and can turn a marginalised protest into a mainstream discussion. It encourages others to join the protest when they see other people they affiliate with joining in. This is why we should focus on building connections with non-activist sympathisers, politically influential audiences and those who are not directly affected by the issue addressed. We should attract and support them to stand against injustice with us.

There are many different ways we can bring what were once minority views into the mainstream. Climate justice campaigns are no longer just supported by extreme environmentalist activists but people from all walks of life. In the 1980s AIDS was a much less understood disease, surrounded by unwarranted fear and paranoia. Princess Diana helped break down barriers of fear by supporting victims, being photographed and filmed offering love and physical touch and saying: 'HIV does not make people dangerous to know. You can shake their hands and give them a hug, heaven knows they need it.'

When the brand Dove advised that women should love their bodies regardless of their size, many people felt permission and confidence to challenge body-shaming by other brands. Even though the brand's priority is for people to buy their products and many people might call this type of advertising 'goodwashing' (see Chapter 5), it also encouraged discussion and reached a wide audience regardless of whether people bought their products. Research which audiences you think might have a lot of influence for your campaign and which audiences other campaign organisations might be struggling to engage with. Don't forget that there are many organisations and activism groups who have resources and activities they can offer to groups such as schools, youth groups, religious communities and other clubs to engage in social change and global citizenship. There is no need to compete with other groups or individuals to engage particular audiences if they can do the job better. Focus on where you can reach audiences that others might struggle to engage and always see yourself as adding to a bigger movement for change with many other different agencies working alongside you.

Audiences to prioritise

Craftivist Natalia wrote in response to one of my blog posts on www.craftivist-collective.com:

> I used to have such a different idea about activism. Up until this year I never thought I could be an 'activist'. I thought a certain type of person was an activist and that I would never be that 'type' of person even though I did find it intriguing. Yes, I admit I thought the stereotype was what it took, i.e. the vegan, who doesn't shave or shower, camps on the street in protest and shouts a lot. It's awful to admit that but that was the idea I had…Finding Craftivism and a few other joyful, gentle approaches to activism has given me so much hope, inspiration and above all LOVE for the world and its complex issues.

Craftivism should be accessible to as many people as possible regardless of existing skill or knowledge. From my experience, there are four groups that craftivism can very naturally and helpfully connect with. However, don't let that stop you looking around your own environment to see which groups and individuals have influence with decision-makers and who you believe you could realistically reach and attract through your craftivism campaigns that others might struggle to connect with. I'm still surprised at how many times a day I am given the opportunity to talk about craftivism and social injustice without forcing it: from baristas at coffee stalls asking me what I am doing today, someone saying they like my homemade craftivism belt to being asked at a train station what a 'pop-up craftivist' is while they point at the suitcase I'm holding. Craftivism is a natural outreach tool but will stick with some people more than others:

1. Craft hobbyists are a natural fit. Fortunately for us, this hobby has been growing steadily over the last ten years and so let's ride this wave where we can! Crafters who are already deeply involved in activism shouldn't be your priority unless you think you could help them increase their impact. Focus on those who are not involved in activism and social justice but have an interest in craft whether they are serious makers, part of a craft group that meet regularly or have taken part in one or two craft activities and are interested in having another go. You might want to gently reach out to influential people you know online who you think might be interested in doing some craftivism and who can share their experience with their followers: creative bloggers, YouTubers, Instagrammers who show their craft projects online or hint that they care about an issue. You can encourage these people to engage with using craftivism. Craftivist Cate heard about my craftivism experiments in the early days from a mutual friend: she follows my projects on my Facebook page and takes part when she can. She wrote in her blog *Steering for NorthArt*:

I'm not a great politician or someone who can lead revolutions. I'm slow-thinking and reflective and quiet. So I do craftivism instead. It's slow and gentle and thought-provoking. It allows me to focus on issues I think are important – and create something that hopefully gets people's attention, that makes them think, or just reminds them that there are others out there who feel the same.[1]

2. Introverts. Offline activism is often loud, performance-based, and involves lots of interaction with the public. That's great for extroverts who gain energy from interaction and stimulation and tend to be more skilled in those areas but it's not always good for introverts and doesn't play to an introvert's strengths. Introverts are possibly the largest group I work with and are often the most wary of taking part in more traditional, extrovert forms of activism. It's difficult to identify introverts and often people aren't sure if they are introverts, but by showing that your activism is quiet, slow and about deep engagement and intimate forms of activism, introverts come out of the cracks and find you. A lot of people who enjoy handicrafts also identity as introverts, as being shy, or both. You can offer introverts the opportunity to have a go at this 'activism for introverts' and see if they find it useful. Stef commented on a blog post I wrote about being an introvert:

I always thought that I wouldn't be able to bring about change because I'm not a big extrovert. I think sometimes the shouty-shouty campaigners/activists can actually put people off becoming involved at times as they feel they have to be or act a certain way in order to create change. I personally volunteered at a campaigns organisation and

I found the people working there to be brash, loud and actually not very friendly which kinda put me off wanting to get involved!

Our gentle protest approach to craftivism purposefully focuses on quiet actions that can be done alone or in groups without pressure of interaction with others: a good fit with introverts. Shy people are not always introverts but craftivism could be a good stepping stone for them to get into other forms of activism if they are nervous to go to a march for the first time. Reaching out to introverts whether they like craft or not could be very mutually beneficial. Susan Cain, author of the acclaimed book *Quiet*, says introverts are 'especially empathetic', think in an 'unusually complex fashion', and prefer discussing 'values and morality' to small talk about the weather – great for conversations with power-holders! Introverts 'desire peace' and are 'modest', such useful traits for non-violent activism. Cain goes on to say that the introvert child is an 'orchid – who wilts easily', is prone to 'depression, anxiety and shyness, but under the right conditions can grow strong and magnificent'. Bear this in mind when reaching out. We need more people to engage in activism and introverts are a third to a half of the world's population and often a large part of the non-activist groups we can reach through our quiet craftivism.*

3. Multipliers are people who know and have influence with a lot of other people, e.g., leaders of local voluntary groups. If you engage them then you might be able to engage their whole group. Focus your attention on reaching out to influential leaders and multipliers

---

* I did a TEDxYouth Talk in Bath in 2016 called 'Activism needs Introverts'. You can find it on YouTube.com/channel/TEDxTalks or put the title in the search tab. Or you can type in the address: www.youtube.com/watch?v=iM5Dl3rLyo8

in your area or field of interest rather than to the vulnerable people affected directly by injustice.* Our focus is to go upstream to where the power is and stop the oppression at its core. We need to get close to those in power to help and show solidarity with the people downstream who are being negatively affected by the power-holders' decisions. Ideally you want to contact influential people who are not directly affected by the injustice you are addressing – people in positions of power (and maybe even responsible for the injustice) will be confused about why they are involved and often presume the issue therefore resonates with and has reached the mainstream. In the book *Responsible Business*, authors Oliver Laasch and Roger Conaway write:

> A first sign of responsible business and products going mainstream happened when Toyota launched the first mass-produced hybrid car, the Prius (1997). Again, it was pop-culture pushing sustainable behaviour and sales. Pictures of celebrities such as Leonardo DiCaprio, Sting, or Cameron Diaz posing with a Prius at the gas station were extremely influential in the commercial success of more than two million cars sold in 2010.

We shouldn't mix up relief work with activism. Every life is as precious as the next, but as craftivists we should reach out to people who have influence with key decision-makers and who we think

---

* Do make sure that people directly affected by the injustice are happy with your project: for example, are they happy in how they are being presented? Make sure their voice is heard so that they feel they are being treated with solidarity not sympathy. Be sensitive to the limitations on their time and energy of being involved, just as you will be with your multipliers' time and energy. If you cannot engage those affected directly, contact a respected organisation working with them to see if they agree with your campaign's approach and communication.

have the time and energy to get involved. There are other incredible organisations and individuals who use handicraft with vulnerable groups to help them grow in craft skill, confidence and wellbeing. Of course we should make sure that those directly affected by injustice are heard and part of solving the situation but I believe it's unfair to expect those directly affected to also find time and energy to fix the problem with little help from others.

Let's also harness the fact that politicians often look to connect with non-political groups in their constituency to help rally support and endorsements for their next election or gain praise for local changes the politician is putting in place. Rightly or wrongly, middle-class,* middle-aged women are an influential audience for politicians in the UK, as they are often seen by politicians as a group that includes mothers who have good contacts with other parents in the area through the local schools and children's activities outside the home, they include women who are believed to be in charge of the household expenditure and who sometimes play an active part in other social groups where they socialise with friends, such as book clubs.

Women's Institutes (WI) have a lot of influence in UK politics and society as a whole. After trying to engage one particular Member of Parliament to no avail, on the global broken food system and the effects it had on his local constituency as part of the Oxfam Grow campaign, I invited him to receive a hamper of tomato jam made by his local WI group (a craftivism project with hand-stitched fabric lids designed to create conversations using a recipe from Kenyan farmer and women's cooperative member Christine)† and to discuss

---

* For the benefit of my readers abroad, in the UK, when I say 'middle-class', I mean 'middle-income'.
† More information on this project can be found at: www.craftivist-collective.com/Christines-tomato-jam

their concerns on the matter. His office got back to me immediately saying he would be there! Find out who it is who has the power to change unjust structures and who your local power-holders listen to. See who you can reach to help use their powerful voice for good.

4. Burnt-out activists. I didn't set out to engage burnt-out activists. My passion has always been reaching out to people who, for whatever reason, haven't engaged a lot in activism before. But after admitting I was a burnt-out activist a lot of people tell me that they are burnt-out activists too, but they don't want to give up on protesting against harmful actions in our world. The approach to craftivism in this book could benefit burnt-out activists and help them ease back into activism in a more sustainable and potentially more effective way. The act of handcrafting can help with self-care because you can use it to be mindful of your physical, emotional and spiritual wellbeing and find ways to look after yourself whilst still being an effective altruistic activist. I call this 'wellmaking'. Craftivist Sue, who bought my *A Little Book of Craftivism*, wrote a positive review of the book, which included the comment: 'It is vital to have activities that nourish us but also continue to get the message out there.'

How to engage

Now that you have some ideas of which audiences to focus on, how do you go about initiating contact with them? The first thing not to do is to oversimplify this craftivism approach: don't slip into encouraging people to do something quick and easy through craft. It's a lie and your audience may feel deceived, which is not a good start to your relationship. You don't have to scare them off by saying it takes a long time and that one value of the craft process is to help us ask ourselves uncomfortable questions. It's important people see (or experience) that our craftivism is about engaging deeply in social change in a safe space using craft as a tool and activism as the goal. Craftivism is one tool in the activism toolkit not to replace other forms but to be used when it is appropriate.

I see engagement in five steps.

1. Research: With the powers of the internet you can find lots of local groups you might not have realised existed. Once you have a realistic list of groups, prioritise those who are most influential for your campaign, do some online research to see what your audience enjoy, who the leader is in the group or which influential person you think you can realistically reach. Put yourself in their shoes and think about how craftivism could benefit that individual or groups.

2. Get noticed: I start by following groups and individuals online to see what they are posting (don't ask to be their Facebook friend – that can be creepy!). I comment on their posts if I like them and praise them for any great actions they've taken and recommend to them anyone or anything I think they might want to be aware of or connect to. That way they get to know you so that when you do introduce yourself it's a warm and gentle approach not a cold call out of the blue.

3. Introducing yourself: Reach out respectfully. Presume people are busy and work from that standpoint. Make your introduction quick so that you're not taking up too much time but also not so little that it sounds rude: introduce yourself, share something about yourself that you think they might relate to, then write clearly what you are offering, the benefits they might gain personally as well as the benefits for our planet. Add a link to more information but then leave the ball in their court. Begging for their help is not attractive. You want them to feel FOMO: the fear of missing out on something interesting and meaningful.

4. Bespoke invite not mass mail-out: If you are trying to reach everyone you won't reach anyone. After interacting with a number of people

who live or work near you, I recommend you set up an invite-only craftivism event introducing people to a particular craftivism project. Quietly send out bespoke invitations to your target list saying that this is a small event for a select few who you think would not only enjoy the event and meet other fascinating people but that you are keen to get their feedback on the project to help you improve on it. Remind them to RSVP as there are limited spaces – scarcity adds value. Make your event cosy and attractive (see Chapter 6) so people feel special and want to tell others about the event they have attended. In your invite and at the event itself, explain what you hope to achieve through your craftivism activities and group and ask for their advice. Not only does it help you improve your craftivism project but you are also acknowledging their wisdom and offering an outlet to share their knowledge. You are encouraging people to become ambassadors for your craftivism activities if they enjoyed the night but without asking them directly and turning a connection into a transaction. It's up to them if they want to suggest you lead a workshop at a group they are part of or write a guest blog about your project to their readers or take part at a level they are comfortable with.

5. Stay in touch. After your event follow up with bespoke emails thanking each individual for coming and sharing their advice. Offer them a way to keep in the loop with future craftivism activities if they are interested and keep interacting with them online and in real life. You might not be in touch regularly but don't forget to treat people with dignity in every interaction. If people demand too much of our time or support, respectfully tell them what you are willing to offer and what you cannot.

I spotted a new and super-cool events series by a company called Crafty Fox Market in London that I thought might involve people who would be interested in craftivism and also looked influential to politicians, the craft community and business people. It was founded by Sinead Koehler. Her events were always busy, with well-curated craft stalls to wander around, DJs playing great music sets, craft activities to do around a few tables, a cafe area: it was a friendly environment in which to meet fellow crafters and always gained media attention. I followed my steps above carefully, making sure I didn't come across as too desperate or demanding (they seemed so popular I guessed Sinead was hounded by requests for craft activities to take place there). One time I paid to have a small sales table as a stepping stone to see if my work fitted the audience – as well as sell some products – and to get the courage to ask if she might consider hosting me to deliver a 'A Heart For Your Sleeve'* workshop at their August 2015 markets: it would be great timing to see if people wanted to take part in the project leading up to the London Climate March and Paris negotiations in December that year. Sinead explained why she accepted my offer of craftivism workshops at both Brixton and Peckham Crafty Fox Markets: 'Not only was Sarah offering a chance for visitors to get hands-on experience and actually make something but it was also a very thoughtful activity which I knew would resonate with our audience.'

Collaborate

Craftivism has opened doors to collaborations with organisations that seemed shut to me when working with other and much larger campaigning organisations. You want your collaboration to be mutually beneficial, a way for you to reach new audiences in social change and a benefit to your collaborator. It can, of course, be argued that all injustices should be addressed but sadly there will always be so many and so little time to address them all. You can't focus on them all, so you have to concentrate on the ones that you feel you can have the most impact

---

* You can find more information on this project at: www.craftivist-collective.com/fortheloveof

on. It can be exciting to get invites to collaborate with non-activist organisations but be careful of whom you lend your support to and work with. It's potentially a high-risk strategy to marry your principles with someone else's objectives, especially if they have commercial goals. Ask yourself whether they are engaging in activism because they care about social change or is their priority that their organisation looks ethical. Research the ethics of the collaborators you work with so that you are not being used for 'goodwashing'.

Don't let collaborators dilute your work by pushing for quick craftivism that is too simplistic, does not involve space for deep engagement in the topic or where you feel censored in telling the truth about the causes of injustices. More often than not you will be asked to engage as many people as possible, so be strong and remind them that your work is about deep engagement with a few people at a time, not shallow and thinly spread. Even charities with good intentions can pressure you into focusing on collecting email addresses of participants (something I don't do) rather than slow genuine engagement in the activity. Hold your ground. You know how to be a craftivist, use these discussions to teach them the ethical and effective ways of craftivism, whether you end up working with them or not. It's an opportunity to teach what you do. Hopefully they will respect you standing by your convictions.

1. Museums and art galleries

   As a craftivist you can reassure publicly funded museums and galleries that you can offer craftivism projects that are not party-political, and you can offer a variety of levels of political activity from focusing on inner-activism, which is a more holistic approach to injustice, to an activity that focuses on a specific injustice issue that has a clear call to action. You can create bespoke projects that could connect to their exhibitions or permanent objects on display

240

and that can also be a springboard for thought on how we can all be the change we wish to see in the world. If they are struggling to bring in new audiences to their space and you believe you can recruit new people to attend a craftivism workshop at the gallery, then offer your support in exchange for engaging people in social change. Through one craftivism workshop I attracted over seventy people to stitch on the roof of the Hayward Gallery one evening in response to the Tracy Emin Retrospective exhibition – it was so busy you could hardly move! The gallery was happy that their space was full of people for the entire three hours. We engaged people who were new to craftivism and activism, as well as new to attending events at the Hayward Gallery.

2. Companies
    You could gently invite companies who have never been political publicly before to join in a craftivism campaign that you think would resonate with their customers. I created a craftivism project for people to do on Valentine's Day: red envelopes contained an alternative Valentine's Day letter, a handmade key ring gift and a sweet. They were hand delivered to gaps in walls, cash-machine slots and shop shelves for people to find. The letter encouraged people to think about how they might express their love, not just for a single person but for the planet, our fellow human beings and future generations. The key ring included the message 'Show Your Love' and was made as a keepsake to encourage the letter-finder.*

    I thought the jewellery company Tatty Devine would be the perfect partner to design the gift I was asking craftivists to make as it was a similar aesthetic. As a fan myself I thought their audience would find

---

* Take part here: www.craftivist-collective.com/Alternative-love-letters-and-gifts

the project fun and fulfilling too. Tatty Devine could offer the project as an activity for their loyal customers and fans to do through their blog and share it on social media to their 30,000 followers. It was a bit of a dream but I had met someone who worked for Tatty Devine. So I gently (and nervously) asked what she thought of my idea. She loved it! And went one step further and let us have a workshop in the basement of their Seven Dials shop the day before Valentine's Day. We made fifty gifts and cards between the fifteen of us (it was a very small basement so we had to cap the amount of people who could attend) and were allowed to leave some of the envelopes in the shop for customers to find on Valentine's Day.

3. Event productions

Being a craftivist can lead to being invited to collaborate on a variety of types of events. I was invited by Future Shorts Ltd to bring craftivism to one of their 'Secret Cinema' productions. We engaged over 5,000 out of 25,000 people during thirty-five sold-out shows over five weeks at their event-production of *The Shawshank Redemption*. It was exhausting and out of my comfort zone but there is nothing like the Secret Cinema, an immersive experience that builds the world of the film around its audience, lifting them from observers to captivated participants.

Our role was to deliver the needlework sessions 'prisoners' could do as part of their rehabilitation. We decorated the room with real testimonies and photographs (in the style of the film's time period) of male prisoners from Wandsworth Prison who worked in their cells embroidering commissions for the charity Fine Cell Work in exchange for payment. The testimonies told of how needlework had increased their confidence, helped manage their anger, depression or anxiety, and helped them rehabilitate and take ownership of the crimes they had committed. 'Prisoners' were encouraged to reflect on the quotes from real prisoners that they were stitching that lay around a hand-printed logo of the fake prison they were in. They were encouraged to imagine how they would feel in prison and how needlework could help their own rehabilitation. Their small pieces of embroidered artwork would later be framed on wooden canvases to be sold to raise money for Fine Cell Work to continue their transformational work.

4. Products for shops

It's not very often (if at all) that you see a tool for activism in a shop, maybe in a radical bookshop but not in a boutique. Offering a ready-made craftivism kit or craftivism tools to help people become craftivists is another form of outreach. Placing such craftivism products in shops also creates another space for engagement in social change where it wouldn't normally happen.

Target apolitical stores to fill the activism void in online and offline stores. I love the fact that the physical presence of my products take up space in a handful (I wish it was more) of boutique shops, craft shops and museum and gallery shops where you wouldn't expect to see activism being thought of or discussed. Barley Massey, owner of craft shop Fabrications which sell many of my craftivism products, comments:

> Sarah's products fit well in our shop and are popular with customers. They are beautifully and thoughtfully presented and provoke questions. They are good conversation starters and I enjoy the discussions that are triggered when visitors see the kits. They are a true gift from Sarah's hands, head and heart, full of wisdom, values and encouragement as we tread the path of 'right action'.

Be proud to be a craftivist

I hear far too often from people that they want to be a changemaker but that they don't fit into activism groups, they're nervous to stand out from the crowd or they don't know where to start. We need to get better at showing that activism can be done in many different ways by many different people in many different places and circumstances. We need confident extrovert activists to use their skills and energy to mobilise people but we also need introverted activists building relationships with people through quiet and deep discussions. Where people feel they can't join in, we need to address this and see where we can help them feel more welcome, more confident, knowledgeable and able to use their existing skills.

Craftivism is one tool in the activism toolkit and for particular people or places it can be a catalyst for change. If done well and offered to particular audiences, it can be one of the most fascinating, empowering and fulfilling tools. Being a craftivist has opened up many more friendly discussions with strangers compared to when I identified as an activist. It's helped me engage with more people from all walks of life and created conversations outside of activism bubbles about how we can all be changemakers in different ways. Your goal shouldn't be to turn everyone into craftivists but to be a tool to open up the possibilities of how people can challenge injustice and be an activist in a way that is effective, sustainable and utilises their skills and character traits. I hope that in the near future when someone says that they are an activist, in whatever shape, that it helps barriers come down not go up.

17
Shareability

Three keys to more abundant living: caring about others, daring for others, sharing with others.

– William Arthur Ward

'Please, friends, I love you but please don't just post harrowing stories on Facebook from around the world without an action we can take. It's disempowering and makes me want to give up on the world. Give us actions to take – campaigns to realistically take part in, links from which to learn more about why it's happening so that we can make sure this doesn't happen in other situations, great charities to support, prayers to pray, etc. Let's do more than shock people into inaction, please, let's offer support and education to help people (inc me) to improve our world. Please let's make hope possible not despair convincing.

That was my response in 2016 to seeing shocking images, videos and news reports of the Syrian crisis. I posted it as a Facebook status update. The response was huge, 100 per cent agreement and gratitude from friends who told me that they felt the same way but were too nervous to say it.

What information we consume and share shapes the way we see the world. So let's be careful and courageous as craftivists. Media and social media have a number of important activist functions: to create awareness, change opinion, provide information, build community, facilitate planning and mobilisation, and offer a call to action. Most campaigners now include on- and offline aspects in their campaign strategy, and so too should we craftivists. It's not enough to share information with people who are following you on social media or people who are your friends on Facebook, we need to intentionally reach out beyond our social bubbles. It's also not enough just to think that sharing social injustices will create change: when news is competing with the latest scoop on an actor's love life, we have to make the story fascinating enough for people to want to share it. We need the issue to touch people's hearts and minds to gain mass support. More than that, we need our activism to be attractive and intriguing so people want to take part out of excitement, not from pity or guilt.

Elma Wheeler was an expert at marketing hot dogs. When asked how he gets a queue outside his hot dog stand and sells so many, he said:

Don't sell the hot dogs, sell the sizzle; the enticing and desirable sounds and smells of the hot dog. Otherwise, you are just selling a dead pig![1]

Ed Gillespie, co-founder of sustainability agency Futerra, tells the story of Wheeler and says it's the 'story's sizzle, salience and social proof that create communication that effectively activates behaviour change beyond the usual'.

We want our craftivism to reinforce how much more awesome we can make our world. With beautiful and unusual images, captivating and hopeful stories and intriguing questions to ponder, as well as positive suggestions for actions, we can engage people in social issues in a way that encourages sharing. We can bring the sizzle (sorry vegan readers)! Otherwise we are just advertising bad news and possibly stimulating despair.

We also often need to help produce a groundswell of support for some particular issues. Political solutions, if they are to be achieved at all, will tend to be short-term unless there is wider support in society. So sharing that groundswell can be an important aspect of such a campaign. The Make Poverty History campaign benefitted greatly from the wide sharing by the public of its slogan, passion and demands and helped create the most robust development plans world leaders have ever made, called the Millennium Development Goals.

Who to share with

Many activism messages tell people what to do. That can be useful at times. I recommend we use craftivism content to share with audiences who prefer being gently led closer to investigate justice and truth for themselves. We can share our beautiful, kind and positive activism with those who feel overwhelmed or nervous of other forms of activism and show them ways they can gently protest and find expression for their concerns and hopes. The more our craftivism weaves into the fabric of popular culture (from books, broadsheets to blogs) the more powerful and useful it can become for our causes.

I've calculated the media and social media reach of some of my craftivism projects in the past and documented the audiences to share the results with politicians and businesses. Sharing this evidence has helped gain more respect, influence with decision-makers we are trying to engage, and it has led to more carefully written responses from those in power as well as continuing engagement with them on the issue. We can use this influence to add to and complement the wider movement for social change and to serve as a springboard for individuals to become changemakers.

What we can share

The Craftivist Collective's motto used to be 'A spoonful of craft helps the activism go down'. Our motto is now 'Changing our world one stitch at a time…' Our craftivism projects can wrap up important, newsworthy stories in a way that becomes more digestible for some audiences. When explaining your craftivism project you can include your motives for the project, the goals you hope to achieve and through what strategy, and point towards where people can find more information on the issue you are addressing.

Always include possible solutions to problems when you share your craftivism project. Awareness without calls to action is not activism, it's just news. You can share your 'crafterthoughts'. Your own concerns, hopes and questions can inspire readers to ask themselves the same questions and engage deeply in the issue using your process as an example of how they can engage in social change too. You can share why you decided to put your craftivism object in a particular place or why you gave it to a particular person and how you did it. That way, you are educating the reader without them feeling like you are patronising or preaching at them. If you experience any direct responses from people offline or online regarding your craftivism object or activity, you can share that too. You might want to document and, with permission, share the conversations you had while you were making your object.

There is so much craftivism content that over time you can share and drip out online in the form of a personal story through different platforms. Our memory can digest and store stories more easily than lots of facts and figures and this way of packaging social action, if executed carefully, can also attract, engage and inspire others to join in the issues you care about.

How to share

To be shareable, craftivism objects should not be displayed in cases like dead butterflies. Our handmade objects are only useful when they become alive, and they only become alive when they are engaging with the world, rather than being passively consumed. Be humble and encourage your audience to decide on their own response whilst still being clear you are addressing an injustice issue. You want your craftivism to encourage thought, discussion and participation, not to create a static statement that preaches at people. It's more worthwhile for people – and more memorable, too – if they come to their own conclusions without being spoon-fed them. It means people are more likely to change harmful habits or thoughts for the long-term.

Your photographs and stories are a vessel to encourage people to think and feel a connection to the issue and to act on it. Therefore, be careful to take high-quality photographs that are sharable in print as well as online. That way your images will be attractive enough to come alive as a catalyst for change.

Where to share

Personal blogs are a place to let a blogger's personality flow. It's a great place for shy or introverted people to speak within their comfort zone. My own craftivism only became noticed and shared with strangers and friends when I started documenting my activities as blog posts that included images of what I was doing, more information on the campaign issue and my strategy, as well as hyperlinks to websites with more information about different ways we can tackle injustice. People started sharing the blog's links and images with their friends and followers to discuss my method, the issue and my crafterthoughts I included in the posts. I received really moving comments and emails on how useful people found them and about the thoughts my blog posts generated in them.

Your blog posts should be a catalyst for thought and conversation with the reader. Let the real you shine through in your posts. It might be that as a parent you are concerned about the effect global-warming will have on your child growing up, or you are a burnt-out activist trying to continue to fight injustice but in a sustainable way. Your unique voice and situation can help readers (or viewers, if you decide to create vlogs instead) connect to you and the injustice issue more deeply. The more honest and vulnerable you are, the more powerful your story can be for readers. Craftivist Alison, author of blog anotherlittlecraftycreation. wordpress.com, wrote a post documenting her participation in our jigsaw project:

> The message I chose to embroider was by Mary Anne Radmacher and says: 'Courage doesn't always roar. Sometimes courage is the little voice at the end of the day that says I'll try again tomorrow.' (Well, just the first four words, for ease of embroidery). I chose it because, as a quiet person myself, it reminds me that you do not have to be loud or shouting to be courageous; everyone can have courage and sometimes it is the quietest people who can be most courageous. I think it fits with the message of the project. Campaigning for worthy causes doesn't have to be about shouting in the streets (something I would never feel confident to do) but hopefully enough little voices can have the same impact.[2]

To help your craftivism reach a larger audience, don't make your blog posts too long (800 words is a good maximum) and focus on one issue at a time. Also think about what key words enable users to find your work online. Think hard about the sort of search terms people will be using to find information on the internet and incorporate these into your title, URL for your blog post and image description, for example: craftivist-collective.com/blog/2012/09/have-you-spotted-any-mini-protest-banners-at-london-fashion-week-2012/

As an active craftivist you can also offer to write a guest blog or be interviewed for a blog or other online platform whose audience enjoy creativity but who might be new to activism or nervous of it. Often bloggers are looking for new content and so they might be grateful for your help, especially if you have great images. As with other media outlets, research which blogs are popular with the audience you want to reach and which ones you think would complement your work. They could become supporters and advocates for your cause and invite you to do more guest posts.

In my experience, craftivists and other bloggers (including lifestyle bloggers, fashion bloggers and 'mummy bloggers') can be anxious about writing about injustices. They don't want to scare off their audience or offer something too serious or political or they feel that it doesn't connect to the themes they write about. By offering them a positive and creative approach to tackling social injustices and a craftivism project to take part in, you can encourage them to support a campaign that is attractive to their audience. Craftivism projects that ask people to add their own voice to the project, and encourage the making-time to be used to think critically about how we can all tackle injustices, can not only create deeper commitment but also produce content that the blogger, in my experience, is proud to share with others as they feel part of a bigger movement for change. Storyofmum.com founder and blogger, Pippa Best, wrote:

> Along with the wonderful guest posts we have shared so far, this campaign has reawakened my desire to change the world

251

in a more conscious way. Maybe because it's creative, beautiful, simple, visual, different. Maybe because it's the kind of thing I like to try anyway. Maybe because my kids are finally in their own room and it's the right time to step up again.[3]

Blog posts often have social media buttons next to them so readers can share the images and easily link to the post on social media. Some people have even stopped blogging and moved over to Instagram and Facebook because sharing can be easier, faster and arguably more engaging than asking people to click through to a blog post.

Social media

Social-media consultant and director of *Craft Blog UK* (one of the most visited craft blogs in the UK) Hilary Pullen says:

> A good marketing strategy should always focus on conversions, not clicks. Your product could be seen by thousands of people but if they don't buy it your marketing campaign has failed. Craftivism works because it's not about the number of voices, or the amount of people who sign, click or donate, it's about making people take the time to start important conversations with each other. If you want to make changes you need to open up a discussion with influential people. Craftivism gets campaigns noticed by influential people and changemakers because it's much more than simply a marketing gimmick. Craftivism engages the campaigners themselves in a way that makes the message they are delivering more powerful. Each piece, delicately hand-stitched, represents an investment of time and deep thinking about the issue and that makes for compelling arguments and great ice-breakers to start those important conversations. I recommend craftivists don't cut corners but see that creating a thoughtful and

beautiful physical craftivism object offline will make their work more shareable online.

One craftivism project can be shared a number of times in different ways through little tweets, Facebook updates, Instagram images and other outlets. Also, by including a website address to more information about your project (such as your blog post link) and adding 'What do you think?' at the end of a post, you can increase interaction and interest. Posts with images or videos tend to be more successful than posts that are wholly text in terms of engagement online as they attract more attention in newsfeeds, whether that's on Twitter, Facebook or LinkedIn. Pinterest, Instagram and Snapchat all focus on images and videos and all of them didn't exist when I started doing craftivism. Don't feel pressured to use all of them (I don't) but find platforms you enjoy using and see how you can use them to share social injustice issues and gather support.

People use Pinterest as a visual search engine: they look for inspiration for their latest projects and products to add to their wish lists. This might be an odd place for activists to look for activism actions but that makes it a great place to use as a craftivist and to attract people to your cause.

You can @ or tag people or organisations into your social media posts as a way for them to notice you if you want to start a conversation with them. I often retweet on Twitter and regram on Instagram other craftivists' work that I like and want to share with a larger audience. Look out for advocates who talk positively about your work. Those who like, comment and share your social media and blog posts are your biggest supporters and should be your biggest focus. Use social media to create a friendly army of advocates because few things are more effective than word-of-mouth marketing.

Hashtags are also a great way to engage a larger audience: adding a hashtag to your social media message and image allows your post to be collected together with all other posts with the same hashtag. This is a great way for you to encourage people to take part in a larger project like the Craftivist Collective #imapiece project (see Chapter 10), which was used 3,273 times by 737 Twitter users reaching 9.6 million people. With every like, share and comment, these interactions can help people grow in confidence and commitment to a cause as well as making them feel part of a community. It's also useful data to share with those in power to show the traction your campaign has received. Craftivist Rachel from Reading tweeted to another craftivist after looking at the #imapiece feed: '@linniekin I'm making one [a jigsaw] for Kate Hoey MP too. Hope it will turn out as good as yours #imapiece'.

You could include #craftivism to showcase your craftivism work to people interested in this area or you could use a popular hashtag to join in a current affairs issue. I created and shared a mini banner at the time #jesuischarlie was trending to join in the conversation and address my concerns. The mini banner message I came up with with my dad said: 'If our lives are ruled by fear we will make innocent people our enemies. If our lives are ruled by love we will make strangers our friends.' You can also follow hashtags like #journorequest as many journalists use social media to find information about products or people to interview. Networking online is crucial to build connections with your audience and with journalists and other influential people.

News outlets

News outlets are often interested in craftivism, as it's a visually stimulating and an unusual way to do activism that is directly relevant to something current and newsworthy. Your craftivism images and activities should be much more time-specific and explicit in their politics for news outlets. For example, you could create a mini banner addressing your concern about modern-day segregation using a timeless quote and put it outside a newly opened expensive members' club on a busy street or an alternative Valentine's card slotted in between two cans of baked beans in a local newsagent on Valentine's Day. You can also use your craftivism photographs to signpost readers to a particular campaign or organisation. My Barbie image with its timeless message has been used to highlight campaigns on gender equality, domestic violence and other issues, and I'm delighted it has helped shine a spotlight on those issues and encourage people to take action regarding them.

Columnists might appreciate your craftivism work and mention your campaign in their column. Sometimes newspapers (especially their weekend supplements) are looking for longer articles and interviews. Articles on new trends are attractive to journalists: if you can show there are three or more groups or individuals working on the same issue then your story may have traction.

Be thoughtful when working with journalists. Not all publicity is good. Often they are looking for quick, simple soundbites to share with their audience. Craftivism should be multi-layered and so don't be tempted to oversimplify it, to stretch the truth, or to play to a stereotype. Journalists might focus on you rather than the issue you are passionate to protest about. Your role as a craftivist is to show that you are an average person who is keen to practise good global citizenship, and craftivism is one way you can protest against injustice. By showing that craftivism is accessible, interesting and fun, as well as worthwhile, it makes what you do seem achievable and hopefully attracts people who might feel intimidated or disinterested in other forms of activism.

Journalists often ask me, 'What campaigns have you won?' It's difficult for any campaign group to claim a win since it's not always clear that you were the main influencer (more on this in Chapter 18). Journalists often don't want to hear this fuzzy answer but it's important to be honest and not set up other craftivists to fail by leading them to think that they will win their campaigns quickly and easily, when in reality that is rare. It can be easy to miscommunicate. If you can, take a journalist to a workshop so they can take part or at least observe people taking part. Remember that the strength of craftivism is its intimacy and the curiosity it can create, its focus on engaging people deeply, not trying to reach everyone with quick and easy actions. You want journalists to hear your passion to tackle injustice, how thoughtful you are about how you can use craftivism for good, and your honesty around the strengths and weaknesses of craftivism.

Magazines and books

Having your craftivism published in books is a great platform to provoke thought and action around social change since they are often used as an activity to slow down and engage deeply in the content. *The State of Craft* by Victoria Woodcock is a craft book featuring over sixty patterns, ranging from pom-pom necklaces to jam-jar lamps. Each project also includes an interview with the craftster for more inspiration. I was invited to submit a project. I made sure that the project and injustice message were universal, timeless, and had attractive images to entice makers to take part in our mini banner project, which is always available to do. Not only does being in a book help craftivism reach out to its readers but being published in a book can give your craftivism credibility and affirm its significance in terms of both activism and craft. Ziggy Hanaor, Director of Cicada Books comments:

> When Victoria Woodcock and myself were working on *The State of Craft*, it was important for us to reflect that embedded within crafting culture there is a certain moral ethos. Craft allows us to feel positive by providing an outlet for our creativity, but also projects that positivity on to the world through reduction of waste materials, and by offering an alternative to disposable consumer culture. We wanted to include Sarah Corbett's work within the Craftivist Collective, as it takes this ethos one step further, and challenges us not just to generate this positivity within ourselves

but to gently challenge others to seek it out. We felt that including her work gave the book a political edge that added a great deal of weight and substance.

Magazines often find it difficult to cover social injustice issues: they tend to work three months in advance and so can't cover current affairs, they have a clear identity of what they can cover to retain their readers, and their advertisers can influence what goes in the magazine and what content might be seen as protesting against their company's practices or political persuasions. Despite this, our craftivism can work within these restrictions for some creative magazines where other forms of activism cannot: it could just be an intriguing image or two in a small news item, a feature on craftivism, a how-to guide for a particular craftivism project readers can take part in or an interview to show readers how to be a craftivist. Without going into detail about a particular political issue, you can encourage magazine readers to think about a gentle approach to protesting against social injustices and help them find out more specific information elsewhere.

It sounds obvious but when we are so passionate to engage people with the injustice issues they can support, we can forget to think about what the publication's priorities are. Don't forget to research which publications you think your craftivism would fit into to reach an audience other forms of activism would not engage. Look at which section craftivism could work best in: it is unlikely you will get an embroidery project in a knitting book or a paper craftivism project in a crochet magazine. Research the circulation of magazines, their audience demographic, their style and content to help you decide which publications to prioritise. One magazine loved my ethos and asked to include some examples of my craftivism in their magazine but once I sent the photographs over they said that the photographs were too bold in colour for their magazine, which had a much softer palette. I reshot some images with softer lighting without harming the activism messages and they used the images happily and are interested in sharing future images too. It challenged me to focus on the style of photographs that the audience prefers, not on my personal preference.

Mollie Makes magazine has been high on my priority list for the last five years. It focuses on engaging 'craftonistas', mostly women under forty-five years of age. The monthly magazine circulation is just under 40,000 in Europe and 100,000 monthly global users visit their website. They also have a large and active social media following: a perfect audience for craftivism and a place where you don't normally see activism shared. I've had my craftivism kits and events covered in the magazine and I have a good relationship with the editor.[4]

In 2016 *Mollie Makes* started a double-page 700-word essay section in the magazine called 'Good Read'. It seemed like a perfect format on which to launch and explain about our new craftivism project 'A Heart For Your Sleeve' (see Chapter 15). I contacted the then editor, Lara Watson, with a short summary of the project, a suggestion of which month they could exclusively launch the project in (September to give time to build momentum and urgency with a deadline to take part before 12 December) and a link to a small photo album of images (I recommend you save your high-resolution photographs on Flickr.com with clear titles, descriptions and information on who to credit the image to. Send a link to a photograph or an album to media contacts rather than email them a large file, which can clog up their emails and annoy them. They can then download the image size they want once they have taken a look). I knew the *Mollie Makes* staff really liked going to London-based Crafty Fox Market events and covering them in their magazine and so I also asked if they were interested in me delivering workshops for this new project in the markets leading up to Christmas, which *Mollie Makes* could partner, promote and support. Lara agreed to both and in addition she also decided to ask five well-known craftspeople to make a heart badge to be included in the article. This helped reach even more people through those crafters' followers because they promoted the project to their audiences online and offline too. This partnership led to readers sharing their green hearts, ideas, making progress and final badges online. This media partnership also helped out the Climate Coalition who became more well known within the UK craft community because of this project.

I have to admit I am nervous about contacting the media asking them to cover my craftivism work. I'm scared of rejection, but the worst they can say is that our work doesn't fit their audience. Remember that they are busy and get lots of requests, but don't forget that your work is about making our world a more creative and compassionate place for all and I don't know any magazine staff or freelance writers who don't want to feel part of that movement. You're offering them a gift with your work and the enjoyment of working together to see how best it can be shared with their audience.

Be mindful of what you share and how you share it
We have to realise and acknowledge that for some media outlets or magazines our craftivism will probably not be as popular as a picture or video of a cute kitten dressed in a cowboy outfit, but that doesn't matter. Don't be tempted to create 'clickbait' content: you might get more attention, shares and 'likes' by promoting simple safe messages that don't ask for a lot of thought or conviction from the viewers but as a craftivist your priority is to engage people more deeply and critically in social change and empower them to take strategic action to tackle the issue. This is a tough task but that is our purpose. If it feels like you are spamming people, then you probably are. You might have lots of ways you can share social change through your craftivism but be careful not to bombard people with information. Quality is always better than quantity. Intrigue is better than an overload of information. Be conversational

POWER IN THE PUBLIC SPHERE

rather than broadcast your message. Share your best content that you truly believe your audience will engage with.

Always ask yourself if you would share what you have posted if you were a reader. Who would you share it with and what thought and conversations could it create? Imagine sitting with a friend, what would make a story of injustice and how to tackle it inspiring, empowering and worth sharing? We listen most to people we know and respect. If they recommend something or discuss something we are more likely to discuss and think about it too and we are more inclined to agree with them than with a stranger. Is our content worth sharing and if so, how best can it be shared?

Share the sizzle

Let's share the sizzle not the dead pig (sorry again vegan readers!). Share your beautiful images, your concerns for others, information on an issue, and always follow it up with suggestions on realistic actions we can take, visions of a better world we can aim towards, and how fulfilling it is to be part of the solution to injustice, not part of the problem. Your stories and crafted objects can be an example for others giving them the inspiration to take part and can even offer a type of permission for people to have a go. They can also be tools for connection with people you know and those you don't, people outside of your natural silo where you can identify common ground through conversation about your craftivism piece.

It can feel like we have a herculean task ahead of us to tackle injustice in the world but if we share and widen engagement that will surely make it harder for those injustices to be ignored.

18
Measuring Success

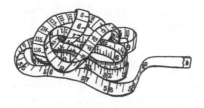

Not everything that counts can be counted, and not everything that can be counted counts.

— William Bruce Cameron

When I first started creating craftivism projects in 2008, the common response was confusion, laughter or opposition. Some self-identified activists told me I was being 'too soft' on power-holders and so I would never make an impact. Some craftspeople told me I was wasting time I could be using to make functional relief objects such as blankets to give to homeless people. Some people were confused about my motivation: craft was far from cool at that time and activism was seen by some as pointless, scary and a chore, so why do it? Some people told me there wasn't a need for what I was doing. I was self-critical too. And rightly so. After all, craftivism existed before I came across it, and even before the word was coined activists had been using craft in different ways for social change going back to the suffragettes, the beginnings of the Labour movement and before. Maybe my 'gentle protest' approach to craftivism wasn't going to be useful or effective, maybe it would even harm campaigning more than help it. I didn't know. But I did know I wanted to find out if using craft in activism in a gentle way could address some of the areas I saw lacking in activism, because very few big social changes happen without some form of activism involved. If my gentle protest approach to craftivism was effective, the results could be transformational, politically and personally. And that's worth trying out.

Why measure?

If you have ever looked at the back of a hand-embroidered artwork it shows you how the neat design on the front has been executed: the strategy of which order the stitches go in, the way the colours weave into each other, the technique chosen to tie up the loose ends, the time and commitment, the thought and care put into the piece and maybe even some hints of mistakes that have been concealed on the back so not to be shown on the front. There are many important reasons why we should take a look at the behind-the-scenes of how we have executed our craftivism.

Measure to learn. We can always improve our practice, especially if we want to continue to use craftivism to campaign for social justice. But we can't improve unless we clearly and as objectively as possible learn from our mistakes and successes. Whether it's the first time you've done some craftivism or whether you are a veteran, you should always evaluate your work and strive to become the most effective craftivist you can be within the personal limitations you have. Whether we like it or not our actions have impact. Reflecting on your craftivism will help you decide whether you should aim for a smaller goal or a bigger impact in your next project; whether you should find a less distracting venue in which to make your object so that you can gain higher quality crafterthoughts; whether you should have chosen a different gift-receiver or another public place to put your piece, etc. Measuring our success – or lack of it – helps us to see how we can hone our craft so we become the best craftivists we can be, now and in the future, to serve those suffering through injustice and to improve our world for everyone.

Measure to share insight. When you evaluate your craftivism, you can then also share your valuable insight with others to help them in their craftivism. Everyone's situation is different, and so there may be an approach that works for you in your area that does not work for someone else or vice versa. But sharing your experience and what you have learnt can inspire and empower others to build reflection and sharing into their craftivism journeys. It helps other craftivists compare your insight with their plans, which can help improve their effectiveness as craftivists. It can also educate any doubters – and there will be doubters! – who think your work is pointless or even harmful. I still have many discussions with people who ask me how my work actually achieves anything. Not only does it interest them to learn about this unusual way of activism, including its strengths and weaknesses, which I'm happy to share with them, but I also gain a lot from these conversations: where I need to improve on my explanation to make it clear what my approach to craftivism is when people seem confused; what triggers excitement or doubt in the people I am talking to, and if they ask a question I can't answer then that gives me some homework to do and may make me think about my craftivism work differently. Encourage constructive, challenging feedback – I always ask students and staff at universities I give lectures in to be devil's advocates and ask me difficult questions so we can all learn. Also, sharing the impact and outputs you've had with the media and power-holders can help strengthen your campaign: the number of craftivism objects made, how many hours of commitment, from where in the world, audience demographic, etc., all of these could influence the outcome from the decision-makers you are conversing with. Richard Reynolds wrote about his own social impact in his book *On Guerrilla Gardening: A Handbook for Gardening without Boundaries*:

> Sow seeds in the minds of others. Don't let what you have learnt rot away when you move on. Pile it onto the collective mental compost heap, a rich resource for fertilising new gardens.[1]

Measure to stay focused. Craftivism can be a challenge to do, and evaluating its effectiveness can be even harder. It's often more attractive to focus on emergency relief or development than advocacy because it's easier and quicker to measure (and justify to others) the impact of your efforts: providing emergency food and shelter are vital for people living in refugee camps. But craftivism is also needed to tackle the root causes of why people flee their homes and how we can help stop the conflict so that more people are not forced to leave their home. We need to measure our success so we do not veer off into transactional, non-activism actions or give too much emphasis to transactional activism.

Measure your impact to help you celebrate your successes big and small. Celebration can keep you motivated to continue to stand against injustice and to strive for a better world when it feels like the injustice you are addressing is just too big to solve. It's also good to celebrate what we have achieved so that when we are tempted to shoehorn craft ideas into a fruitless craftivism project, we have the motivation to focus on craftivism projects that actually made positive social changes not just raise awareness of an issue.

Measure your impact to help plan future craftivism activities. It's irresponsible of us to waste physical resources, our energy and our limited time on craftivism that is ineffective or, even worse, harmful when those resources could be used in better ways. It can feel like a chore to evaluate your impact but thoughtful measuring helps not hinders our work. It's vital.

How to measure your success

Throughout your process, at key moments (such as after a workshop) and at milestones (such as receiving a response from a power-holder you have contacted), as well as at the end of your project, make time to reflect and assess your work by asking yourself some questions. For example:

- Did you meet your objective?
- Did something or someone block you from reaching your goal? If so, should you have chosen a different route or can you divert your plan to a different route to continue your work?
- If you didn't reach your goal, where on the spectrum from A to B did you get?
- Was it worth your time, resources and energy doing it?
- Was the response what you expected or do you need to communicate it differently so your campaign does not get misunderstood or misinterpreted?
- If you held a craftivism event, did people go off on a tangent rather than addressing your crafterthought questions? Was that because your instructions were not clear enough or do you need to facilitate the session more carefully?
- If the object you made was for a power-holder or an influential person, did you receive any feedback? Did you ask them for constructive criticism that you and other craftivists could learn from?

Hopefully those questions above, and other questions you can think of for yourself that are specific to your project, will help shine a spotlight on what worked, what didn't, and show you how you could improve your future craftivist projects. Jim Coe, campaign evaluation specialist, told me once over a coffee:

You need to be clear what your objectives are so you can check in to see if you are on the right track, but just as important is finding the space and time to reflect on your findings. People always want to know what tools they can use to monitor and evaluate, but really you just need a pencil and some paper, and some good questions. It's the thinking that is the important bit in evaluation.

Always be aware that reflection and evaluation of our craftivism work is an art not a science. When it comes to measuring success, knowledge really is power and planning to evaluate your work from the start is paramount.

Be clear about your goals

If we are clear in our objectives from the start, we can effectively collect the right data and feedback. During our project we will be more aware of external factors that may have influenced our results, and we can plan the monitoring and evaluation of our craftivism objectives into our strategy. This allows us to measure what we have achieved against the clear goals we set, and then we're more likely to see some of the impact we have made (often not all of the impact is visible).

Objects such as banners, posters or placards alongside performance, music and visual arts have always been used as a catalyst to engage in public debate on injustice issues, but unfortunately throughout history there has not been much evaluation of the impact objects have made in protests. That's not very useful for our craftivism work but there is value in collecting quantitative data on the reach and uptake your object has had with people, organisations and the media in order to see where you can improve, and to share that information to help existing and future craftivists. For example, in the early days of my craftivism journey, many craftivists around the world came across my mini banners online and were inspired to make their own. I observed that craftivists often struggled with creating an intriguing message to stitch, many were unclear of the purpose of the banners or the best places to hang them in order to have the biggest impact. I reached out to ask what they were trying to achieve and how I could help. The feedback led me to make ethical mini banner DIY craftivism kits to help craftivists make the project as effective as possible. The kits include clear objectives, tips, instructions, message suggestions, crafterthought questions to reflect on before and during the making, woven labels to attach to the mini banners to help create a supporter journey for the viewers and a postcard to keep, which is a photograph of a mini banner hung up in a public place to offer more direction on where to hang their own banner. I'm now on my third and final version of the kit after analysing feedback and seeing completed mini banners made from version one and two kits, and it's definitely producing better understanding and results.

Assessing, not just collecting

Measuring for a craftivist is about assessing data, not just collecting it. Data on its own won't tell you everything but the collection of good information in combination with thoughtful interpretation leads to good understanding. There is increasing pressure in advocacy to try and show concrete results from your actions. Don't obsess over data collection: focus on what you want to achieve, measure what you can, but be aware that you can't measure everything. Your craftivism is more than a list of transactions, it's about creating transformations in ourselves, others and our world. And these transformations are often invisible, impossible to measure quickly, and, in fact, tend to be immeasurable anyway. It's these changes in hearts and minds that create the most long-lasting positive change, so that is our priority. See your impact as like an iceberg – there is a small amount of data above the water showing some impact you are having, such as how many people took part in your craftivism project, the number of people who read your blog about your craftivism or the amount of likes it had on social media. But it's the impact under the water that can be the most transformational. Looking in too reductionist a way can mean that you miss out on seeing the wonderful impact you might have had. The thing is to be clear about what's important and look for signs that you are on the right path, or not.

Does the data indicate part of a deeper engagement, commitment and change towards justice? The answer may often be 'we don't know'. That's when we can ask ourselves to measure the impact differently: each invite may bring up a different answer. Is it worth wearing your green heart on your sleeve to stand up for what you want protected in this world and intrigue viewers in a way that might create conversations on climate change with you? Absolutely. Is it worth making a gift for a power-holder whose actions concern you? If you do it with courage, care and commitment to building a respectful relationship with them, yes, it is. If you make it with a disrespectful message stitched on or no clear social injustice link and then throw it in their face and don't stay in touch with them, then don't do it. It could harm the craftivism approach and if your object has the Craftivist Collective label stitched onto it, it could harm any potential future communication the Craftivist Collective initiates with that power-holder – they might refuse to connect because of a previously disrespectful action such as the above. Is it worth doing a one-off workshop in a public museum or art gallery? Sometimes yes, sometimes no. I would argue that it is *if* you believe you are the best person available to deliver a thoughtful craftivism workshop, *if* that venue is asking for your skill in an area in which they feel they are lacking and you can educate them or even train them up in, *if* you can address social injustice issues that the organisation does not address, *if* it will reach people who are not already engaged in the issue or an audience who are particularly influential for the issue you are addressing, *if* it will reach a large audience during the workshop and/or through their promotional information and *if* you have the time and energy to deliver it well. Each invite may bring up a different answer. And perhaps your last question should be the most difficult one: what would the world be missing without the craftivism I had done?

Success isn't always obvious

Activists' success can look like nothing has happened, because it's halted rather than created change: e.g., stopping an animal species becoming extinct, stopping more people working in sweatshops, stopping the drilling through the arctic circle for oil. Don't be disheartened. When it comes to craftivism, our work will not stop a war on its own but we should see our actions as part of a bigger campaign picture and acknowledge that we are just one tool in the toolbox. Other approaches are needed to complement our work and vice versa. You might not think that you have achieved a lot by shopdropping 'Mini Fashion Statements' in pockets of unethically made clothes, but isn't it better to do it than nothing? You may never know the impact you have had but you might have stopped someone buying a shirt they didn't need, made them consider saving up to invest in one that would last longer. They might have asked the store manager what the scrolls mean, which their manager might then report to a higher level to be addressed, or you might introduce someone to the Fashion Revolution campaign who then goes on to be a proactive member of that movement for change. Was it worth the recycled paper used, the ribbon, your time carefully handwriting the messages and your own engagement in the issue to provoke thought on the clothing industry? I believe that the potential positive impact a craftivist object can achieve for you and others outweighs the harm it might create if it's made to the best of its potential. Some people might think that your little craftivism actions are small drops in the ocean but as Mother Teresa taught us: 'The whole ocean is just millions of drops.'

Throughout your measuring, don't forget that what might seem like a small activism action for one person might be a huge leap and achievement for someone else. Some of my proudest successes are when I've helped people lobby their local politician for the first time and then they go on to do more lobbying. My projects often give people the confidence to attend their first non-violent protest march, or learn the habit of being more intentional in what they buy or how they treat people through their company. My craftivism has helped to strengthen and grow some existing campaigns and even helped 50,000 people gain an important increase in their wages, encouraging more companies to do the same. On the flip side, if you are working with experienced activists you should expect a more strategic and robust craftivism project than when working with novices, just as you would expect a better running technique delivered by a trained marathon runner compared to an amateur very new to running long distances.

Our evaluations must also take into consideration uncertain claims of causality in politics, business, and in everything that is happening in the world. The nature of activism is that events sometimes evolve rapidly and in a non-linear fashion. An effort that doesn't seem to be working might suddenly bear fruit. Or your craftivism campaign might gain traction but then suddenly lose momentum. Your action might be in place to be covered in your local newspaper one day but then it's left on the cutting-room floor twenty minutes before it goes to print because something seen as more newsworthy happens. Was it still worth taking the action even if people don't read about it in the paper? Yes. Could you have had a plan B to share your action in other media outlets such as online websites, blogs, social media or even the local community paper or church newsletter? Only you will know.

Success in implementing a new model for change

Change is just as likely to happen through inspiration and the use of a catalyst as through imposition. Martin Luther King was inspired by Gandhi's tactic of non-violence; Gandhi was inspired by Tolstoy's non-fiction book *The Kingdom of God is Within You* and by the suffragette movement. We are all influenced by others, sometimes knowingly, sometimes not. Sadly there will always be poverty, suffering and injustice in our precious world. Ideas and alternative models to the status quo can quietly inspire and empower others as soon as they are created, or they can lie dormant but gain traction and relevance centuries later. Knowing that I am limited in my own capacity because I cannot clone myself to achieve more in the same time, one of my high-priority goals with this gentle protest approach to craftivism was to share my craftivism methodology and personal case studies with both the charity sector and individuals to encourage them to implement a form of activism into their campaigning because I knew I wouldn't have the time or capacity to deliver the campaigns myself.

Changing policy or behaviour through specific political craftivism projects is not the only way to succeed as a craftivist. Teaching others how to do effective craftivism is a success if they then use your methodology to deliver positive social change too. Professional campaign staff of charities often tell me that they and their colleagues follow my craftivism work and have been inspired and challenged to think through ways to campaign that they may have not thought about or tried before. Some charities are now including more creative activities to engage people in social change in a slower, more deeply engaging way. Some charities are using more positive messages to encourage rather than demonise power-holders. Some charities are looking at ways they can make sure that some of their campaign activities harness the skills and energy of introverts not just extroverts. Head of campaigns and engagement at BOND,* and author of thoughtfulcampaigner.org Tom Baker writes:

---

* BOND is the UK membership body for organisations working in international development or supporting those that do through funding, research, training and other services. They have over 450 members, ranging from large agencies with a worldwide presence to smaller, specialist organisations.

I've been a 'professional' campaigner for over ten years. Campaigning can often feel like you're on a treadmill without a stop button – you just have to run faster and for longer – but I've seen how craftivism has helped to remind us that it's good to slow down, to take time to consider why we're doing what we're doing, and recognise that heading out onto a march or demonstration isn't for everyone. I think it's had a profound impact on our approach to campaigning across the sector.

You can have impact working behind the scenes with a group or organisation as a consultant. While writing this chapter I have decided to spend some of my time working with a large UK national mental health charity to help them create a craftivism project, which is part of a fundraising activity they want to link to activism and deeper engagement in the issues. There are so many campaigns to focus on, why am I focusing my time on this? Well, not only is mental health not an area we have covered in the Craftivist Collective but more importantly in my eyes, this is an unusual project for charity-sector staff who want to include activism through craft in future fundraising projects. If I can help create a successful product not just in terms of fundraising money for the charity's work, but also show that activism and fundraising can complement rather than compete or conflict with each other, then this model could be used by other charities to create similar projects. This means that this project can have impact beyond its immediate objectives and possibly be scaled up to reach more people. If it doesn't work, this new project will still create learning that will be useful for the charity and the charity sector and maybe even beyond. It might be that there are local organisations near you that you think you could advise and work with to create craftivism activities they can use to strengthen their existing social-change work.

Sprouting success

Making sure that our intentions resonate with people is intrinsic to the craftivism approach in this book. I always hope that my craftivism work will reach beyond my immediate circle of influence and grow organically in people. Some fruits of your labour often pop up in places you have not planned. People often congratulate me for the fact that Malala Yousafzai, joint winner of the Nobel Peace Prize in 2014, attended one of my talks and workshops, and Russell Brand, the actor, comedian and activist, called in to the end of one of my workshops with his mum to watch what we were doing, asked thoughtful questions and took away my little book and kit to go through (the workshop was ending and the venue closing so sadly he couldn't take part). It's a big compliment, it can add credibility to your work and it can attract more people to take part in craftivism. These events are often perceived as big successes, but I would say they are small ones: Malala doesn't need craftivism to reach audiences and speak to power-holders; Russell Brand doesn't need my help to get his voice heard. It has, however, undoubtedly made a wide audience aware of my form of craftivism, something that I had not planned for.

It's worth noting any results that you did not expect. They might help you plan more robust craftivism projects in the future. For example, I created a bespoke project for the UK charity World AIMS (World Action in Methodist Schools). It not only became their most popular event ever with secondary school students across the UK but organically it engaged parents, which was not part of my plan and which had not happened for World AIMS before. Some schools even set up after-school craftivism sessions so that students, parents and teachers could stitch together. Sarah Corris, the global education project manager for World AIMS, writes:

> It created the perfect forum for young people to really engage with an issue. And unlike other forms of activism, it created a safe environment for staff, students and parents to relate to one another

about the pressing issue and reflect before reacting. The process requires and provides real thinking time, allowing all involved to channel their voice through their own unique creativity. I think that is why it was our most popular campaign activity.

Many further education colleges and higher education universities across the world include the craftivism projects and methodology in this book (and I hope this book is helpful for them too!) on some of their courses, from textiles to product design, courses which have not covered social change in the curriculum before, as well as in courses such as social studies, media and politics amongst others. Dr Kristy Holmes, Assistant Professor and Chair of the Visual Arts Department at Lakehead University, Canada, messaged me out of the blue to say:

I'm an art history professor and my students are doing this as a project for my course. Very excited about it. Thanks for all your wonderful work, I talked a lot about the Craftivist Collective in my unit on Craftivism, the students (and I) were really inspired by what you're doing. For some, it helped give clarity to the meaning behind their practice and for others it showed how small steps can lead to big change. Lots of students have referenced the experience in project work and it was hugely inspirational to us all.

I never expected an email like the above but more and more have popped into my inbox over the years. Do not underestimate the influence you can have on people through your craftivism work and the craftivism you share. You might be surprised what emails end up in your inbox. I've received emails from different people who have told me that they've come across groups, from students to elderly ladies, doing craftivism who have all said that they wouldn't be doing it if they hadn't seen examples of what to do from my work. After working on my first craftivism book – *A Little Book of Craftivism* – the managing director of Cicada Books, Ziggy Hanaor, had this to say:

> When I asked Sarah to pitch a craftivism book to me, she had a clear sense of what the book could be, which I could immediately envisage: a small book of sixty-four pages with a warmth and accessibility that reflected the projects that the Craftivist Collective had produced. It was certainly one of the most rewarding titles I've worked on. To some degree the making of the book felt like a piece of craftivism in and of itself. Discussing how best to communicate ideas of gentle activism through the text and images was a thought-provoking and inspirational process that I still bear in mind when I am in times of crisis within my work.

I write a monthly newsletter read by a few thousand people around the world. It's not a long newsletter and it's not to a huge readership in some people's eyes, but it aims to update people on craftivism projects they can take part in, what we have been successful in achieving in the last month, thoughts to reflect on in the coming month and often spotlights non-craftivism resources I think craftivists might find useful to help them become more effective global citizens. I don't ask for or expect replies from people. I can see from the statistics from the newsletter service provider how many people open up the newsletter and click on the different links and resources, which helps me see which posts resonate with people and which do not (always evaluating!). But receiving emails, like this one below from Craftivist Greta, help me gain more insight into the impact my newsletters can have:

> Each of your newsletters has brought quotes, resources, and ideas that have really spoken to me, and I just wanted to tell you

'Thank you!' I know it can be hard to measure the kind of work you're doing, but it has had a real impact on me.

I save feedback emails into a 'Happy Folder' in my email account and letters and cards in a physical box, so when I am doubting the effectiveness of my craftivism work (which I do regularly!) I can read through them again and see the pieces of craftivism are having an impact. I keep constructive criticism too, and try to address it in my work. If you ever doubt your effectiveness I recommend you save feedback (positive and negative) to reflect on, especially to help you shape your future craftivism activities as well as to keep you motivated to protest against injustice gently.

Personal impact

One area of craftivism that you can measure in much more depth than any other area is how craftivism has affected you, as a maker, gift-giver, culture jammer and observer. Have you used the act of making a craftivism object as an opportunity to engage more deeply and critically in social change? Have you used the making process to understand and reflect on the complexities of injustice and how you might be entangled in parts of the problems and solutions? Have you changed the way you think or behave with the help of your craftivism activity or object?

My gentle protest approach to craftivism is about allowing the maker and observer to take ownership of the process of engaging in the issue. It does not force people into transactional activism actions but focuses on offering the possibility of personal and societal transformation. This means that people can engage at any level – it's out of my control. It's up to you how much you use craftivism as a catalyst for personal development and therefore how impactful craftivism is on you. Don't forget that heart work is hard work. Be prepared to feel challenged throughout the process if you want to gain the most from craftivism, but don't forget that your craft is a comfort during these sometimes uncomfortable times.

Success in personal sustainability

If we want a more sustainable world, achieving it without burning out is essential. Craftivism can be a costly endeavour in terms of emotion, energy and time. There are always going to be injustices in the world that need to be addressed but we need to do a manageable amount well rather than a lot badly. Always ask yourself beforehand if your craftivism campaign is needed. It might not be or you might need to improve your strategy. Do you need to do it or can someone else? You might need to focus on one element of the campaign and ask for help with other elements. Do you have more influence in one area of injustice rather than another so should focus where you have the most potential power? Don't become a burnt-out craftivist. I have a fridge magnet with a quote next to a photograph of the women's rights activist Gloria Steinem that reads: 'The truth will set you free. But first, it will piss you off.'

The truth behind injustice should piss us off, but if a craftivist becomes burnt-out, stressed, overworked, cynical, obsessed with their work or too ill to perform it, we limit our impact and can put people off joining a movement for social change. Feeling bad does not change the world, positive action does.

The problem with activists is that we are instinctive dreamers of the better world, and we are naturally impatient for a better world and sometimes our impatience and our ambition become greater than our ability to think rationally and logically about what is achievable. Sometimes we think too small for our craftivism and miss out on having a greater impact, sometimes we think too big and forget that if we had focused on doing something smaller we could have made a bigger difference. We shouldn't feel guilty for enjoying craftivism. The key to avoiding burn-out is to develop personal habits and practices that nurture and sustain us, to make time to dance and laugh with loved ones as well as also making time to pick up our craftivism tools to eradicate injustices. Numerous studies confirm that engagement in causes greater than the individual self is strongly linked to overall life happiness and satisfaction.* Being a craftivist can be a powerful antidote to feelings of powerlessness, meaninglessness, isolation and boredom.

Craftivism can help us feel connected and engaged in our world, and remind us that we can help shape the world into a brilliant place for us all. Don't give up: have the humility to accept the messiness of our world and its people, be sure of your position to pursue your goal with dignity and persistence, accept what gives you energy in your craftivism actions and what drains you of energy, where you can make a big difference and where you are not needed so that you can use that time to rest, recreate or focus on a different craftivism project. Being a sustainable craftivist not only helps you continue your work but also inspires and educates others as to how they can act out their values in thought, word and deed too, which is much more than fun, it's fulfilling and can improve our world.

Move beyond success

People are at the centre of our craftivism work, and that makes our craftivism results difficult to measure. Even with the most robust systems of collection we are never certain of our impact. We can't change people; they have to change themselves. Sometimes people tell you if and how your craftivism has affected them, sometimes they don't. Sometimes they lie and say that it had no impact because they don't want to encourage you, and sometimes they lie to say it has changed their ways because they want to please you. Sometimes they don't know yet or will never know if your work has affected their hearts, minds and behaviour. Sometimes your work affects them subconsciously. Sometimes people will be influenced by your work but not credit you. Politicians or companies may give a number of reasons for why they have made a change and may

* www.pbs.org/thisemotionallife/topic/altruism/altruismhappiness

be reluctant to tell you if your campaign has been successful because they don't want you to use your knowledge to protest against them in the future or share your winning tactics with others. People might pick and choose from my methodology, which can be frustrating when I see the flaws but I have to let go and let people follow their own path without me trying to take over. We've talked about measuring success and why that's important but don't get hung up on collecting as much data as possible. Allow people to take ownership of the way they use your craftivism resources and activities in their journey. Asking for feedback too quickly (or at all) can stunt participants' critical thinking or even be counter-productive. No matter what happens in our craftivism campaigns we should always deliver our campaigns with openness, connectedness and love rather than conflict. Fran Peavey coined the phrase 'heart politics' to describe this:

We ask questions and explore. It's not a fix but a sharing. We explore alternatives and meaning. We hope things move on some levels though it is not always evident what shifts occur.[2]

Our activism actions should not be about winning or losing, who is right and who is wrong, or about if we are the most popular craftivists. Our actions are about serving and being in solidarity with other human beings suffering from the results of injustice, about how to improve our world and, where we can, about how to work with others to do that together. There is often no one fix or solution. Sometimes goals take decades to achieve – civil rights, LGBT rights and women's rights campaigns, and even now these goals still haven't been fully achieved and in some areas can feel even more at risk of being taken away by current or future people in positions of power. We might have the most robust strategy we have ever created for one craftivism project that has worked in the past but an external factor could derail our plans or speed up our success. Our own environment and the wider world is always changing and that will affect our craftivism results, but we shouldn't let that put us off doing our craftivism. We cannot save anyone alone. Victories are often only temporary but if we can continue to regularly spread our influence and protest against the injustices we see then we can make it harder for injustices to creep back in and we can be part of the solution to injustice rather than part of the systemic problem. We need to see our vision of a utopia as a journey, not as a destination, because although it's not something we can ever hope to reach on earth, that shouldn't stop us from trying!

Keep looking up

When I despair, I remember that all through history, the way of truth and love has always won. There have been tyrants and murderers, and for a time they can seem invincible, but in the end they always fall, always.

I cling to these words from Mahatma Gandhi. If your craftivism changes the way you behave for the better, that is a success. If your craftivism changes the way your friend behaves, that is a double impact. If your craftivism helps to change the way 10 per cent of the population of the country in which you live behave then that can create a new status quo! Craftivism can't fix all of the world's problems but it can be a useful tool in the activism toolkit *if* we use it wisely and continue to sharpen it. Craftivism can not only make a difference at the time of your activity and provoke thought and action by its finished object, but the documented images and words can have ripple effects now and in the future (that's my hope with this book).

One person alone cannot change the world. Emmeline Pankhurst, Aung San Suu Kyi and Nelson Mandela are all considered civil rights leaders of movements that changed the world, but on their own they wouldn't have been able to achieve what they did. It doesn't matter if you are a craftivism group leader or a group member or a lone craftivist, a creator of new craftivism projects or a participant in existing ones, we can all be part of the change we wish to see in the world through learning from past craftivism and activism campaigns, thinking critically and focusing on a strategic gentle protest approach to activism.

We should always be motivated by our values and weave our principles through all that we do. Everyone has a part to play in improving our world using their unique talents and opportunities. We should quietly organise and work hard for what we believe is right. The world will always have poverty and suffering in it but as James Baldwin says, 'Not everything that is faced can be changed, but nothing can be changed until it is faced.'

Every act of craftivism we do should be done in good faith but we should also accept that we don't have complete control over the results of our labour. We just have to hope and employ the wisdom and experience we have at our disposal to be as strategic as possible in order to reach realistic goals and answer the question: does our work and the way we exercise power promote life in a beautiful, kind and fair way?

We should cherish every smile of appreciation, every word of encouragement, every thank you. When you struggle to see the impact your craftivism activity is having, see these as well deserved reward for your craftivism endeavours. Your little successes should spur you on to bigger but realistic challenges and increase your confidence and courage to protest against injustice. Keep learning from your craftivism activities and look for the ripples, but don't be disappointed if you don't see them immediately. Don't forget that Rome was not built in a day. It took around ten years just to build the Colosseum! Don't expect to achieve big things quickly. Arrogance is toxic and can set you up to fail and so don't focus on the winning. If the world ends tomorrow, would you still behave responsibly towards others and our planet? Commit to the power of gentleness, be open to success and willing to learn from failure and remember that whatever you do, you are a valued human being, whether your craftivism bears fruit or not.

Since starting on my craftivism journey in 2008 I have suffered less scepticism year-on-year and I have seen much evidence that craftivism can be transformational, politically and personally, if delivered effectively. Author Rebecca Solnit in her book *Hope in the Dark* comments:

> Ideas at first considered outrageous or ridiculous or extreme gradually become what people think they've always believed. How the transformation happened is rarely remembered.[3]

So let's be disciplined to hone our craft. Let's be flexible with our strategy, assess the data we have collected to gain wisdom and keep a strong moral compass throughout. As I've mentioned before, being a craftivist is a journey not a destination. The path might be uneven, rocky, wiggly, behind fog or steep at times but it is also full of beauty, joyful moments, enlightening viewing, and gives us a direction in which to travel with a sense of solidarity and a purpose beyond ourselves. Some craftivists will dip in and out of campaigns. Some groups will last for one session, others for years. But I haven't yet met a craftivist or a supporter of our gentle protest approach to craftivism who regrets their involvement. So let's pick up our tools and let's see what we can create…

Epilogue

'The saving of our world...will come, not through the complacent adjustment of the conforming majority, but through the creative maladjustment of a nonconforming minority...Human salvation lies in the hands of the creatively maladjusted,' preached Martin Luther King Jnr in his sermon 'Transformed Nonconformist'.*

To be a craftivist is not just to be someone who likes craft: it is to be someone who hones their craft to question injustice, encourage peace and show ways to achieve a better world for everybody involved. The test of whether we truly want a better world is in the doing – through action. So are you ready to stretch out your hands and open up your craftivism toolbox?

In the craftivism toolbox you will find:

Scissors to shape the future into a more harmonious world.

Thread to weave intimacy through protests where there is currently enmity.

---

* *Strength to Love* by Martin Luther King, published by Fortress Press (copyright 1963 © Martin Luther King). First Fortress Press edition, 1981, p. 27. Fortress Press, Philadelphia. Printed in the United States of America.

A needle to stitch love and kindness through structures that are lacking.

A seam-ripper to cut through the knots, tangles and seams that hold systems of oppression in place.

A pattern to follow with courage, care and compassion where a robust plan of action is needed.

So, craftivists, let's use craftivism as a form of gentle protest. Let's use our craftivism to practise what we preach: creating a world with beauty, kindness and fairness. Let's use craftivism as a way to stand up against injustice for the introvert as well as the extrovert, for the crafter as well as the banner-waver, for the reflective among us as well as those who want to dive straight in.

Let us all pick up our tools and be effective change*makers*.

Wellmaking Clinic

Being the change you wish to see in the world is good for your own individual wellbeing as well as the wellbeing of society. But sometimes, when we are passionate about an injustice, we forget to look after ourselves. Here are some prescriptions for whatever is making you concerned or anxious. They are all accessible and enjoyable as well as manageable for even the busiest people.

- **Feeling too sad to do anything?** Each morning start your day by thinking about what you are grateful for and write it down in a gratitude journal or on a piece of paper you then put in a gratitude jar. Gratitude affects our physical health, psychological wellbeing and our relationship with others. By writing what you are grateful for and keeping it, you are reminding yourself of the goodness in our world, not just focusing on the bad.

- **Feeling overwhelmed?** Start with daily actions and habits you can change. Draw a straight line across the middle of a piece of landscape A4 paper from left to right and plot out an average day to assess what areas in your life you can improve. For example: can you move your home energy supplier to a greener one? Can you buy your food and necessities more ethically? Can you intentionally smile at those you interact with during your day, from bus driver to bartender? Can you car-share or cycle to work to lower your carbon footprint?

- **Feeling powerless?** Find a good resting place and read an issue of *Dumbo Feather* magazine cover to cover. It's full of interviews with inspiring people who use their passions and talents to make a positive difference in the world. Not only will this magazine remind you that there are wonderful people in the world tackling injustices so you don't have to do it all but you can learn from their journeys, helping you on your journey as a changemaker.

- **Impatient for change?** One evening, cosy up with a cup of tea, popcorn and watch Steven Spielberg's film *Lincoln* (2013). This slow-paced, beautiful film teaches us how President Abraham Lincoln abolished slavery in America over time, with patience, humility and gentleness with those who disagreed with him. I also recommend the films *Selma* and *Gandhi*.

- **Feeling anxious?** *Flow* is a Dutch quarterly magazine about positive psychology, mindfulness, creativity and the beauty of imperfection. It encourages us to do things differently and make new choices. It also includes free paper-craft resources and activities.

- **Too angry to think straight?** Go on a run or power walk. Release your anger in a safe way. Come back to your activism plans with a clear head and a kind heart.

- **Struggling to empathise with people in positions of leadership who are doing harm?** Watch the film *Coriolanus* directed by and starring Ralph Fiennes, and set in the modern day. Learn why Coriolanus believes violence is the correct answer and what motivates his actions to help you exercise intelligent empathy.

- **Feeling hopeless?** Subscribe to the quarterly magazine *Positive News,* a constructive journalism magazine, reporting on people and initiatives that are creating a sustainable and fair world. It aims to help create a more responsible and balanced media by sharing good news written by journalists. Make time to read it slowly without distraction so that you can learn about the good things that are happening in the world.

- **Struggling with in-depth books on injustice?** Start with accessible and attractive comic books to increase your knowledge and understanding of global issues. *Pedro and Me: Friendship Lost and What I Learned* by Judd Winick is a small comic book about HIV in the 1990s. Art Spiegelman's *Maus I* and *II* is a story of the Holocaust. *The Complete Persepolis* (volumes 1–4) by Marjane Satrapi is set during the Islamic Revolution in Iran.

- **Getting itchy fingers and want to *make* change with your own two hands?** Put the kettle on, make a cup of tea and open up one of my craftivism kits (www.craftivist-collective.com/shop or buy from your nearest independent stockist) and see where it takes you.

Notes

Introduction
[1] Greer, B., 'Craftivism', *Encyclopedia of Activism and Social Justice* (SAGE Publiations, 2007). Also www.craftivism.com/definition

Part I: Definitions

Chapter 1: Craftivism
[1] www.craftivism.com/blog
[2] Korn, P., *Why We Make Things and Why It Matters: The Education of a Craftsman* (Vintage, 2017), p. 31.
[3] Rorty, R., *Philosophy and Social Hope* (Penguin, new edn 1999), p. 24.
[4] Ricketts, A., *Activists' Handbook* (Zed Books, 2012).

Chapter 2: Gentle Protest
[1] Goleman, G., *Emotional Intelligence: Why It Can Matter More Than IQ* (Bloomsbury, 1996), p. xii.
[2] See www.ted.com/talks/scilla_elworthy_fighting_with_non_violence/transcript

Part II: Power in the Process

Chapter 3: Slow Activism
[1] Honoré, C., *In Praise of Slow: How a Worldwide Movement is Challenging the Cult of Speed* (Orion, 2005).

Chapter 4: Mindful Activism
[1] Langer, E. J., *Mindfulness* (Harvill Press, 1991).

Chapter 6: Communal Crafting
[1] Parker, R., *The Subversive Stitch: Embroidery and the Making of the Feminine* (I. B. Tauris, 2010).
[2] Crawford, M., *The Case for Working with your Hands: Or Why Office Work is Bad for Us and Fixing Thing Feels Good* (Penguin, 2010).

Part III: Power in the Product

Chapter 9: Graceful Activism
[1] Hyde, L. *The Gift: Imagination and the Erotic Life of Property* (Vintage, 1983), p. 68.
[2] Goleman, D. P., Emotional Intelligence: *Why It Can Matter More Than IQ for Character, Health and Lifelong Achievement* (Bloomsbury, 1996), p. 106.
[4] Ibid., p. 96.
[5] Dr Frank Bernieri quoted in ibid., p. 116–7.
[6] Peavey, F., *Strategic Questioning: Insight and Action, How to Discover and Support a Life of Integrity and Commitment to Change* (New Society Publishers, 1994), p. 30.

Chapter 10: Compete with Beauty
[1] www.wired.co.uk/article/meet-bruce-mau-he-wants-toredesign-the-world
[2] Rawsthorn, A., *Hello World: Where Design Meets Life* (Penguin, 2015), p. iii.
[3] Koren, L., *Wabi-Sabi for Artists, Designers, Poets and Philosophers* (Stone Bridge Press, 1994).
[4] Grudin, R., *Design and Truth* (Yale University Press, 2010), p. 8.
[5] Rothenburg, D., *Survival of the Beautiful: Art, Science and Evolution* (Bloomsbury, 2011), pp. 5–6.
[6] Rawsthorn, A., *Hello World: Where Design Meets Life* (Penguin, 2015), pp. 188, 252.

Chapter 11: The Message
1 Hyndman, S., Why Fonts Matter (Virgin Books, 2016), p. 80.
2 Garfield, S., *To the Letter: A Journey Through a Vanishing World* (Canongate, 2013), p. 20.

Part IV: Power in the Public Sphere

Chapter 13: Intriguing Craftivism
1 Arendt, H., *The Life of the Mind* (1978).

Chapter 14: Pretty Protests
1 www.listsofnote.com
   Lists of Note is a beautiful and intriguing website by Shaun Usher, who has put together three beautiful books published by Unbound: *Letters of Note, More Letters of Note and Lists of Note*.

Chapter 15: Wearing your Convictions
1 Van Der Linden, S., 'Exploring Beliefs About Bottled Water and Intentions to Reduce Consumption: The Dual-Effect of Social Norm Activation and Persuasive Information', *Environment and Behavior* (2013). eab.sagepub.com/content/47/5/526
2 Phrase coined by Dr Christine Shaw-Checinska at her TEDxEast-End 2015 'Disobedient Dress: Fashion as everyday activism'. See www.youtube.com/watch?v=63-9YIVAhpI
3 Ribeiro, A. with Blackman, C., *A Portrait of Fashion: Six Centuries of Dress at the National Portrait Gallery* (National Portrait Gallery, 2015).
4 Hodder, I., 'The Contextual Analysis of Symbolic Meaning' in S. M. Pearce, ed., *The Interpreting Objects and Collections* (Routledge, 1994), p. 12.
5 Quote came via text message, 24 August 2015.
6 www.tomofholland.com/category/remaking

Chapter 16: Reaching Out
1 www.facebook.com/CraftivistCollective/
2 Laasch, O. and Conaway, R., *Responsible Business, A Textbook for Theory, Practice and Change* (Editorial Digital del Tecnológico de Monterrey, 2016), p. 37.

Chapter 17: Shareability
1 This story came from Ed Gillespie's YouTube video, 'Stories, Sizzle, Salience and Social Proof': www.youtube.com/watch?v=u_chRVbjhgM
2 For Alison's full post, see anotherlittlecraftycreation.wordpress.com/2013/02/19/
3 See Pippa's story at: www.storyofmum.com/content/changetheworld piecebypiece
4 www.immediate.co.uk/brands/mollie-makes-2/ABC Jan-Dec 2013

Chapter 18: Measuring Success
1 Reynolds, R., *On Guerrilla Gardening: A Handbook for Gardening without Boundaries* (Bloomsbury, 2014), p. 244.
2 Peavey, F., *By Life's Grace: Musings on the Essence of Social Change* (New Society Publishers, 1994), p. 7.
3 Solnit, R., *Hope in the Dark, Untold Histories, Wild Possibilities* (Canongate Books, 2016), p. xiv.

Acknowledgements

A huge thanks to the craftivists around the world for being part of the Craftivist Collective, sharing your projects and crafterthoughts and encouraging others to join in our gentle protests. Without your eagerness to join in with the projects and the thoughtful questions you ask on how to be an effective craftivist, I wouldn't have had the courage and agency to write this book. I'm honoured to be part of this growing community.

A huge appreciation goes to those in the charity sector who encouraged me to keep asking challenging questions about activism techniques, have the courage to try out my craftivism and gentle protest ideas and make time for me to talk through my analysis with them: Tom Baker, Rachel Collinson and Duane Raymond, among others.

To those who 'adopted a craftivist' (me!) so that I can continue my work – your financial support is invaluable.*

Thank you to my patient and kind editor Justine Taylor for her time, skills and for many times gently saying 'I think you might be overanalysing that', with a smile on her face.

I am so proud to be related to my family and blessed to have such amazing friends; your unwavering support and encouragement have been and continue to be my safety net on this unusual journey.

* www.craftivist-collective.com/adopt-a-craftivist

Unbound is the world's first crowdfunding publisher, established in 2011.

We believe that wonderful things can happen when you clear a path for people who share a passion. That's why we've built a platform that brings together readers and authors to crowdfund books they believe in – and give fresh ideas that don't fit the traditional mould the chance they deserve.

This book is in your hands because readers made it possible. Everyone who pledged their support is listed below. Join them by visiting unbound.com and supporting a book today.

Liz Aab
Elizabeth Abbott
Hannah Abbott
Lois Acton
alabamathirteen
José Alejandro
Jon Alexander
Max Alexander
Sarah Allen
Tom Allen
Joanne Ames
Martin Amor
Billie Anderson
Rohan Anderson
Karen Apps
Natalie Arif

Katie Elliott Armitage
Joanne Armstrong
Stephanie Arnold
Suzanne Arnold
India Aspin
Tim Atkinson
Madeleine Ayling
Alison Backhouse
Carole Backler
Karen Badenoch
Helen Baggaley
Jemma Bagley
Adam Bailey
Rachel Bailey
Jessica Bain
Nicki Bair

Demelza Baker

Tom and Demelza Baker

Jessica Ball

Laura Ball

Helen Ball - Social Know How CIC

Annie Banham

Janice Barrett

Lizzie Barrie

Liam Barrington-Bush

Susan Barry

Maddy Baxter

Jo Bayly

Emily Beardsmore

Jane Beasley

Sarah Beeston

Ben & Sarah

Nancy Bennie

Michaela Bere

Kate Berry

Stephanie Bescoby

Katy Bevan

Deena Beverley

Shanna Bhambra

Nikki Bi

Zoe Bicat

Laura Billlings

Jo Blakey

David Brickey Bloomer

Maya and Rhea Boodhun

Chloe Booth

Eric Booth

Kristin Booth

Wendy Bourton

Genevieve Brading

Jayde Bradley

Olivera Bratich

Marta Brebner

Kaye Brennan

Karina Brisby

Michael Brooks

Alison Bruce

Margaret Brunger

Nigel Bryant

Judith Bryson-Meehan

Kathleen Buckley

Steven Buckley

Kate Bull

Alex Bunn

Ali Burdon

Dan Burgess

Angie Burke

Debbie Burnham

Leigh Burrows

Mike Butcher

C A

Rhiannon Cackett

Emilia Caddick

Charlotte Calkin

Jacqueline Calladine

Eleni Calligas

Fabienne Katy Camm

Hilary Campbell

Iain Campbell

Jill Cansell

Beth Capper

Lily Caprani

Anna Carey

Carla Carpenter

Daniel Carpenter

MK Carroll

Ingrina Carson

Emily Carter

Philippa Carter
Kelley Carmichael Casey
Heather Cawte
Jamie Chalmers
Elaine Chambers
Sharon Chambers
Heather Champ
Naveed Chaudhri
Joy Cherkaoui
Donna Cheshire
Joanna Chittenden
Namrata Chowdhary
Sam Kennedy Christian
Anne Clark
Charlotte Clark
Penelope Clayden
Catherine Clements
Joanne S B Clements
Vicki Clough
Katy Cocklin
Jim Coe
Stevyn Colgan
Teresa Collenette
Gillian Collins
Rachel Collinson
Alice Condé
Victoria Conmy
AJ Conroy
Nikki Cooper
Stephanie Cooper
Aaron Copeland
Emma Corbett
Henry Corbett
Jane Corbett
Patricia Corbett
Thomas Corbett

Gemma Cowin
Plum Cox
Craftspace
Charlie Craggs
Jaime Creeth
Liz Crichton
Tessa Crichton-Miller
Lisa Cromar
Julia Croyden
Matthew Currey
Neil Currie
Daniel Curtis
Emazing Curvytents
Ellie Cusack
Andrea Østmo da Costa
Antonio Da Cruz
Sarah Daly
Gareth Dauncey
Lauren Davidson
Emma Davies
Harriet Davies
John Davies
Rhian Davies
Nyree Davis
Jill Dawsom
Anna Day
Jess Day
Guido de Graaff
Jean de la Haye
Sophie Deen
Anne Delnevo
Krys Dembinska
Pete Dennis
Moxie DePaulitte
Una Devine
Deborah Doane

Rebecca Dobson
Paul Douglas
Dawn Downes
Rosie Downes
Alexi Duggins
Katherine Dunhill
Melanie Dunkley
Gemma Dunning
Erica Durante
Naomi Dyer
Natasha Dyer
Education Services 2010
Hana Eggleston
Cora Eley
Annie Elisabeth
Lynsey Ellard
Emma and Alice
Joan Endres
Chris English
Frida Engström
Viv Ervine
Rebecca Evans-Merritt
Om Farrand
Joan Fawcett
Charlotte Fereday
Taylor Fields
Anna Fisk
Brian Fitzgerald
Tal Fitzpatrick
Sofie Flaeten
Donna Fleming
Em Fleming
Malcolm Fleming
John-Paul Flintoff
Bellatrix Foe
Lorna Fogden

Karin Folkesson
The folks at WarmthandWonder.co.uk
Simone Foote
Janey Forshaw-Smith
Maya Forstater
Hannah Fortune
Jane Foster
Sarah Francis
Tracy Frauzel
Sophie Freeman
Yvonne Fuchs
Alice Fuller
Abigail Funnell
Jacqui G
Lorna Gaffney
Gardenia Fair
Kizzy and Myles Gardiner
Wendy Gardiner
David Garratt
Claire Garside
Anna Gavurin
Doug Gay
Dr Sarah Gee
Sarah Gee
Heidi Geis
Sophie Geschke
Dinah Gibbons
Jane Gibbs
Liz Gibson
Beverley Gilbert
Ed Gillespie
Sarah Gillett
Girls Friendly Society
Melanie Godecki
Belinda Gordon
Mary Gordon

Jen Donkin Gourley
Amanda Graupner
Sarah Green
Trust Greenbelt
Helen Greenwood
Betsy Greer
Emily Griffith
John Griffiths
Tim Griffiths
Debbie H
Fiona Habermehl
Sarah Haggie
Freya Hall
Joe Hall
Joel Halliday
Charlotte Halstead
Rin Hamburgh
Nuala Hamilton
Natasha Hanckel-Spice
Masahiko Hand
Nick Hand
Jenny Harper
Sarah J Harper
Lynn Harrigan
Bethan Harris
Louise and Mark Harris
Sam Harvey
Robyn Hawkins
Kathryn Hay
Sarah Haynes
Beverley Haywood
Olivia Hebblewhite
Margaret Heffernan
Rachel Heicher
Tina Helfrich
Audrey Helm

Helen Hennerley
Gaelle Henriet
Wiebke Herding
Cecilia Hewett
Bonnie Hewson
Lara Hill
Eva Hoffmann
Emma Holland-Lindsay
Sarah Hollingworth
Lucy-Anne Holmes
Emma Homent
Charlotte Hooson-Sykes
Rob Hopkins
Susie Horne
Margaret Hossack
Catherine Howarth
Gillie Howarth
Sophie Howarth
Greta Hughson
Lisa-Raine Hunt
Philippa Hunt
Jo Hunter
Rachel Hurdley
Emma Hurrell
Becky Hurst
Emma Ibbetson
Sophia Ireland
Minna Jaakola
Andy Jackson
Ema Jackson
Annette James
Curtis James
Emmy Jane
Janis Jefferies
Alison Jeffers
Annie Jefferson

Hilary Jennings
Nicky Jerrome
Ali Jinnah
Mairi Johnson
Alli Jones
Andrea Jones
Andrew & Sarah Jones
Ann Jones
Connie Jones
Emma Ashru Jones
Helen Jones
Catherine Joyce
Helen Judges
George Julian
Elisa Kärki
Mona Kastell
Stacey Pedersen Keating
Jenny Kehoe
Ruth Kelly
Hilary Kemp
Frank Kennedy
Helen Coates Kenner
Laura Kerr
Dan Kieran
Kate Kilpatrick
Nina Kin
Lara Kinneir
Martin Kirk
John Kjellberg
Mieke Klaver
Lorna Knight
Sandra Knott
Marianne Nødtvedt Knudsen
Hannah Kochmann
Sinead Koehler
Anna Komar

Lerryn Korda
Roman Krznaric
Louise Kulp
Hannamari Kumpusalo
Yoko Kuramoto-Eidsmoe
Hannah Lamdin
Georgie Laming
Stephanie Landymore
Christine Lang
Paul Langley
Sue Langridge
Bethan Lant
Jenny Linnea Lantz
Gemma Latham
Sarah Laurenson
Eileen Laurie
Max Lawson
Maggie Le May
Emma Leaf-Grimshaw
Agatha Lee
Lisa Lee
Penny Leeman
Luke Leighfield
Emma Lennox
Aino Lepistö
Tim LeRoy
Fritha Lewin
Craig Lewis
Jessica Lewis
Mary Lewis
Sarah Lewis
Sian Lile-Pastore
Alexandra Lilley
Clare Linton
Josie Long
Look Lane Ltd

Sandra Lopacki

Emmy Lou

Ellen Loudon

Anita Loveland

Siw Lövkvist

Victoria Lowry

Danielle Lowy

Clare Lucas

Pamela Luckock

Eleri Luff

Jen Luk

Elin Lundell

Kuan Luo

Patricia Lynch

Clare Lyons

Janice Macaulay

Sue MacFarlane

Ann Mackey

Eilidh Macpherson

Eleanor Madley

Francesca Cambridge Mallen

Sandra Markus

Jo Marshall

Kate Elizabeth Marshall

Jacqui Marson

Richard Martin

Ruth Martin

Amy Mason

Laura Mason

Barley Massey

Iona Mathers

Cherie Matrix-Holt

Susanna Matthan

Carol Maurer

Peter May

Elle McAll

Joan McAlroy

Catherine McAtier

Lorna McBride

Linda McClintock-Tiongco

Michelle McCormick

Lou McGill

Alyce McGovern

Heather Mclay

Belinda McLean

Laurie McNeill

Jess McQuade

Clare Mead

Kate Megan

Sue Mellis

Andy Middleton

Sarah Milan

Phil Millar

Ann Mills-Duggan

Branislava Milosevic

Becky Minehart

Andy Minnis

Kate Mitchell

Ray Mitchell

John Mitchinson

Stephanie Moffat

Sarah Moon

Sarah Moore

Ariel Moreton

Hannah Morley

Roger Morris

Tess S.N. Morris

Annalise Moser

Much Ado Books

Mia Mueller

Bernd Müller

M. Geneva Murray

Nathalie Nahai
Lisa Nathan
Carlo Navato
Lucy Neal
Philip Nevin
Rachel Newsome
Melanie Nicholls
Miriam Nicholson
Paula Niemi
Alexander Noble
Jo Norcup
Jane Norris
Anne Norton
Timothy Notenboom
Jean O'Brien
Michaela O'Brien
Tríona O'Connell
Kevin O'Dell
Kath O'Donnell
Kim O'Driscoll
Dominic O'Reilly
Catherine Oakes
Malin Ögland
Erik Olesund
Team Oliver
Alice Owen
Henry Owen
Jean Owen
Emma Page
Kate Page
Sarah Page
Irini Papadimitriou
Elizabeth Parkhurst
Clive Parkinson
Amelia Parsons
Liz Pearce

Heidi Pearl
Lucy Pearson
Megan Pedersen
Teri Pek
Nick Pennell
Jess Perriam
Abigail Perrow
Tasha Peter
Craig Philbrick
Ben Phillips
Steph Phillips
Louise Phin
Jill Pickering
Sarah Plumer
Kate Poland
Justin Pollard
Pom Pom Quarterly
Dulseigh Pomerance-Trifts
Beki Pope
Diane Porter
Ruth Potts
Alison Collison Powell
Kit Powney
Melissa Poynton
Lorna Prescott
Hannah Preston
Jo Price
Sarah Price
Cressida Pryor
Hilary Pullen
Chiara Quaglia
James Qualtrough
Charity Quin
Clare Radford
Faith Radford-Lloyd
James Ramsay

Ché Ramsden

Tracy Ramsey

Heather Ratcliff

Duane Raymond

Rachel Rayns

Eddie Rego

Renee Renee

John and Vanessa Rew

Richard Reynolds

Richard and Lyla Reynolds

Bethan Joy Richardson

Ellen Richardson

Stine Ringnes

Claire Ritchie

Ann Roach

Christine Roberts

Sian Roberts

Jane Robertson

Julie Robertson

Laura Robertson

Alayne Robin

To Robin from Audra

Zoe Robinson

Susan Rochester

Maru Rojas C

Yvette Noblesse Rombouts

Pauline Ronksley

Jon Ronson

Ellen Rosewall

Carrie Ross

Jenny Ross

Julian Rosser

Jennifer Roth

Keira Esse Roth

Susan Rovira

Gabi Rowe

Vivienne Rowett

Julia Rowntree

Hilary Roy

Bernadette Russell

Gabriella Russo

Brid Ryan

Lucy Ryder

Alison Saint

Annie Salmon

Salon London

Sara Sara

Jonathan Satchell

Ceri Saunders

Peter Saunders OBE

Lisa Scandrette

Gemma Scattergood

Jennie Carvill Schellenbacher

Marjolyn Schreuder...urban nomad

Lucy Scott

Lynsey Searle

Angela Secker

Pamela Sedgwick-Barker

Caroline Sefton

Karen Selley

Sarah Shafer

Nikki Shaill

Jo Shaw

Katie Shaw

Vyvian Shaw

Nic & Mark Shayler

Ann Sheppard

Kate Shurety

Cate Simmons

Robert Simpson

Pia Sjöstrand

Ellie Skinner

Lydia Slack
Slartibartfast
Sophie Slater
Susan Slater
Robyn Slator
Wendy Slattery
Nicola Slawson
Katie Slee
Charlotte Slinger
Anita Smith
Anna Smith
Hannah Smith
Kim Smith
Laura-Jane Smith
Matthew Smith
Rachel Smith
Vicki Smith
Rachel Smith-Evans
The Snail of Happiness
Debbie So
Carry Somers
Hanna Sorrell
Ishah Speers
Eva & James Spens
Sally Spens
Joshua Stacey
Amanda Stagg
Kirsty Stanley
Emily Steedman
Amelia Steele
Jeff Steer
Katrin Steiger
Victoria Stephens
Rachel Stevens-Hall
Esther Stevenson
Catherine Stewart

Tree Stitchless
Amanda Stocker
Emily Stone
Natasha Stone
Sally Stone
Lottie Storey
Katie Stowell
Jane and Gav Strange
Katy Styles
Ruth Sullivan
Cathy Summers
Veronika Susedkova
Michelle Sutherland
Fran Swaine
Laurel Swift
T C
Caroline Taraskevics
Glen Tarman
Rachel Tavernor
Gavin Taylor
Patricia Taylor
Pete Taylor
Rachel Taylor
Susana Tempel
Jane Thakoordin
Angharad Thomas
Glyn Thomas
Katharine Thomas
Tamsin Thomas
Laura Thomson
Sarah Thorp
Clare Thorpe
Miranda Threlfall-Holmes
Anne Thwaites
Kathryn Tindale
Sonja Todd

Caroline Tomes
Solitaire Townsend
Michael Townsend Williams
Laura Trevelyan
Niki Tucci
Karen Turnbull
Karen Turner
Sarah Turner
Teija Turtio
Deborah Twigger
Emma Tyrrell
Jill Tytherleigh
Jenny Unsworth
Tom Van Deijnen
Vancouver Craft Festival Society
Nigel Varndell
Janet Vaughan
Cecily Vessey
Janet Voyce
Wendy Waghorn
Rachel Wakefield
Jonathan Wakeham
Inge Wallage
Wendy Ward
Tricia Warden
Carol Warrington
Lara Watson
Jane Watterson
Sara Watts
Katherine Webb
Sue Webster
Alice Wenban-Smith
Miranda West
Georgina Westley
Jane Wheeler
Hannah Whelan

Grace Whowell
Rachel Wickert
Hester Wijk
Gill Wildman
Elizabeth Wilkinson
Linsey Williams
Elysia Willis
Victoria Willis
Andy Wilson
Amber Wingfield
Ross Wintle
Nicolò Wojewoda
Julian Wood
Lesley Wood
Seán Wood
Pauline Woods
Sal Woodward
Caroline Woolfenden
Jane Workman
Christine Worrall
Anne Wright
Grace Wroe
Martin Wroe
www.anne-murray.com
Angie Wyman
Tracey Yates
Peter Yeo
Bek Yip
Kerry Yong
Wendy Young
Holly Zaher
Alfred Zollinger